WORDSWORTH AS CRITIC

Wordsworth
as Critic

W. J. B. OWEN

UNIVERSITY OF TORONTO PRESS

Reprinted in Canada 1971
ISBN 0-8020-5201-0

This work has been published with the help of
a grant from the Humanities Research Council of Canada
using funds provided by the Canada Council.

The aim of this book is to show the growth of Wordsworth's think-ing about the theory of his art; the demonstration is based primarily upon his formal critical essays, but it draws, naturally, on personal statements about poetics and about the growth and constitution of the poet's mind in *The Prelude*, in other verse, and in letters. The growth which I trace is ragged, but organic; proceeding by a series of prunings of, and grafts upon, material previously established. The basic material from which the process begins is, of course, the Preface to *Lyrical Ballads* of 1800, and, because of the primary nature of this document, my discussion of it and of its immediate descendant of 1802 is on a larger scale than that of the later critical essays. Most of this discussion appeared as the Introduction to my edition of the Preface (Copenhagen, 1957); it has been adapted to my present pur-pose and slightly reduced in length. I have taken the opportunity to consult various accounts of the problems raised by the Preface which have appeared in the last ten years, notably the helpful essays of Stephen M. Parrish, and I hope I have taken note of such of my reviewers' criticisms as I could accept; but on the whole I have found little reason for any basic revision of the analysis of the Preface which I offered in 1957. I have separated this analysis from my text, apparatus, and commentary of 1957 the more willingly because of the appearance of Paul M. Zall's *Literary Criticism of William Wordsworth* (Lincoln, 1966), which, by reprinting the texts of 1800 and 1802 in full, gives implicit approval to my claim that

Wordsworth's revisions and additions of 1802 differ significantly in intention from the text of 1800, and which includes the drift of some parts of my commentary in its own annotations. But from time to time I have given references to my commentary, so that these pages shall not be overburdened with complex discussion of difficulties of interpretation or with lists of sources and analogues.

Chapters VI–IX of the present book emerge from the task which I share with Professor Jane Worthington Smyser of editing Wordsworth's prose works for the Clarendon Press. Two of the documents studied are familiar to readers of Wordsworth if only because they have been regularly reprinted in collected editions of his *Poetical Works* since their first appearance in 1815, and one of them, the Preface of 1815, has recently been discussed in some detail.[1] The third text, the threefold *Essays upon Epitaphs*, is less familiar because the first Essay is buried amongst Wordsworth's notes to an unpopular poem, *The Excursion*, and because the second and third Essays have been as effectively concealed, in a corrupt text, in Grosart's and Knight's editions of the *Prose Works* (London, 1876, 1896), in Nowell C. Smith's *Wordsworth's Literary Criticism* (London, 1905), and in Zall's collection.

With a few exceptions, the primary documents are cited below in the text of Zall's edition, and references are given to his book. The Preface to *The Borderers* and the second and third *Essays upon Epitaphs* are cited in the text of the forthcoming Oxford edition, but references are given to Zall where he prints the relevant passage, and to Knight's edition of the *Prose Works* where Zall is deficient. Where my text of these works differs from Zall's (or Knight's), notice is given by means of an asterisk prefixed to the quotation. Because no currently available text of these works is wholly accurate, and also because Zall usually prints the earliest rather than the latest versions of the various documents published by Wordsworth, the texts in this book will differ from time to time from those in common

1/James Scoggins, *Imagination and Fancy: Complementary Modes in the Poetry of Wordsworth* (Lincoln, 1966), especially Chapters 4 and 5.

use. Zall's headnotes give more or less adequate information on the dates and occasions of the works studied here; I have therefore omitted discussion of these matters, except where some background information seemed necessary to the understanding of the document, as in the case of the Preface of 1815.[2]

I am indebted to the institutions and scholars who made possible my edition of the Preface to *Lyrical Ballads*, and to Messrs Rosenkilde & Bagger for permission to draw largely on that edition; to the Trustees of Dove Cottage and to Yale University Library for permission to quote unpublished material; to Cornell University Library; to the Humanities Research Council of Canada and to the Publications Fund of the University of Toronto Press for grants in aid of publication; to McMaster University for research grants.

W. J. B. Owen

2/I have discussed the occasion and general intention of the *Essay, Supplementary to the Preface* in my paper, "Wordsworth and Jeffrey in Collaboration," *R.E.S.*, N.S., xv (1964), 161–67. My attention in this book is confined to a limited area of the Essay.

✳ Contents

✳ Abbreviations

Abrams = M. H. Abrams, *The Mirror and the Lamp: Romantic Theory and the Critical Tradition* (New York, 1953).

Barstow = Marjorie L. Barstow, *Wordsworth's Theory of Poetic Diction* (New Haven, 1917).

Biog. Lit. = S. T. Coleridge, *Biographia Literaria*, ed. J. Shawcross (Oxford, 1907).

C.L. = *Collected Letters of Samuel Taylor Coleridge*, ed. E. L. Griggs (Oxford, 1956——).

C.N.B. = *Notebooks of Samuel Taylor Coleridge*, ed. K. Coburn (London, 1957——).

Collingwood = R. G. Collingwood, *The Principles of Art* (Oxford, 1938).

C.R. = *Correspondence of Henry Crabb Robinson with the Wordsworth Circle*, ed. Edith J. Morley (Oxford, 1927).

Dennis = *Critical Works of John Dennis*, ed. E. N. Hooker (Baltimore, 1939, 1943).

Duff = William Duff, *Essay on Original Genius* (London, 1767).

E.Y. = *Letters of William and Dorothy Wordsworth: The Early Years*, ed. E. de Selincourt. Second edition, revised by Chester L. Shaver (Oxford, 1967).

Garrod = H. W. Garrod, *Wordsworth: Lectures and Essays* (Oxford, 1923).

Gerard, *Genius* = Alexander Gerard, *Essay on Genius* (London, 1774).

Gerard, *Taste* = Alexander Gerard, *Essay on Taste* (London, 1759).

Hartley = Joseph Priestley, *Hartley's Theory of the Human Mind* (London, 1775).

Havens = Raymond Dexter Havens, *The Mind of a Poet* (Baltimore, 1941).

H.C.R. = *Henry Crabb Robinson on Books and their Writers*, ed. Edith J. Morley (London, 1938).

[Johnson,] *Lives* = Samuel Johnson, *Lives of the English Poets*, ed. G. B. Hill (Oxford, 1905).

Journals = *Journals of Dorothy Wordsworth*, ed. E. de Selincourt (London, 1941).

Knight = *Prose Works of William Wordsworth*, ed. W. Knight (London, 1896).

Lovejoy = Arthur O. Lovejoy, *Essays in the History of Ideas* (Baltimore, 1948).

L.Y. = *Letters of William and Dorothy Wordsworth: The Later Years*, ed. E. de Selincourt (Oxford, 1939).

Mackenzie = Agnes Mure Mackenzie, *The Process of Literature* (London, 1929).

Moorman, *Early Years* = Mary Moorman, *William Wordsworth. A Biography. The Early Years* (Oxford, 1957).

M.Y. = *Letters of William and Dorothy Wordsworth: The Middle Years*, ed. E. de Selincourt. Second edition, revised by Mary Moorman and Alan G. Hill (Oxford, 1969–70).

P.L.B. = *Wordsworth's Preface to* Lyrical Ballads, ed. W. J. B. Owen (Copenhagen, 1957).

Prel. = *The Prelude*, ed. E. de Selincourt. Second edition, revised by Helen Darbishire (Oxford, 1959). The text of 1805 is cited unless otherwise stated.

Priestley, *Oratory* = Joseph Priestley, *A Course of Lectures on Oratory and Criticism* (London, 1775).

P.W. = *Poetical Works of William Wordsworth*, ed. E. de Selincourt and Helen Darbishire (Oxford, 1940–49, and revised issues of various volumes).

Raleigh = *Johnson on Shakespeare*, ed. W. Raleigh (London, 1908).

S.C. = S. T. Coleridge, *Shakespearean Criticism*, ed. T. M. Raysor (London, 1960).

Scoggins = James Scoggins, *Imagination and Fancy: Complementary Modes in the Poetry of Wordsworth* (Lincoln, 1966).

Sharrock = Roger Sharrock, "Wordsworth's Revolt against Literature," *Essays in Criticism*, iii (1953), 396–412.

Smith = Elsie Smith, *An Estimate of William Wordsworth by his Contemporaries* (Oxford, 1932).

Whalley = George Whalley, *Poetic Process* (London, 1953).

Zall = *Literary Criticism of William Wordsworth*, ed. P. M. Zall (Lincoln, 1966).

The titles of standard works of reference and of periodicals are abbreviated in commonly accepted forms. Wordsworth's texts are cited, where possible, from Zall, and references are given to his book by page number and line number, in these forms: 23.20 = page 23, line 20; 16.1–2 = page 16, lines 1–2; 21.28–22.1 = page 21, line 28 – page 22, line 1; 10.8, 16, 20 = page 10, lines 8, 16, and 20.

The Preface to *Lyrical Ballads* exists in two main versions: that of 1800, and that of 1802, which, with minor revisions, is the basis of Wordsworth's final text of 1850. The major difference between the two versions is in the addition, in the text of 1802, of a lengthy passage (Zall, pp. 47–54) which is best known for its discussion of the question, "What is a Poet?" (48.28). The added passage, and some related matter in the Appendix on poetic diction (Zall, pp. 63–67), also added in 1802, introduce ideas which cannot be wholly reconciled with the original version of 1800; it will therefore be convenient to discuss the version of 1800 first, and to consider Wordsworth's later ideas separately.

1 *The Theme of the Preface of 1800*

The main object of the Preface of 1800 is to define and defend a particular rhetoric: to assert the poetic value of "a selection of the real language of men in a state of vivid sensation" (16.1–2) and of "the language of prose" (23.20). "Poetic value" is estimated by a standard known in classical times and constantly emphasized in eighteenth-century aesthetics: the permanence of the artist's appeal. Yet Wordsworth's viewpoint is strikingly different from that of the mere critic of the eighteenth century, who urged that the classics must be great because they had survived in men's esteem for generations or centuries;[1] rather, Wordsworth's aim is to define a rhetoric, to be used now, by the practising poet of 1800, such that his appeal to his readers' taste will be as nearly permanent as may be. Moreover, such a standard of value was for Wordsworth in 1800 of considerably wider application than to literature alone. It is closely connected with his sense of the value in the permanence of "nature," in the several senses in which Wordsworth uses that word. Thus the "passions" of the boy Wordsworth were "intertwined," "Not with the mean and vulgar works of Man, But with high objects, with enduring things, With life and nature." At Cambridge, he had from geometry "a still sense Of permanent and universal sway," an image of God; and he (or "a Friend") mused "On Poetry and geometric Truth, The knowledge that endures ... And their high privilege of lasting life." The "steady form" of the mountain, the "forms Perennial of the ancient hills," give "to the mind ... a pure grandeur," diffusing "Composure and ennobling Harmony" even in "the press Of self-destroying, transitory things" in the city. Nature

> "Holds up before the mind, intoxicate
> With present objects and the busy dance
> Of things that pass away, a temperate shew
> Of objects that endure, and ...
> Disposes her ...
> To seek in Man ... what there is
> Desireable, affecting, good or fair
> Of kindred permanence."[2]

Wordsworth finds relief from his sense of social evil in his time in "a deep impression of certain inherent and indestructible qualities of the human mind, and likewise of certain powers in the great and permanent objects that act upon it which are equally inherent and indestructible" (21.28–22.1). His acceptance of nature as his guide

1/So, most notably, Johnson's Preface to Shakespeare (Raleigh, p. 9). The most remarkable later expression of this view is probably Arnold's Preface of 1853, which seems to rely on Wordsworth for some of its phrasing.
2/*Prel.*, 1.431 ff., VI.151 ff., v.64 ff., VII.721 ff., XII.33 ff.

after whatever crisis he passed through in the middle nineties includes an acceptance of "the language ... of life and nature" (29.35–36) for poetry; and poetry becomes "the history or science of" – the permanent truth about – "feelings" (13.27).[3] Thus the attempt to define a permanent rhetoric is for Wordsworth a means of aligning poetry with nature, of giving it, as far as possible, a form as "steady" and as "perennial" as that of the mountain.

To this comprehensive motive behind the Preface all other motives suggested by Wordsworth, and more especially by his critics, are eventually subordinate. It is true that Wordsworth wished to celebrate the virtues of the statesman of the Lake District or of his counterpart of the Southwest, and, perhaps for the sake of a kind of decorum, to use their language; but because their way of life was, he thought, natural and permanent. It is true that he revolted against the diction of Pope and Darwin; but because it seemed to him unnatural and impermanent. It may even be true, in a sense, that he wished to celebrate the common man because of a pressing desire to use his language; but because he thought that language natural, and therefore most likely to be permanently effective.[4]

Accordingly, the motive is stated plainly in the first operative paragraph of the Preface of 1800, and is repeated in the last: "Several of my Friends are anxious for the success of these Poems from a belief,

3/For a fairly full list of such passages, see Havens, pp. 302–3, and his index, s.v. *Enduring*; for a wide-ranging general discussion, see David Perkins, *The Quest for Permanence* (Cambridge, Mass., 1959), especially Chapters I–III; and on Wordsworth's wider concern with the opposed notions of Permanence and Mutability, see Charles J. Smith, "The Contrarieties: Wordsworth's Dualistic Imagery," *PMLA*, lxix (1954), 1181–99.

4/The three points indicated have been alleged as motives behind *Lyrical Ballads* and its Preface: the first and third, for instance, by Lascelles Abercrombie, *The Art of Wordsworth* (London, 1952), pp. 81 ff., 87; the second by Wordsworth himself, in *Prel.*, XII, written five years after the Preface. The motives, considered singly, are insufficient: one may disapprove of Pope's or Darwin's rhetoric and yet not write *Lyrical Ballads*; one may write about rustics in the diction of the eighteenth century if one will; and one may use the common man's language and yet not write about rustics. On Wordsworth's personal motives for writing the experimental ballads, see my edition of the text of 1798 (London, 1967), Introduction, sec. IV.

that if the views, with which they were composed, were indeed realized, a class of Poetry would be produced, well adapted to interest mankind permanently ... " (16.21–24). "... it has been ... my present aim ... to offer reasons for presuming, that, if the object which I have proposed to myself were adequately attained, a species of poetry would be produced, which is genuine poetry; in its nature well adapted to interest mankind permanently ... " (32.17–23).

Wordsworth is aware that poetic fashions change: "It is supposed, that by the act of writing in verse an Author ... not only ... apprizes the Reader that certain classes of ideas and expressions will be found in his book, but that others will be carefully excluded. This exponent or symbol held forth by metrical language must in different æras of literature have excited very different expectations ... " (17.13–19). The lesser writer is misled by the poetic fashions of his day: *" ... a man called to a task [writing an epitaph] in which he is not practised may have his expression thoroughly defiled and clogged by the style prevalent in his age; yet still through the force of circumstances that have roused him, his under feeling may remain strong and pure. Yet this may be wholly concealed from common view" (114.13–18).

It seems to follow that the style which was once fashionable, but which is no longer so, lacks the quality which makes for permanent appeal, or smothers that quality under a mass of other and undesirable qualities dictated by the fashions of the age. At particular periods, particular words, idioms, turns of expression – a particular "language"[5] – are felt to be "poetical." Whence it would seem to follow again that to escape the impermanence which change of poetic fashion appears to confer, the poet may either devise a language which is permanently "poetical," or he may devise one which is never "poetical" and thus not subject to change of poetic fashion. The remainder of Wordsworth's discussion of the language of poetry (that is, most of the Preface of 1800) is, in effect, a claim that it is possible to do both these things, as it were, at once. He sets about

5/On the meaning of *language*, see *P.L.B.*, Commentary, nn. on 16, 183–88, 255–56, 274–76, Appendix, 56–57.

rejecting the obviously "poetical" (as it appears to him at the end of the eighteenth century), and attempts to show that the language which remains is suitable for poetry: in that it is permanent – the language of rustics; and in that it is free from "poeticisms," which confer impermanence, and is, sometimes at least, found in good poetry – the language of prose.

II *Permanence*

The notion of permanence is first developed with respect to Wordsworth's subject-matter:

"Low and rustic life was generally chosen because in that situation the essential passions of the heart find a better soil in which they can attain their maturity, are less under restraint, and speak a plainer and more emphatic language; because in that situation our elementary feelings exist in a state of greater simplicity and consequently may be more accurately contemplated and more forcibly communicated; because the manners of rural life germinate from those elementary feelings; and from the necessary character of rural occupations are more easily comprehended; and are more durable; and lastly, because in that situation the passions of men are incorporated with the beautiful and permanent forms of nature." (18.5–16)

In this portrait, the rustic is seen as a "pure archetype of human greatness" (*Exc.*, III.951), an undiluted, uncompounded essence of humanity, ideal man, or the nearest approximation to that ideal which is likely to occur; and he is contrasted, by implication, with the sophisticated product of the city.[6] His characteristics recommend his language to the attention of the poet: for various reasons, "such a language arising out of repeated experience and regular feelings is a more permanent and a far more philosophical[7] language than that

6/The unresolved comparatives point to an unmentioned "elsewhere," presumably the city: cf. *Prel.*, XII.119–26, 201–3.

7/On *philosophical* see *P.L.B.*, Commentary, n. on 106; Zall, 18.fn.8.

which is frequently substituted for it by Poets" (18.24–26). Wordsworth is saying that in a rustic environment the basic, and permanently surviving, passions of mankind, "such as exist now and will
probably always exist" (20.21), "the general passions and thoughts
and feelings of men" (text of 1802, 54.8–9), will be more powerful,
and less liable to suppression, than in other environments; they will
be simple (that is, one-fold, "pure," uncontaminated by – as we say
– conflicting passions); and the man who gives vent to them in words
will, because his theme is thus "simple," because his attention is not
distracted by side issues, use a language entirely adequate to his
subject-matter – a "philosophical" language.

These ideas can perhaps be illustrated by Wordsworth's treatment
of "the maternal passion" (20.4) in *The Idiot Boy.* Betty Foy's
"maternal passion" is obviously "mature," if not over-ripe, and
negligibly "under restraint"; it is "simple," since it is clearly uninfluenced by the pressure of such feelings as shame which (Wordsworth told John Wilson in 1802) induce "gentlefolks" to dispose of
imbecile children (73.17–19); and her language, if not exactly
"forcible," at least expresses her obsession with a single theme.
Moreover, her "manners"[8] clearly spring from her maternal passion.
A difficulty arises, as Coleridge seems more or less to have seen
(*Biog. Lit.*, ii.35), in that the rustic environment of the poem has
little or no bearing on Betty's character. Her maternal passion, as
Wordsworth admits without noticing it in his letter to Wilson (73.15
ff.), is a virtue closely connected with economic necessity. Wordsworth has, in a measure, protected himself by his use of the phrase
"Low ... life"; but it is not clear that Betty's passion for Johnny has
any essential connection either with "the necessary character of rural
occupations" (unless their main characteristic is the poverty of those
who follow them) or with the "beautiful and permanent forms of
nature."

The notion that those who follow "rural occupations" are neces-

8/See *P.L.B.*, Commentary, n. on 93. As applied to an individual, the sense is
perhaps "habitual behaviour or conduct" (*O.E.D.*, sense 4.a).

sarily more "natural," are purer types of humanity, than are city-dwellers, is common and probably false.[9] False or not, the belief is in part the basis of Wordsworth's attempt to describe the language he proposes to use in his poetry. Wordsworth believes that he can discover in a rustic environment a man, a feeling, and a language of which the purity, the simplicity, is analogous to these attributes as they apply to the notion of a chemical element;[10] or, at least, that the closest approximations to such a man, a feeling, and a language which are possible to our experience are to be found in such an environment. Moreover, the drift of his argument is presented as a quasi-logical statement: simple people have simple feelings, and therefore use a simple language to express them.[11]

None of this, in spite of the tone of Wordsworth's language, is self-evident to the modern reader. It was not self-evident to Coleridge, who thought that mountainous districts do not necessarily breed high-minded inhabitants, and that rustics do not speak a plain language, but a broken and halting one (*Biog. Lit.*, ii.32, 44). In the Preface, Wordsworth offers no evidence at all for the "maturity" and "simplicity" of the rustic's feelings. In *The Prelude*, he claims that he found his ideas true from his own experience in the Southwest and in the Lake District (Book XII, *passim*). The evidence is insufficient to prove the general proposition which Wordsworth here advances. If it is true that the rustic's feelings are simpler than those of the townsman, it does not follow that he contemplates them "more accurately" than the townsman contemplates his. If it is true that he contemplates them, accurately or at all, it does not follow that the rustic communicates them "more forcibly" or more plainly than the townsman. It is presumably true that, if a man has a simple feeling, he will give more adequate expression to it than he would if his

9/See Havens, pp. 590–91, n. on *Prel.* (1850), XIII.102, for a convenient brief discussion.

10/Walter Raleigh's apt analogy: *Wordsworth* (London, 1903), p. 172.

11/Thus, in a parallel passage in *Exc.*, 1.340 ff., it is clear that we may interpret thus: "[feelings] That ... Exist more simple in their elements And [therefore] speak a plainer language," but not thus: "[feelings] That ... Exist more simple in their elements And [contrary to expectation] speak a plainer language."

attention were distracted by other feelings; but the judgment is valid only with respect to the varying emotional states of the individual. It is clear that Wordsworth is dealing with analogies rather than with proofs. What sort of language he is trying to describe we shall see more clearly if we consider his views on the influence of natural environment on the "passions of men" and the expression of them.

"Low and rustic life," says the Preface, "was generally chosen [for the subject-matter of *Lyrical Ballads*] ... because in that situation the passions of men are incorporated[12] with the beautiful and permanent forms of nature." This obscure statement is clarified by a passage in a letter to Coleridge of 1799:

"I do not so ardently desire character in poems like Burger's, as manners, not transitory manners reflecting the wearisome unintelligible obliquities of city life, but manners connected with the permanent objects of nature and partaking of the simplicity of those objects. Such pictures must interest when the original shall cease to exist. The reason will be immediately obvious if you consider yourself as lying in a valley on the side of mount Ætna reading one of Theocritus's Idylliums or on the plains of Attica with a comedy of Aristophanes on your hand. Of Theocritus and his spirit perhaps three fourths remain of Aristophanes a mutilated skeleton. ... But I may go further read Theocritus in Ayrshire or Merionethshire and you will find perpetual occasions to recollect what you see daily in Ayrshire or Merionethshire read Congreve Vanbrugh and Farquhar in London and though not a century has elapsed since they were alive and merry, you will meet with whole pages that are uninteresting and incomprehensible." (*E.Y.*, p. 255)

Wordsworth has discovered that the poet will be intelligible to a wider public, and to more generations of the public, if he deals with material which is basic in human experience and therefore of widespread and permanent interest. Stated thus, the discovery turns out to be a commonplace; but the argument by which it is made is per-

12/Apparently = "associated": see *P.L.B.*, Commentary, n. on 96.

haps unusual.[13] Wordsworth is claiming for rustic life a stability in natural environment and in "manners" (which he considers to be closely connected with natural environment) – a stability such that the environment and manners portrayed by Theocritus can be recognized, more or less, at a considerable remove in time, "in a valley on the side of mount Ætna"; or even, at a remove in time and also in space, in eighteenth-century Ayrshire or Merionethshire. On the other hand, in Athens or London, no such stability is to be found: for in cities natural environment does not shape manners since there is none to shape them;[14] consequently, the literature based on urban manners will lack widespread and permanent appeal.

Such a view, in so far as it is applied to natural environment itself, is sufficiently clear: so long as a mountain (say) is considered to be, in some sense, a poetical object,[15] then the more or less permanent nature of the mountain will confer a similar persistence of interest on the poetry which deals with it. The other part of the notion, that natural objects confer a similar stability on the manners they are said to induce in those who live near them, begs a question. Part of the business of *The Prelude* is to answer the question. But when John Wilson asks it in 1802, Wordsworth answers him half-heartedly. He writes cautiously, admitting that "we cannot perhaps observe" the formation of a particular national character under the influence of a particular natural environment "in our own island at the present day, because, even in the most sequestered places, by manufactures, traffic, religion, law, interchange of inhabitants, etc., distinctions are done away which would otherwise have been strong and

13/Johnson's observations on pastoral poetry in *Rambler*, 36, are not dissimilar; as his views on the "stile which never becomes obsolete," in the Preface to Shakespeare (Raleigh, pp. 19–20), resemble Wordsworth's on the language of rustics.
14/*Prel.*, XII.202–3: "cities, where the human heart is sick, And the eye feeds it not, and cannot feed."
15/In the *Guide to the Lakes* Wordsworth mentions "those stronger emotions which a region of mountains is peculiarly fitted to excite" (Knight, ii.33). On the rise of the prestige of the mountain as a subject for poetry, see Marjorie Hope Nicolson, *Mountain Gloom and Mountain Glory* (New York, 1963).

obvious" (70.13–17). The theory would be true if some inconvenient facts did not prove it false. Civilization has, regrettably, spoiled a simple, clear-cut analogy, a rigid parallelism, between character and environment: a notion which has obvious affinities with Wordsworth's ideas about a simple man, simple feelings, and a simple language expressing those simple feelings, which were discussed above.

The most important element in the passages under examination is the notion of *permanence*. Wordsworth seeks to write a poetry the subject-matter of which shall be of permanent interest; he seeks, similarly, to use a language which shall be permanently intelligible, or as near that as possible. For such a subject-matter, and Wordsworth's conviction that the language used will always convey the matter as directly as it is now conveyed to the poet and his immediate audience, guarantee for him the permanent value of the poetry. Such a subject-matter Wordsworth thinks he can find in rustic subjects; because, clearly enough, though he does not trouble to say so in the Preface, "rural occupations" (as he thinks) have been, are, and will continue to be the mainstay, the one essential element, of the continued existence of humanity; in a word, because "rural occupations" provide us with food and clothing and other "animal wants."[16] Wordsworth sees in the farmer of the Southwest and in the statesman of the Lake District, in those whose occupation lies "Among the natural abodes of men, Fields with their rural works" (*Prel.*, XII. 107–8) – he sees here "men as they are men within themselves" (*ibid.*, 225), men whose occupation is the one essential task of humanity, men who, in doing what they do, are doing all that is necessary to qualify them for the title of *men*. This view is plausible only within a limited view of history. Our "animal wants" have been supplied by means other than agricultural pursuits, and some will be

16/*Prel.*, XII.94. The point is clearly made in a work Wordsworth almost certainly knew, Jacques Delille's *Discours préliminaire* to his translation of the *Georgics* (1769), in *Œuvres* (Paris, 1836), p. 299: agriculture is "le premier de tous les arts, celui qui nourrit l'homme, qui est né avec le genre humain, qui est de tous les lieux, de tous les temps."

supplied by other means in the future; are so supplied now, by (for instance) synthetic clothing materials. And if we grant, as obviously we must, that such inroads made by technology are slight compared with the continuing importance of agriculture, it does not follow, and has not followed since 1800, that agriculture persists in the form which Wordsworth valued. His letter to Charles James Fox shows that he saw, in the decline of the statesman, the beginning of the process which proves his theory of permanence untrue in the longer view; but he saw it, perhaps inevitably, with a short-term view. He saw it from the point of view of the individual concerned; not as a process which would create a new way of life in England, different from that of the past though not necessarily worse, but rather as the destruction of the moral and social values of a particular way of life which he believed was the sole permanently necessary way.[17]

The language which expresses this way of life he considered to be similarly permanent. It is "the best part of language" (18.20) because it is thus permanent, because it answers the needs of this permanently necessary way of life. It has survived, he says, "universally intelligible" from Chaucer's day (18.fn.9). He presumably conceives it as whatever "language," whatever stable corpus of vocabulary, idiom, syntactical method, and the like, has survived in English from Chaucer's time – that is, probably, from the earliest stage of English with which Wordsworth was acquainted – until 1800. And by "the best objects from which the best part of language is originally derived" Wordsworth evidently means those quasi-permanent elements of rustic life to which this language gives names and expression: those human passions, habits, occupations, and environment[18]

17/He complains to Fox of "a rapid decay of the domestic affections among the lower orders of society," and argues that, by evils consequent upon industrialization, "the bonds of domestic feeling among the poor ... have been weakened, & in innumerable instances entirely destroyed." He gives instances; concludes that there is among his neighbours "an almost sublime conviction of the blessings of independent domestic life ... this spirit is rapidly disappearing, [and] no greater curse can befal a land"; and claims that the "domestic affections" are particularly strong among the "rapidly disappearing" statesmen (34.31–36.19).
18/See *P.L.B.*, Commentary, n. on 100–1; Zall, 18.fn.7.

which are sufficiently basic, important, and permanent in human experience to ensure that the corresponding elements of language do (more or less) survive: the "repeated experience and regular feelings" (18.24–25) which the Preface attributes to the rustic.

All this is, at best, only partially true. The obverse of the footnote of 1800 on the permanence of Chaucer's language is revealed in Wordsworth's note of 1820 introducing his version of *The Prioress's Tale*: "In the following Poem I have allowed myself no further deviations from the original than was necessary for the fluent reading, and instant understanding, of the Author: so much however is the language altered since Chaucer's time, especially in pronunciation, that much was to be removed, and its place supplied with as little incongruity as possible."[19] The modernizations, written a year after the Preface, confirm these statements: the printed text, further from Chaucer's words than Wordsworth's manuscript, retains many bald transliterations, some of which misrepresent Chaucer's intention and others of which are merely unidiomatic archaisms. It may, indeed, be admitted that a good many basic elements in English and pre-English *vocabulary* are comparatively permanent (though many others are not); but to claim that the other elements of "language" show stability is merely to contradict the written evidence of Old English, or of Latin as compared with the modern Romance languages. And in the limited field of vocabulary, it is by no means proved that the "repeated experience and regular feelings," which Wordsworth, with some justice, regards as the basis of a stable language, are more especially the property of the rustic than of any other man.[20] It is probable that Wordsworth eventually tended to

19/*Miscellaneous Poems* (London, 1820), iii.114.
20/That is, the rustic's language is no more "natural" than his occupation, environment, and the characteristics which are alleged to result from these. In the text of 1802, references to "natural" language are more frequent than in 1800 (47.30, 48.6, 49.33, 53.29; 63.18, 64.10, 65.2, 65.7, 67.25). This expansion is incautious, since no language is "natural" in the sense that it is instinctive utterance: convention rules "the language of men" as it rules poetic diction, which is "unnatural" only in the sense that its conventions differ from the more widely accepted conventions of "the language of men."

such a view himself, for he continues, especially in the additions made to the Preface in 1802, to speak of "men" and their language, but not about rustics. More significant still is the complete omission from the *Essays upon Epitaphs*, in which, as we shall see, Wordsworth handles with much greater assurance this and other major ideas of the Preface, of any attempt to define a permanent language in sociological terms.

III *The Language of Prose*

The second stage of Wordsworth's attempt to define his language – the language of permanent poetic appeal – consists of two parts: a definition by negatives, and a positive identification of his language with "the language of prose." The one is complementary to the other: Wordsworth says, in effect, that if a style, or a language, lacks certain conventional poeticisms (which are unnatural and confer impermanence on language), it is, essentially, the language of prose. The connection is not made specifically at the proper point;[21] but it must be granted if the abruptly introduced subject of the language of prose is to have relevance to the argument. At this stage, too, "the language of men," and specifically the language of rustics, once it has served as the norm against which conventional poeticisms are measured, conveniently slips out of sight in the text of 1800, appears again only twice (28.37, 29.35–36), insignificantly, and is replaced as an effective element of the argument by "the language of prose." The identification of "the language of men," or of a selection of it, with "the language of prose" is never made except by remote implication.

The conventional poeticisms which Wordsworth proposes on the whole to reject from his language are: "personifications of abstract ideas"; "what is usually called poetic diction," which seems to include "phrases and figures of speech which ... have long been regarded as the common inheritance of Poets"; and "many expressions

21/The proper point would have been at about 23.6.

... which have been foolishly repeated by bad Poets" (22.10, 22.20–21, 22.35–37, 23.1–3). Some distinction seems to be intended between the second and third of these, but what it is the Preface does not make clear.

The special consideration given to the figure of personification is noteworthy. Wordsworth's suspicion of it can often be detected behind his criticism of verse the defects of which are not so immediately obvious to his reader as they are to him.[22] In the text of 1802, however, it is regarded as admissible when "prompted by passion" (44.35), and thus falls into line with other figures.

Wordsworth's objection to personification and poetic diction is that they do not "make any regular or natural part" of "the language of men" (22.13–15): they are not part of that common, quasi-permanent corpus of English which was defined earlier. Yet since a language is poorly defined by stating what it is not, or what it does not contain, Wordsworth makes two further efforts towards a general definition in positive terms. He seems to be in difficulties. He does not know how, he says apologetically, "without being culpably particular," to define his style, except by giving, not a definition of it, but an account of how he sets about writing: "I have at all times endeavoured to look steadily at my subject." He follows this up with another virtual negative: "consequently I hope it will be found that there is in these Poems little falsehood of description," and another vagueness: "my ideas are expressed in language fitted to their respective importance" (22.26–33). This is not very impressive or precise. It was, perhaps, genuinely difficult for Wordsworth to frame an adequate general definition, in positive terms, of the permanent elements of English. The task would be slightly less formidable in the present century with the aid of the *Oxford English Dictionary* and the records on which such a work is based; but Wordsworth had no comparable apparatus. The best he can do, when he is not using

---

22/In Gray's sonnet (23.29–24.5), personification is explicit or implicit in the first, second, fourth, fifth, ninth, and eleventh lines; in the extract from Johnson (66.3–18), in the seventh, ninth, and all succeeding lines; on the extract from Cowper (66.29–67.8), see *P.L.B.*, n. on Appendix, 140–46.

the roundabout terms which deal with the language of rustics, is to note that some parts of Chaucer are "universally intelligible" in 1800: he has at his command, in effect, a limited part of the historical information supplied by *O.E.D.* He gropes for something more tangible, and finds it in the solution to a kind of equation: if from the language of poetry, as it is usually defined, one subtracts conventional poeticisms, the remainder is the language of prose. Three problems present themselves: the source of such an equation; the validity of the solution; and the critical value of the solution if it is valid.

We need to look for a source of the equation because of the abrupt introduction of "the language of prose." No earlier passage has hinted that "the language of prose" is relevant to the discussion; on the contrary, no standard except "the real language of men" has been proposed; and even now, as we saw above, no attempt is made, unless by remote implication, to claim that "the real language of men," purified or not, is identical with "the language of prose."

Two works which Wordsworth probably knew might have provided the hint for formulating the equation in the terms suggested. The first is the first prose Interlude to Erasmus Darwin's *Loves of the Plants*. The object of this dialogue between Poet and Bookseller is to discover "the essential difference[23] between Poetry and Prose." According to the Poet, it is "that Poetry admits of but few words expressive of very abstracted ideas, whereas Prose abounds in them": "And as our ideas derived from visible objects are more distinct than those derived from the objects of our other senses, the words expressive of those ideas belonging to vision make up the principal part of poetic language. That is, the Poet writes principally to the eye, the Prose-writer uses more abstracted terms." One means of achieving this end is the use of "Personifications and Allegories," because "These are other arts of bringing objects before the eye; or of expressing sentiments in the language of vision."[24]

Here is a passage which specifically claims that personification is a

23/Wordsworth's phrase, 24.11, 13.
24/*The Loves of the Plants* (3rd ed., London, 1791), pp. 48–49.

mark of poetical style which distinguishes poetry from prose. Wordsworth, looking for a general definition of the language which does
not use personifications, might well have been led to the use of its
terms, and so to the statement and solution of the equation given
above. This is further suggested by the phrasing of 1802: personifications "are utterly rejected as an ordinary device to elevate the style,
and raise it above prose" (44.30–31).

The second work concerned is the article, "Is Verse Essential to
Poetry?" which appeared in *The Monthly Magazine* for July 1796,
and which, as Miss Barstow showed,[25] Wordsworth almost certainly
knew. The drift of this paper is not the same as Wordsworth's: it
purports to show that the term *poetry* can reasonably be applied to
what we may, for convenience, call "poetic prose," and that it ought
not to be confined to works in verse. But some of its statements,
read without due regard to context, have a superficial relevance to
Wordsworth's argument:

"The character of poetry, which may seem most to require that it
be limited to verse, is its appropriate diction. It will be admitted, that
metaphorical language, being more impressive than general terms, is
best suited to poetry. That excited state of mind, which poetry supposes, naturally prompts a figurative style. But the language of fancy,
sentiment, and passion is not peculiar to verse. Whatever is the
natural and proper expression of any conception or feeling in metre
or rhyme, is its natural or proper expression in prose. All beyond
this is a departure from the true principles of taste. If the artificial
diction of modern poetry would be improper, on similar occasions, in
prose, it is equally improper in verse. In support of this opinion, the
appeal may be made, not only to the general sense of propriety, but
to those perfect models of fine writing, the Greek poets. The language of these great masters is always so consonant to nature, that,
thrown out of rhythm, it would become the proper expression of the

25/Barstow, pp. 120 ff. The article was written by one William Enfield: see
Arthur Beatty, *William Wordsworth: His Doctrine and Art* (2nd ed., Madison,
1927), p. 56, and Lewis Patton, "Coleridge and the 'Enquirer' Series," *R.E.S.*,
xvi (1940), 188–89. Wordsworth received the issue in question from James Losh:
see Moorman, *Early Years*, p. 309, and my review, *R.E.S.*, N.S., x (1959), 95–96.

same sentiment in prose. If modern poetry will seldom bear to be brought to the same taste,[26] it is because the taste of the moderns has been refined to a degree of fastidiousness, which leads them to prefer the meretricious ornaments of art, to the genuine simplicity of nature."[27]

It will be seen that, while the author recognizes that "the artificial diction of modern poetry" may be "improper," he yet concedes that poetry (in verse or prose) has a diction "appropriate" to itself. One may, he says, use the figurative language of passion[28] in prose as well as in verse; one does not require the "passport" (*P.L.B.*, p. 138) of metre in order to be justified in using it. One may, says Wordsworth, use the language of prose (undefined – except that it must be "well-written" – and hence to be interpreted in the broadest sense) in verse, presumably to express passion: a noticeably different proposition. The proposition as Wordsworth states it may be supported if care is taken to ignore the qualification always implied in the Enquirer's discussion: that the prose he has in mind is "metaphorical" and "figurative," in fact "poetic." Such prose, he says, is better without the "artificial diction of modern poetry." Wordsworth has already decided that "artificial diction" is improper in verse; the Enquirer's statement, read without due regard to context, appears to support the definition of the language of poetry as that of (any sort of "well-written") prose. Because of its "meretricious ornaments," modern poetry cannot be "thrown out of rhythm" and yet remain "the proper expression of the same sentiment in prose." It seems to follow that such poetry as Wordsworth's, which lacks "meretricious ornaments," could suffer such a change without damage, and that its language must be proper to prose. But of the Enquirer's qualification,

26/A misprint anticipating "taste" five words further on; Miss Barstow reasonably suggests "test."

27/*Monthly Magazine*, ii (1796), 455. Cf. Dennis, i.24:

"*Beaum[ont]*. Why, will you allow nothing to be said in Verse that may not be said in Prose too?

"*Freem[an]*. Yes, an Expression may be too florid, or too bold for Prose, and yet be very becoming of Verse. But every Expression that is false English in Prose, is barbarous and absurd in Verse too."

28/On the conventionality of this idea, see *P.L.B.*, Commentary, n. on 290 ff.

that the prose he envisages is to be "poetic," there is no sign in Wordsworth's discussion in the text of 1800.

In sum: the tendency of the two passages from Darwin and *The Monthly Magazine* is to suggest to a not too careful reader that the language of poetry differs from the language of prose in its use of "personifications," "artificial diction," and "meretricious ornaments"; since Wordsworth has decided that his poetry will not use these devices, it is an easy step for him to draw upon the terms of these discussions, and hence to arrive at a definition of the language of poetry based on the equation stated above.

To assess the validity of the solution is more difficult. It is true, as Wordsworth says, that some critics find and censure "prosaisms" in verse (23.9–12). They may, from at least one point of view, be justified. These lines from *The Prelude* of 1805, for instance, though possibly serviceable as part of a poem, do not seem to be poetry:[29]

> "Through those delightful pathways we advanc'd,
> Two days, and still in presence of the Lake,
> Which, winding up among the Alps, now chang'd
> Slowly its lovely countenance, and put on
> A sterner character. The second night,
> In eagerness, and by report misled
> Of those Italian clocks that speak the time
> In fashion different from ours, we rose
> By moonshine, doubting not that day was near."
>
> (VI.617–25)

This is prosaic, and, as Coleridge says of another poem, "justly blamable ... because the words ... would find their appropriate place in prose, but are not suitable to *metrical* composition."[30] But not wholly for this reason: also, perhaps rather, because "the *matter* ...

29/I use Coleridge's distinction, *Biog. Lit.*, ii.8–11.

30/*Biog. Lit.*, ii.60. The phrase "and the order of the words," here omitted, is inapplicable mainly because Wordsworth has distorted prose order *metri causa*. *Countenance* is perhaps vaguely "poetic," but not more so than *bosom*, which Wordsworth uses of a lake in prose and verse (Knight, ii.31, 37).

is contemptible" (30.18–19). What powerful feelings overflow here? Who can visualize, or who can suppose that the poet took due notice of, "delightful pathways" or the "lovely countenance" of an Italian lake? If this is not the jargon of the guide-book and the inarticulate English tourist, at any rate it is the language of prose, which here describes accurately neither the scene nor the traveller's reaction to it, but merely records the fact of travel or the fact that some Italian clocks may mislead the unwary.

By contrast, the famous description of the Simplon Pass (*Prel.*, VI.556–72) presents not only the natural spectacle but also what it did, and meant, to the poet's mind. The idea of eternity suddenly rendered intelligible in the "types and symbols" excites the poet's mind, producing a purposeful selection of imagery well adapted to illustrate the illuminating paradox of energy released and renewed so continuously that a certain "peace" is imposed on the scene: a notion epitomized in the bold figure, "The stationary blasts of water-falls." This too is "the language of prose," in so far as it contains no "artificial diction"; but the poet's excitement drives him to use metaphor which is neither conventionally poetic nor, probably, wholly suitable for prose. *The Monthly Magazine*'s Philo-Rhythmus perhaps illuminates: "Rhetorical prose, poetic prose, plain prose, and prose run mad, are all well understood by persons conversant with literature, nor does any confusion arise" (ii [1796], 533). The description of the Simplon Pass uses "the language of [poetic] prose," the account of Maggiore and Italian clocks uses "the language of [plain] prose"; and this is the difference between them which is felt and understood by most readers: a difference which can be detected, at the simplest level, from the presence in the one passage of trope and the sense of its justifying passion. In fact, "prose" and "the language of prose," terms which must have seemed to Wordsworth to offer the prospect of a solidly positive definition of the language of permanent appeal, are seen to be equivocal. But without further qualification they will probably be taken to mean "plain prose," and its appropriate "language," the object of which will, in general, be to convey "Matter of Fact, or Science" (47.fn.2; cf. 24.fn.15), and not poetry, the "overflow of powerful feelings."

A third case arises when we consider such a line as the admired "And never lifted up a single stone" (*Michael*, 466). Here too is "plain prose"; but the effect differs from that of the account of Maggiore. The difference lies in the fact recorded: the matter is not, in this case, "contemptible." The fact is significant and eloquent; it says more than itself. It says, without saying it in words, that Michael was broken, that a great spirit at times acknowledged defeat. The fact says this, and the line which records the fact must, in a sense, say it too. The line says it by oblique statement, almost by understatement. This sort of understatement, which records the fact without its implications, the pathetic without the pathos, the awful without the awe, is, perhaps, Wordsworth's most characteristic device of rhetoric. It is, perhaps, what he mainly meant by "the language of prose." It is the rhetoric of most of the lines of Gray's sonnet of which Wordsworth approves (23.29 ff.).[31] But it is a peculiarly dangerous form of rhetoric; for, once the fact recorded is seen to be insignificant, incapable of saying more than itself, the record ceases to be oblique statement and becomes direct statement, a prosaism, the language of "plain prose."

If, then, we grant Wordsworth's proposition that a conventional poetic diction is undesirable, because impermanent in its appeal, we may conclude that his solution to the equation stated above is valid. But as a critical doctrine, and even as a definition of Wordsworth's language, the equation is of small value. As a critical doctrine, because it merely repeats Wordsworth's postulate: it serves merely as a caveat against conventional poeticisms; as a definition of Wordsworth's language, because, again, it merely repeats his postulate: it

---

31/The lines use oblique statement since they consistently omit to mention the fact of death. The most impressive epitaph that Wordsworth ever met with was *"nothing more than the name of the Deceased with the date of birth and death, importing that it was an Infant which had been born one day and died the following" (Knight, ii.186). He may have learned the technique of reticence as much from the ballads as from "men" or "prose."

means no more than that his language avoids conventional poeticisms. It makes no positive statement on what the language of prose is; nor could it make any positive statement, because there is prose and prose, and because "the language of prose" is a term insufficiently precise to define any particular sort of prose or any basis common to all sorts. The language of prose is no more stable than the language of poetry. Within any age, it varies according to function; from age to age, it varies, as does the language of poetry, according to the taste of the time. Yet Wordsworth uses the phrase as if it denoted a definable essence of rhetoric, a stable idiom, "pure" like the passions and language of the rustic, a permanently normative mode of expression. It is not so; and, accordingly, in recognizing, in the three passages of Wordsworth's verse examined above, the presence of the language of prose, we have been engaged in recognizing, as the feature common to all three, the absence of conventional poeticisms. The equation is, in fact, in spite of its appearance, a negative doctrine and a negative definition.

iv   *The Impermanence of Language*

The negative and roundabout terms of the argument nevertheless hint at a conceivable and indeed a usable rhetoric, which seems to be exemplified in some poems of 1800 and thereabouts (such as *Michael* and some of the "Poems on the Naming of Places"), and which, like most others in English poetry, has its successes and failures. Apart from the question of its permanence, this language risks failure more often than some others. For success, as poets in the classical tradition, especially, well knew, depends upon the nice adjustment of style to subject-matter, and Wordsworth's theory allows the poet the minimum range of styles. This limitation seems inevitable when the theorist sets out to define, not styles congruous with various subject-matters, but one "language" which shall be the language of all poetry. In practice, Wordsworth's language is often "philosophical," removing obstacles of verbiage between the eye and the object, between the mind and the fact presented; but it tends to adopt the same monotone whether it is used, successfully, to present the significant fact with fine precision (Michael did not build the sheep-fold), or, unsuccessfully, to present the insignificant fact with cruel clarity (Italian clocks mislead; Alpine insects sting, *Prel.*, vi.642–43; a name is forgotten, *Prel.*, ix.483–84). Wordsworth is aware that he "sometimes ... may have written upon unworthy subjects" (29.7–9), though he evidently does not consider the possibility very real; yet, in view of the comparative inflexibility of his style, no poetry relies for its success so heavily upon its subject-matter as Wordsworth's.

But the language of *permanent* poetic appeal is not defined in positive terms by the Preface. It is improbable that it ever can be, or that the poetry of permanent appeal which Wordsworth sought to write can ever be written. For any class of words, any turns of expression, any "language" which the poet thinks capable of conveying what Wordsworth calls "excitement," will eventually come to be felt as stereotyped, stale, and impotent to convey excitement. Thus the twentieth century does not, on the whole, consider individual words or particular classes of words, regardless of context, as especially potent in poetry; yet Wordsworth, with the backing of associationist psychology, evidently considered that particular words could be so felt: "The end of Poetry is to produce excitement in coexistence with an overbalance of pleasure. ... But if the words by which this excitement is produced are in themselves powerful, ... there is some danger that the excitement may be carried beyond its proper bounds" (26.14–21).[32]

The passage appears to imply that, for Wordsworth, some individual words provoked powerful emotional responses, and that he expected these responses to be duplicated in his reader; yet, because such words were, to Wordsworth, the "prose" names of the things

32/Hartley thought that "the very words, *burn, wound, &c.* seem ... to excite ... a perception of the disagreeable kind" (Hartley, p. 50). See *P.L.B.*, Commentary, n. on 565–68, and cf. Burke, *On the Sublime and Beautiful*, Part v, in *Works*, Bohn ed., i (London, 1886), 169–81.

denoted, as well as provokers of poetic "excitement," he evidently expected that their "power" would be permanent. The result may be seen in Wordsworth's handling, in particular, of the vocabulary of emotion, analysed some years ago by Josephine Miles.[33] According to this theory, emotion named is emotion conveyed, and Wordsworth's "Oh pain it was To part" (*Prel.*, IX.726–27), for instance, ought to be as potent a leave-taking between lovers as, say, Shakespeare's picture of injurious Time with his robber's haste (*Troilus and Cressida*, IV. iv.42–48). We do not find it so; and in such a case Shakespeare's figure seems more likely to have permanent appeal than Wordsworth's language of prose. The adjective in Wordsworth's "delightful pathways," naming an emotion, was perhaps a "powerful" word to the poet; to us it is a colourless term of vague commendation. Clearly, such usages, typical, we may suppose, of "the language of prose," do not make for permanent appeal in the poetry which relies on them to convey excitement. The mere development of English vocabulary, recorded in historical dictionaries and elementary Histories of the Language, is sufficient to defeat Wordsworth's purpose. On the other hand, where "the language of prose" seems to be permanently powerful, as in that line from *Michael*, it may be surmised that the permanence arises, not so much because the line uses the language of prose, as because the language of prose is here capable of oblique statement; because the line is, in its context, as it were figurative, and continues to be felt as such.

Thus Wordsworth's hope of "a class of Poetry ... well adapted to interest mankind permanently" is unrealized in terms of his theory. For his poetry dates as much as any other poetry, and, while this is no particular censure of Wordsworth's poetry, the dating proves the theory untrue. In its *obiter dicta*, and especially in its psychological approach to metre, seemingly new at the time, the Preface of 1800 is more immediately successful. The main argument fails, not unnaturally, to prove an impossible thesis. Wordsworth is aware less of

---

33/*Wordsworth and the Vocabulary of Emotion* (Berkeley and Los Angeles, 1942).

the failure of his theory than of the possible failure of his practice (29.5–17); and his confidence in success both present ("were I convinced [that certain expressions] were faulty at present") and permanent ("and that they must necessarily continue to be so") is more obvious than his fear of failure. The poet's problem, which, from the nature of the case, he is unlikely to solve, is different: it is the probability that "expressions" which are satisfactory "at present," to the poet and perhaps to his contemporary audience, may become unsatisfactory in the future; ceasing to be felt as "powerful," or to produce "instant understanding," or both, and thus defying the poet's hope of permanently direct appeal.[34] Recognizing this, and the corollary that rhetorics other than Wordsworth's have been and will be acceptable, we do not share Wordsworth's confidence that he had discovered the essence of poetry, any more than we share Johnson's in Dryden's "poetical diction ... those happy combinations of words which distinguish poetry from prose" (*Lives*, i.420); and we attribute whatever permanence of appeal Wordsworth's poetry may have to reasons other than those advanced in the Preface. For language, even when not vulgar and mean, is yet among the works of man, enduring by growth and change; and that variety of it which shares the steady form of the ancient hills is usually reckoned to be dead.

34/Cf. W. H. Auden, "The Poetic Process," *The Listener*, liii (1955), 1110: "the poet had always to assume that the history of the language is at an end. ... This assumption is necessary but ... not always valid."

Two ✳ The Theory of Metre

In the Preface of 1800 Wordsworth's discussion of metre arises naturally from the equation of the language of poetry with the language of prose.[1] Seeing that he has laid himself open to a charge of inconsistency by admitting such an artificiality of language as metre, he sets about attempting to explain the inconsistency away.

Wordsworth's first arguments draw upon the same ideas as those which have been employed to defend his use of "the language of men" and "the language of prose": those concerning permanent and widespread appeal. Metre is useful to the poet in "heighten[ing] and improv[ing] the pleasure which co-exists with" passion (25.12–13), and its usefulness is proved by "the concurring testimony of ages" and by "the consent of all nations" (25.12, 25). These ideas recur, in unemphatic forms, during the discussion: "words metrically arranged will long continue to impart ... pleasure" (26.11–12); "verse will be read a hundred times where ... prose is read once" (28.21). But the argument shortly drifts away to more complex aspects of the subject.

The first of these is nevertheless connected with the starting-point of Wordsworth's argument on the possibility of permanent poetic appeal. It is commonly held, he has said, that metre is an "exponent or symbol" (17.17), a "symbol or promise" (64.34) of an "unusual language"; but the unusual language has varied from age to age

1/Difficulties in connection with the linking in the text of 1802 are discussed below, Chapter IV, sec. i; and see *P.L.B.*, Commentary, n. on 277 ff.

(17.17–22), and is therefore impermanent in its appeal. This view – that "Poets ... from the [mere] circumstance of their compositions being in metre, it is expected will employ a particular language" (text of 1802, 53.31–33) – is, Wordsworth affirms, false: his use of metre puts no such obligation on the poet. In the complex of elements which is the total effect of poetry, metre is seen by Wordsworth as a stable element, contributing a constant effect which is pleasurable: "the charm which ... is acknowledged to exist in metrical language" (25.25–26). The words used by the poet, the style he chooses to adopt, would with propriety be the same whether the writer chooses to use prose or verse (25.22–23, 67.29–31). The total effect of the composition will not, indeed, be the same whether the writer uses prose or verse, for metre is considered capable of adding "pleasure"; but "the difference can only lie in the superstructure" (115.7–8).[2]

The image implied in the sentence just quoted and by similar phraseology elsewhere – metre conceived as a (desirable) addition, almost by way of ornament, to a structure (of language) already serviceable in its own right – is replaced in the subsequent discussion by a conception of metre and of other elements of poetry as possessing a quality akin to the notion of *sign* in elementary mathematics; or, rather, of these elements as connected with, or producing, emotional effects which may be so conceived. Such a notion allows Wordsworth to describe the total effect of poetry as analogous to the result of adding the various terms in a complex expression, some of which are opposite in sign to others.[3] The notion is similar to, and may have been derived from, Corollary 9 to Hartley's Seventh Proposition, in which the ideas of "sensible pleasures" and "sensible pains" are supposed to cancel one another out when in mutual asso-

2/See *P.L.B.*, n. on 277 ff., for similar phrases. The proposition is strongly denied by Coleridge (*Biog. Lit.*, ii.50 ff.), who argues for an interaction between language and metre, though not, to be sure, for the use of a conventional diction: "I write in metre, because I am about to use a language different from that of prose" (p. 53), namely, the figurative language of passion. Shawcross's note on this passage seems to attribute to Coleridge just that proposition of Wordsworth's which Coleridge is engaged in denying.

3/An instance of Wordsworth's interest in contrarieties; see Chapter I, sec. i, n. 3, above.

ciation, leaving as a net result what Wordsworth calls "an over-balance of pleasure" (28.6).[4]

This notion begins to appear when Wordsworth makes a final effort to answer objections saying that "more will be lost from the shock which will be ... given to the Reader's associations [by a failure to use 'artificial distinctions of style'] than will be counterbalanced by any pleasure which he can derive from the general power of numbers" (25.31–33). Some poems (traditional ballads?) which deal with "more humble subjects, and in a more naked and simple style" than *Lyrical Ballads*, "have continued to give pleasure from generation to generation" (26.1–4).[5] Such poems, runs the implication, since their ability to please by reason of subject-matter and style is necessarily small, must owe much of their appeal to the use of metre: metre is the major factor making up the "overbalance of pleasure" which the poems are said to achieve.

More specifically, the *regularity* of metre is conceived as a quality of (say) positive sign which may "temper and restrain" the irregularity (conceived as of negative sign) of "excitement," an "excited state" of mind, or "passion"; metre has in it a quality of "normality" which, in a measure, cancels the "unusual and irregular state of the mind" (26.16) which poetry sets out to produce; or, rather, cancels any undesirable excess of "unusualness" and "irregularity." Such a quality appears to be attributed to metre on two grounds: of its own nature, it is "something regular" (26.22), and, by association, it is connected with "a less excited state" (26.23).[6] Similarly, in the

4/Hartley (p. 27) unconvincingly explains that the "overbalance" is in practice pleasurable (though, presumably, in theory it might be painful) because "our sensible pleasures are far more numerous than our sensible pains; and tho' the pains be, in general, greater than the pleasures, yet the sum total of these seems to be greater than that of those; whence the remainder, after the destruction of the pains by the opposite and equal pleasures, will be pure pleasure." So Wordsworth, in general terms, alleges that man "in his ordinary life" finds "every where objects that immediately excite in him sympathies which, from the necessities of his nature, are accompanied by an overbalance of enjoyment" (51.24–31); and here, in particular, he assumes that poetry (at any rate successful poetry) will achieve "an overbalance of pleasure."

5/That is, have achieved permanent poetic appeal.

6/How it acquires such associations, and, especially, how it acquires

complex effect of poetry metre is a positive factor of *pleasure* which tends to cancel out the excessive pain which may be produced by powerful descriptions of passion (26.18–20, 26.25–32, 28.6–13).

Again, where the poetry is not characterized by "passion," where the poetical complex does not contain the "negative" terms indicated above, then metre will be the main factor contributing to the reader's pleasure. This is the state of affairs in "lighter compositions" (28.14), or when the poetry deals with "the plainest common sense," as in the case of Pope (28.23).

Some light is cast on this curious and somewhat obscure description of the workings of metre by two passages inserted into the argument in the text of 1802: 56.23–34 and 58.19–21. They deal with a characteristic which, in a measure, involves and generalizes the two conceptions, regularity and pleasure, indicated above: the artificiality of metre, its "unnaturalness" or "unreality." The language which Wordsworth proposes to use in his verse is characterized by its naturalness or "reality"; hence (presumably by a mode of operation similar to the Hartleian arithmetic described above), "the tendency of metre [is] to divest language in a certain degree of its reality, and thus to throw a sort of half consciousness of unsubstantial existence over the whole composition" (56.25–27); its tendency is to impart to the reader "an indistinct perception perpetually renewed of language closely resembling that of real life, and yet, in the circumstance of metre, differing from it so widely" (58.19–21). Metrical language, merely because it is metrical while a wholly "natural" language is not, assures the reader that he has, after all, to do with a work of art; that the passions of which he reads are not "real," though the quasi-natural language of passion might have led him to suppose that they were; in short, metre assures the reader that he is reading poetry and not a report of real life. This is not to say that the passions will not be felt; but they will not be felt as totally painful.

Such a notion is probably intelligible and even familiar to the modern reader. It seems similar to Johnson's account of the effective

associations with an "unexcited" state of mind (26.23; in the text of 1800 only), are not made clear; see *P.L.B.*, Commentary, n. on 568–80.

realism of drama which springs from his exposure of the fallacy of the unities. "The delight of tragedy proceeds from our consciousness of fiction; if we thought murders and treasons real, they would please no more. Imitations produce pain or pleasure, not because they are mistaken for realities, but because they bring realities to mind."[7] Wordsworth is saying that, in the poetry which deals with passion, metre ensures that the reader does not mistake the poet's imitation for reality; or, from the Coleridgean point of view, metre is a means of ensuring that poetry is perceived as an imitation and not as a copy.

At first sight it might seem that Wordsworth has blundered in dissociating such an effect of metre from a similar effect which might be produced by an artificial diction.[8] If the artificiality of metre produces such an effect, why should not the effect be produced or enhanced by the artificiality of poetic diction? The answer lies in the need for contrast: the realism of "the language of men" or "the language of prose" needs to be offset by the artificiality of metre, and vice versa. Once the two elements "language" and "metre" are seen both to be artificial, the contrast will disappear together with the connection of the one element with "nature" and "real life." The contrast can be maintained only if the poet uses such a language as Wordsworth endeavours to define earlier in the Preface, and if he then "superadds" to it the artificiality of metre. The total effect of the poem is defined by the aesthetic principle[9] "the pleasure which the mind derives from the perception of similitude in dissimilitude"

7/Raleigh, p. 28. Closer to Wordsworth is Priestley, *Oratory*, p. 264: "the strong sensations, excited by scenes of terror and compassion [in tragedy], are so much diminished by a conviction of their being only imaginary, as to fall within the limits of pleasure: since pleasure hath been defined to consist of sensations moderately vigorous, and pain of sensations exceeding that degree." Metre is a means towards this conviction: "several circumstances, which every moment demonstrate the scene to be no reality, have a good effect. Otherwise *prose* would be universally more agreeable than *verse*, because no person ever speaks seriously in verse" (p. 266). See *P.L.B.*, Commentary, n. on 607.

8/Cf. Shawcross in *Biog. Lit.*, ii.281; Garrod, p. 156; and a review of the *Poems* of 1807 in *Annual Review and History of Literature*, vi (1807), in Smith, p. 87. To the contrary, *C.L.*, ii.814 (19 July 1802): "wild Ducks *shaping* their rapid flight in forms always regular (a still better image of Verse)."

9/When Wordsworth first introduces this idea, he seems to be thinking mainly of the effects which may be produced by the varying of the metrical form

(27.14–15). Wordsworth's language is in itself "similar" to that of real life, but in that it is metrical it is "dissimilar." The use of a language widely different from that of real life would render the principle inapplicable.

Less satisfactory than Wordsworth's account of the regularizing effects of metre is his claim that metre can, on occasion, "impart passion to the words" (26.32–27.6).[10] For, in terms of the earlier discussion, it would seem that, if the usual effect of metre is to tone down, to regularize, and to discipline, the only result in the case envisaged will be to flatten even further the already flat effect of "words ... incommensurate with the passion, and inadequate to raise the Reader to a height of desirable excitement" (26.33–35). If, again, the usual effect of metre is to impart a positive element of pleasure, this may, no doubt, be achieved but seems to have no particular bearing on the subject of "passion." For passion in the earlier discussion is, on the whole, associated with pain; yet here Wordsworth seems to find "something which will greatly contribute to impart passion to the words" in "the feelings of pleasure which the Reader has been accustomed to connect with metre in general." Moreover, part of the regularizing effect of metre as discussed earlier was said to arise from a "feeling [of pleasure? (cf. 27.2, 57.10)] not strictly and necessarily connected with the passion" (56.22–23). The best that can be made of the theory as stated thus far would seem to be that, in the case envisaged, metre will contribute to the total effect "pleasure" or "pleasurable excitement."

We may come a little closer to Wordsworth's intention by observ-

against an established metrical norm. Cf. Hartley, pp. 262–63: "That the versification has of itself a considerable influence, may be seen by putting good poetical passages into the order of prose. And it may be accounted for from what has been already observed of uniformity and variety, from the smoothness and facility with which verses run over the tongue, from the frequent coincidence of the end of the sentence, and that of the verse, at the same time that this rule is violated at proper intervals in all varieties, lest the ear should be tired with too much sameness." Wordsworth may, however, intend a wider application; certainly the principle is implied in 58.19–21, cited above.

10/Similarly, metre enables Pope not only to make "the plainest common sense interesting," but also "frequently to invest it with the appearance of passion" (28.23–24).

ing, first, the phrase "the feeling, whether chearful or melancholy, which [the reader] has been accustomed to connect with that particular movement of metre," and, secondly, Wordsworth's account of the effect he expected from the metre of *The Thorn*. Consideration of these passages will show that the seeming confusion of thought arises, in part at least, from an insufficiently marked shift of emphasis: a shift from a discussion of the effects of metre in general to one of the effects of particular sorts of metre. Particular sorts of metre may, it appears, achieve particular effects by association. The poet who deals with a "chearful" passion and whose language is "incommensurate" with that passion will, if he knows his business, use a metre with "chearful" associations; and he will proceed similarly, *mutatis mutandis*, if he deals with a "melancholy" passion.[11] The cheerful or melancholy associations, Wordsworth appears to claim, will attach themselves to the words; the pleasurable associations of metre *qua* metre will, presumably, attach themselves to the whole composition in accordance with the previous discussion; thus the mixture of passion, or excitement, and pleasure which is typical of successful poetry will, in a measure, be achieved.[12]

In his note on *The Thorn*, Wordsworth admits that, for the sake of dramatic propriety ("while I adhered to the style in which such persons describe"), he has used language "incommensurate with the passion, and inadequate to raise the Reader to a height of desirable excitement." In order to "impart passion to the words," Wordsworth has used a "Lyrical and rapid Metre," so that the poem will "appear to move quickly," though in fact, and with dramatic propriety, it moves slowly.

Wordsworth appears to mean that the "rapidity" of the metre will

11/"Chearful" is not, of course, a mere synonym for "pleasurable," and a "melancholy" metre is quite capable of giving "pleasure."

12/The oddness of the discussion is increased by the parenthesis "what it must be allowed will much more frequently happen" (26.32–33); whence it appears that, from the point of view of language, most poems are failures, and struggle to a kind of half-success only with the aid of metre. The number of poems from which the association of cheerfulness or melancholy can be developed must be small. The remark probably anticipates the observations on the general inadequacy of the poet's language which were added in 1802.

carry associations of excited and urgent utterance, which will be attached to the words of the poem even though these "move slowly," that is, fail to come to the point of the story and are repetitious (again with dramatic propriety) and longwinded. Hence the "words, which in [the] minds [of persons such as the imaginary Captain] are impregnated with passion," will "convey passion to Readers who are not accustomed to sympathize with men feeling in that manner or using such language" (13.6–15).[13]

It is, no doubt, true that excited speech is often rapid; as the rapid rhythm of the *scherzo* of the average symphony tends to be more exciting, or to express excitement more obviously, than the slower movement of *largo* or *andante*. It seems likely, then, that Wordsworth succeeds in his aim if his metre does, in fact, appeal to the reader as "rapid." The inevitability of such an appeal is taken for granted in the note; but not necessarily with justification, for the speed at which poetry is read is not governed by any actual or implied metronome markings. In spite of these difficulties, it is probable that many readers do, in fact, find the metre rapid. In regular English iambics, a line shorter than pentameter tends, perhaps, to be felt as "short," hence as "quickly completed," and hence, again, as "rapid." Wordsworth's four-stress line, with two three-stress lines to the stanza, meets this requirement. A fairly frequent caesural break in the middle of the four-stress line produces a suggestion of yet shorter lines ("She was with child, and she was mad"; "Her looks were calm, her senses clear"). The unrhymed lines perhaps keep the reader's attention moving forward in search of rhymes which are expected but do not occur.[14] On the whole, Wordsworth's theory seems here to have had a fairly successful application.[15]

13/Garrod's attempt (p. 166) to interpret this note in the sense of the tempering of painful passions seems contrary to the natural interpretation both of the note and of the obviously parallel passage in the Preface, 27.5–6, with its unequivocal phrase "impart passion to the words."

14/Wordsworth began the poem in octosyllabic couplets (*P.W.*, ii.240, textual n. to ll.1–22), which jar to a stop as each is completed; the present stanza-form is certainly an improvement towards maintaining the movement of the poem.

15/We are not here directly concerned with the ultimate success or failure of *The Thorn*. The sense of failure which it gives to many readers probably arises

Elsewhere, no such effects are discernible. The prosy parts of Wordsworth's blank verse, especially, appear to gain no advantage from being in metre;[16] if anything, the verse-form, associated in the minds of most readers with the grandeur of Milton, merely draws attention to the poverty of the matter, by raising expectations of Miltonic matter and thought which never arrive.[17] Combined with quasi-Miltonic language, it may produce the effects aimed at by parodists like John Philips, when wit, humour, or mere lightness of touch does not seem to be part of Wordsworth's intention. The regularity of the metre achieves only a sense of control when there is nothing in the matter which needs controlling. Any "pleasure" which the reader feels at the outset is apt to be replaced eventually by the recurrence of the awkward question: "Why have you written in verse?" And the "indistinct perception ... of language closely resembling that of real life, and yet, in the circumstance of metre, differing from it so widely," is apt to provoke, not a "complex feeling of delight," but a "sense of oddity and strangeness"[18] at the difference thus arbitrarily imposed by the poet when nothing seems to justify it. In short, Wordsworth's practice sometimes suggests that he thought any prose language improved by "fitting [it] to metrical arrangement" (15.3–16.1), even when the absence of passionate language was due, not to the inadequacy of the language to the passion, but to the absence of passion itself. Such a case is not, indeed, envisaged in the theory here discussed; but if it occurs, and if Wordsworth's theory truly describes the regularizing, pleasurable, and associational effects of metre, the regrettable results indicated above seem bound to follow.

from a sense of divided interest, between the portrayal of the supposed narrator and the story of Martha Ray. See pp. 91–92 below.

16/Consider, for instance, *Prel.*, vi.617–25, cited above, p. 20; or the versified account of the passions and language of rustics in *Exc.*, i. 341 ff., compared with the prose of the Preface.

17/Such an association might be blunted for a contemporary reader familiar with the traditional eighteenth-century philosophical poem in blank verse. On the varying levels of the style in *The Prelude*, see Herbert Lindenberger, *On Wordsworth's Prelude* (Princeton, 1963), Chapter i.

18/*Biog. Lit.*, ii.54, on the rhymes in *The Sailor's Mother*.

Wordsworth's theory of metre is, as he admits (27.8 ff.), incomplete. He says nothing of the art of poets such as Spenser and Milton in employing rhythms unusual in their metrical context to emphasize the meaning of words; or of the skill of such as Shakespeare and Donne in adapting the rhythms of verse to those of colloquial speech. Wordsworth is not lacking in such skills, but his emphases are too often crudely indicated by the italics of written prose. Yet he probes, more deeply than any considerable earlier critics,[19] into the psychological bases of the effect of ordinary metrical patterns, and makes some valuable discoveries about them. He could hardly have foreseen, any more than he foresaw that the language he called "prose" would not be as permanent in its appeal as he thought, that in a century or so many poets would, as often as not, reject these patterns as being unsuitable to what they had to say.

19/A hint of Wordsworth's theories is to be seen in Dennis, i.364–65: "great Passions naturally threw [the ancient Greeks] upon Harmony and figurative Language, as they must of necessity do any Poet, as long as he continues Master of them. Which is known by Experience to all who are Poets; for never any one, while he was wrapt with Enthusiasm, or with ordinary Passion, wanted either Words or Harmony; and therefore Poetry is more harmonious than Prose, because it is more pathetick. ... And in Poetry, they who write with a great deal of Passion, are generally very harmonious. ... At the same time 'tis a little odd to consider, that Passion, which disturbs the Soul, should occasion it to produce Harmony, which seems to imply the Order and Composure of it. Whether this proceeds from the secret Effort that the Soul makes to compose it self, or whatever the Cause is, the Effect is certain. But as Passion, which is the Disorder of the Soul, produces Harmony, which is Agreement; so Harmony, which is Concord, augments and propagates Passion, which is Discord. ... Numbers are proper to move Passion, and for that reason are inseparable from Poetry, which has no other design." Again, "Harmony may be said to be both the Father and the Child of Passion; 'tis produced by it, and begets it; and the more pathetick any Discourse is, the more harmonious it must of Necessity be" (i.376). Harmony to Dennis means, or includes, metrical form: four elements of it are "Number, Measure, Cadence, and Rime" (ibid.). We may have here an elementary statement of Wordsworth's views on metre both as a tempering agent and as a generator of passion.

Three ✳ "The Spontaneous Overflow of Powerful Feelings"

Wordsworth's proposal to base his subject-matter on the behaviour of a particular social class to which he himself does not belong, and to use or imitate the language of this class which is not his own language, implies a theory of poetry based on the concept of "imitation."[1] The subject indicated by the heading of the present chapter is considered by Wordsworth in two brief and obscure passages in the text of 1800 (19.15–33 and 27.27–28.6) which have no marked relevance to the generally mimetic theory of that text; but it requires discussion here since it suggests a theory of poetry congruous with that advanced in 1802, and since it appears to look forward to Wordsworth's later view of the Imagination which is hardly touched upon in the Preface to *Lyrical Ballads*.

1 *"Feelings Connected with Important Subjects"*

Wordsworth distinguishes his poems in *Lyrical Ballads* from certain contemporary work by claiming that "each of them has a worthy *purpose*" (19.9–10). He hastens to add that he did not always begin "to write with a distinct purpose formally conceived; but I believe

---

1/See Abrams, pp. 8–14. Except in discussing the specific Coleridgean distinction between imitation and copy, I adopt Professor Abrams' usage, in which "imitation" and related terms correspond rather to Coleridge's conception of copy than to his conception of imitation.

that my habits of meditation have so formed[2] my feelings, as that my descriptions of such objects as strongly excite those feelings, will be found to carry along with them a purpose" (19.10–14). Feelings "strongly excited" are those "powerful feelings" which may overflow as poetry;[3] whence it appears that only such "objects" as may be connected with "a worthy *purpose*" are competent to excite in the poet feelings sufficiently strong to serve as the basis of poetry. Mere strength of feelings, the feelings of a man "possessed of more than usual organic sensibility," are not a sufficient basis for poetry; they must be modified by "long and deep" thought (19.14–20).

The purpose at which Wordsworth aims is subsequently stated: it is "to illustrate the manner in which our feelings and ideas are associated in a state of excitement ... to follow the fluxes and refluxes of the mind when agitated by the great and simple affections of our nature" (19.36–20.2). It is, in fact (as appears more clearly from the examples given in 20.6 ff.), to define "general truth," the norm of human emotional behaviour,[4] and to show that particular incidents are congruous with it. The obscure passage 19.20–33, which is evidently intended to amplify 19.10–14, is meant to show how mental habits are formed in the poet such that, when his feelings have been "strongly excited," they have *ipso facto* been excited by something which has inevitable connections with general truth. We shall examine the passage in accordance with this general intention.

A preliminary difficulty arises from an ambiguity in Wordsworth's use of the word *feeling* and its plural. In 19.13, feelings are "excited": they are regarded, therefore, as faculties, analogous to the physical senses, which respond to stimulus from without – from the "objects"

2/This word is represented by "prompted and regulated" in the texts of 1836-50. "Formed" means "determined the shape of," or, without the metaphor, "determined the nature of." In the revised reading, "prompted" means, presumably, "stimulated" (as from repose) to receive the "excitement" of "objects"; "regulated" means, perhaps, "determined the intensity of," with relation to some scale of values, as a clock is regulated by making it work faster or slower in accordance with a standard of time.

3/The implications of this view of the origin of poetry are discussed in Chapter IV below.

4/See Chapter IV, secs. vi and vii, below.

of 19.13.[5] Similarly, in the second *Essay upon Epitaphs*, feelings are "recipient ... powers" (114.9–10). We shall indicate this sense in the discussion below by writing "[1]feelings." At 19.20, however, we hear of "influxes of feeling," as if feeling were a stimulating agent entering the mind; this sense we shall indicate by writing "[2]feelings."[6] An influx of [2]feeling thus causes, or is the same as, excitement of [1]feelings. The "feelings" of 19.16 hover between these two senses: for *overflow* may be used of that ([2]feeling) which overflows its container (the poet? or his [1]feelings?), or the container itself ([1]feelings), which cannot contain all that is put into it. The sense intended in 19.25 cannot be determined immediately.

With these distinctions in mind, we may attempt to detect the processes described in 19.20 ff. The first two are easily seen:

(1) In the mind are "thoughts" which represent past influxes of [2]feelings, that is, past cases of excitement of [1]feelings.

(2) Contemplation of the relation of these thoughts one to another produces knowledge of what is important. This seems to be the exercise of what the Preface of 1815 calls "Reflection, – which makes the Poet acquainted with the value of actions, images, thoughts, and feelings; and assists the sensibility in perceiving their connection with each other" (141.1–4).[7]

In less Wordsworthian terms, these two stages may, perhaps, be

5/Not necessarily material objects: see *P.L.B.*, Commentary, n. on 100–1; Zall, 18.fn.7.

6/This ambiguity is probably inherent. My pen *feels* hard, but my fingers *feel* its hardness. The indifferent use of the same verb with either percept or percipient as nominative reflects the difficulty in Wordsworth's use of *feeling* here.

7/Presumably the process also enables us to discover what is unimportant; but the subsequent fate of thoughts and feelings connected with the unimportant is not adequately described. The clause "feelings connected with important subjects will be nourished" (19.25) might imply that other feelings will perish of starvation; the later reading, "our feelings will be connected with important subjects" (42.17–18), is vaguer. Cf. *H.C.R.*, p. 166: "Wordsworth, in answer to the common reproach that his sensibility is excited by objects which produce no effect in others, admits the fact and is proud of it. He says that he cannot be accused of being insensible to the real concerns of life. He does not waste his feelings on unworthy objects."

summed up as the evaluation of past emotional experiences by a process of introspection which works upon the memory of the experiences.

At this point, the imprecision of Wordsworth's account becomes critical. Thus: (*a*) "this act" (19.24) may mean (i) "contemplating" (19.22), (ii) "contemplating [thoughts]" (19.22–23), (iii) "discover-[ing] what is ... important" (19.23–24), or (iv) the complex act denoted by the second and third of these. (*b*) The word "feelings" (19.25) may mean "past ²feelings" (represented, now, by thoughts), "present ²feelings" ("continued influxes of feeling"), or "¹feelings" ("recipient ... powers"), to which a definition in terms of time is irrelevant. (*c*) In the phrase "feelings connected with important subjects," the intended emphasis may lie on (i) *feelings* (rather than thoughts), or on (ii) *important* (rather than trivial).

From this confusion no certainty can emerge, but if we have regard to the general intention which is suggested by 19.10–14, the following interpretation may be offered: Contemplation of thoughts is a means of recognizing that certain past ²feelings arose from important subjects, or of recognizing the importance of the subjects from which certain past ²feelings arose. On the basis of a sufficient number of instances, recognition of the importance of these subjects prompts the poet to encourage such ²feelings as have, in the past, been connected with important subjects, that is, prompts his ¹feelings to react strongly to such stimuli as have produced such ²feelings in the past.[8] Moreover, the repeated recognition of this connection between such feelings and subjects gives the poet such confidence in the inevitable, or usual,[9] connection between his powerful feelings and important

8/The reading of 1802, "our feelings will be connected with important subjects," may be construed: On the basis of a sufficient number of instances, recognition of the importance of these subjects, and of the connection between powerful past ²feelings and important subjects, suggests to the poet that any such ²feelings to which he may be exposed on any particular occasion may likewise be connected with important subjects.

9/At 29.5–9 Wordsworth concedes that his "associations must have sometimes been particular instead of general," so that the connection may not always be inevitable.

subjects that he may take for granted that on any particular occasion the connection does indeed exist,[10] and that consequently his feelings, if on any particular occasion they are powerful, are a suitable basis for an important poem.

Thus far of the poet. The reader is evidently supposed to follow a path parallel to the poet's: to have his ¹feelings excited by the poet's description of "objects" and by his utterance of "sentiments";[11] and he will, presumably, arrive at a sense of the "importance" of the subject with which these ²feelings are connected; especially "if he be in a healthful state of association" (19.31), that is, if his associative trains are normal and similar to the poet's.[12]

What standard of "importance" Wordsworth has in mind is not made clear in this passage, except in so far as it is the "general truth" indicated in 20.1 ff., and expounded more fully in the additions of 1802. Elsewhere, there are suggestions of moral value involved in the perception of general truth in particular instances such as poems may record. Such seems to be the implication of 48.15 and 48.25–26 ("moral feelings ... corrected and purified" by the right-minded experience of art);[13] of some lines in MS. W of *The Prelude* (*Prel.*, p. 621): the poet

> "is one whose habits must have needs
> Been such as shall have fitted him no less
> For moral greatness;"

and especially of Wordsworth's letter to John Wilson:

"a great Poet ought ... to *rectify* men's feelings, ... to render their feelings *more sane, pure, and permanent.* ... It is not enough for me

---

10/From the imaginative life arises "Emotion ... Most worthy then of trust when most intense" (*Prel.*, XIII.115–16). The wider application of this principle seems to be questioned in the *Ode to Duty.*

11/"Every thought prompted by passion, is termed a *sentiment,*" says Lord Kames, *Elements of Criticism* (5th ed., Edinburgh, 1774), i. 451.

12/This is perhaps the view stated in 1815: "As the pathetic participates of an *animal* sensation, it might seem – that, if the springs of this emotion are genuine, all men, possessed of competent knowledge of the facts and circumstances, would be instantaneously affected" (185.1–4). See pp. 215 ff.

13/See *P.L.B.*, Commentary, n. on 302.

as a Poet, to delineate merely such feelings as all men *do* sympathise with; but it is also highly desirable to add to these others, such as all men *may* sympathise with, and such as there is reason to believe they would be *better and more moral* beings if they did sympathise with." (72.16–19, 74.33–75.4)[14]

The poet, we gather from such passages, is a moral being,[15] he is morally right in perceiving the general truth of human conduct, and he aims to improve the moral standards of his readers by inducing them to perceive general truth also.

ii "*Emotion Recollected in Tranquillity*"

Wordsworth's observations on this subject (27.27–28.6) occur as an *obiter dictum* in his account of the pleasurable effects of metre. The stages of the process of composition which he indicates may be thus defined:

(1) A primary emotion, presumably felt on some particular occasion.

(2) A recollection of it "in tranquillity": the poet remembers that on such and such an occasion he felt such and such an emotion.

(3) A metamorphosis of the state of tranquil recollection to a state of actual emotion. The secondary emotion thus arising appears "gradually"; it is "similar [kindred 1802] to" the primary emotion of 1.

(4) "In this mood successful composition generally begins."

(5a) Composition proceeds "in a mood similar to" that of 4.

(5b) In the mood of 5a, "the emotion ... , from various causes is qualified by various pleasures."

Of these, 1–3 seem familiar enough in common experience: recollection of a personal loss recreates the attendant sorrow; recollection

14/My italics except in "*do*" and "*may*."
15/See especially the identification of literature with morals in the second *Essay upon Epitaphs* (113.19–114.12).

of an insult recreates the consequent anger. Difficulties arise in stages 4 and 5. A distinction seems to be intended between the mood relevant to beginning a poem and the mood relevant to proceeding with it. If no distinction were intended, we should expect some such phrasing as: "In this mood successful composition begins and is carried on," or merely: "In this mood successful composition is carried on." We need to know, if possible, the nature of the distinction. It is to be found, if anywhere, in stage 5b: stage 5 differs from stage 4 in that, at stage 5, "the emotion [of stage 4] ... is qualified by various pleasures [which are not present at stage 4 itself],"[16] and which, perhaps *a fortiori*, are not present at stage 1. If this interpretation is correct, the substitution of *kindred* for *similar* in 1802 is perhaps intended to denote a closer relation between the moods of stages 1, 3, and 4 than between the moods of stages 4 and 5, and, again *a fortiori*, than between the moods of stages 1 and 5.

What are the "various pleasures" by which the recollected emotion is qualified? They presumably include, in some measure, those which Wordsworth expects the reader to feel from the presence of metre in a poem (28.6–13). Nevertheless the pleasures arising from metrical form seem to be attributed to the reader rather than to the poet, and to be conceived as in the nature of a compensation offered to the reader for pleasures which the poet feels but which, from the nature of things, the reader cannot feel. We must look elsewhere for an account of pleasures specifically the poet's.[17]

16/These particular pleasures are evidently not present even if the emotion of stages 1 and 4 should happen to be a "pleasant" one: they are relevant to the act of composition rather than to the emotion.

17/In a passage dated (?) 1808, Coleridge discusses "that pleasurable emotion ... which arises in the poet himself in the act of composition." He reaches the conclusion that it is "that sort of pleasurable emotion, which the exertion of all our faculties gives in a certain degree; but which can only be felt in perfection under the full play of those powers of mind, which are spontaneous rather than voluntary, and in which the effort required bears no proportion to the activity enjoyed" (*S.C.*, i.147–48). The "faculties" concerned are "a more than ordinary sympathy ... a more than common sensibility [and] a more than ordinary activity of the mind in respect of the fancy and the imagination" (i.147). This account is not very lucid, but is worth recording, since it begins with what look like remi-

A fairly late sonnet draws attention to the poet's satisfaction in "the sense of difficulty overcome" (28.7), not in connection with metrical language, but with the finding of the *mot juste*:

> "How oft the malice of one luckless word
> Pursues the Enthusiast to the social board,
> Haunts him belated on the silent plains!
> Yet he repines not, if his thought stand clear,
> At last, of hindrance and obscurity."[18]

The poet finds pleasure merely in achieving a successful "incarnation of the thought" (125.27).[19] Here, evidently, is a pleasure which is particularly attributable to the poet in the act of composition: the reader may find pleasure in the *mot juste*, but he cannot know the pleasure which arises from its achievement after, perhaps, many unsuccessful efforts towards it.

In Wordsworth's conception of language as "an incarnation of the

niscences of Wordsworth's antithesis of poetry and science (24. fn.15), and since the faculties just cited resemble the endowments of the poet as Wordsworth gives them in the Preface of 1802 (48.29 ff.). Clearer is *Biog. Lit.*, ii.15, of Shakespeare, in *Venus and Adonis*, "himself meanwhile unparticipating in the passions, and actuated only by that pleasureable excitement, which had resulted from the energetic fervor of his own spirit in so vividly exhibiting, what it had so accurately and profoundly contemplated." Similar is Gerard, *Taste*, p. 3: "We have a pleasant sensation, whenever the mind is in a lively and elevated temper. It attains this temper, when it is forced to exert its activity, and put forth its strength, in order to surmount any difficulty: and if its efforts prove successful, consciousness of the success inspires new joy"; and so Gerard, *Genius*, p. 67. Coleridge's "himself meanwhile unparticipating in the passions," suggesting that the poet has progressed from the feeling of an emotion to the understanding of it, seems to run counter to Wordsworth's "emotion ... does itself actually exist in the mind," but other Coleridgean accounts do not; for instance, *Biog. Lit.*, i.59: "the union of deep feeling with profound thought"; *C.L.*, ii.812: "every phrase, every metaphor, every personification, should have it's justifying cause in some *passion* either of the Poet's mind, or of the Characters described by the poet." See also n.23 below.

18/*Misc. Son.*, ii.xix; *P.W.*, iii.29–30. Cf. Landor's "Verses Why Burnt," in *Works*, ed. Welby and Wheeler, xv (London, 1935), 234: "How many verses have I thrown Into the fire because the one Peculiar word, the wanted most, Was irrecoverably lost."

19/Cf. 125.8–11: "those expressions which are ... what the body is to the soul, *themselves a constituent part and power or function in the thought*" (my italics).

thought" we may find ground for an expansion of our ideas on the poet's pleasures. Such a metaphor implies that the "thought" does not achieve a wholly intelligible mode of existence until it is embodied in its appropriate language; until the poet, as the phrase goes, "knows what he wants to say." To discover "what he wants to say," and how he knows it, we must recall the earlier discussion of "the spontaneous overflow of powerful feelings" (19.10–33). From this passage it appeared that the "powerful feelings" of a poet "possessed of more than usual organic sensibility" are subjected to an automatic process of evaluation. The poet's habits of mind are, indeed, such that his feelings are powerful only when connected with "important subjects," in particular with "the great and simple affections of our nature" (20.2), with "general truth," the norm of human behaviour. We are justified, therefore, in inferring that the emotion which is recollected in tranquillity is, in some sense, already evaluated, already known to be "connected with important subjects."

The qualification "in some sense" is needed because Wordsworth says that he did not always begin to write a poem "with a distinct purpose formally conceived" (19.11); but it is clear that, unless the emotion has been at least subconsciously recognized as relevant to an "important subject," Wordsworth would not, in terms of this discussion, have been concerned to make a poem from it. Since, however, he was, obviously, aware of the "purpose" of a poem when he had written it, and therefore of the importance of the subject with which the poem deals, it seems clear that the writing of a poem must make explicit to the poet the importance of the subject, at the beginning of the composition perhaps only dimly sensed.[20]

Our conception of the composition of a typical Wordsworthian poem may thus be amplified somewhat as follows: The poet's feelings are excited on some particular occasion by some external source. *Ex hypothesi*, the source has some connection, perhaps latent, with an "important subject": were it not so, the poet's feelings would not be excited, at any rate sufficiently "powerfully" to produce, eventually,

20/For similar accounts by other poets and critics, see sec. iii below.

a "spontaneous overflow of powerful feelings." At some later stage, the emotion is "recollected in tranquillity"; in the interval, the emotion has been evaluated, consciously or otherwise, as "important," that is, "connected with important subjects."[21] The mood of tranquillity is replaced by a re-creation of the primary emotion;[22] this, it would appear, provides the impetus to composition. The composition once under way, the poet appears to be in the position of at once feeling the emotion and perceiving (or discovering) its significance.[23]

From several points of view not specifically mentioned by Wordsworth in this passage, such a state of mind might be described as pleasurable. It is probable that any writer who deals with a subject he thinks important feels satisfaction at the sense of complete mastery of it. From points of view more specifically Wordsworthian, we may observe that this clarifying of the significance of the poet's subject and of the emotion which the subject excites is *knowledge*: knowledge of "general nature" (52.8–9), of "the universal intellectual property of man" (117.34),[24] of the norm of human nature; and that, to Wordsworth, "we have no knowledge, ... no general principles drawn from the contemplation of particular facts, but what has been built up by pleasure, and exists in us by pleasure alone. ... The knowledge ... of the Poet ... is pleasure" (51.13–16, 52.12–13). We may observe further that the perception of significance involves a process of generalization, of perceiving "those points of human nature in which all men resemble each other" (*L.Y.*, p. 127); and that such

21/There is no evidence to show that, as is sometimes assumed, it is during this period of tranquillity, immediately preceding composition, that the evaluation takes place (so, probably, Garrod, p. 160).

22/If we could assume complete integration between the texts of 1800 and 1802, we should naturally suppose that this process was the same as the "conjuring up" of passion of 49.3 ff. No particular difficulties arise from such an identification, but no light is cast by it on the present problem.

23/Cf. *P.W.*, v.344: "A vivid pulse of *sentiment and thought* Beat palpably within us, and *all shades Of consciousness* were ours" (my italics); *Biog. Lit.*, ii.12: "a more than usual state of emotion, with more than usual order; judgement ever awake and steady self-possession, with enthusiasm and feeling profound or vehement."

24/Cf. *P.W.*, v.344: "oft have we ... Looked inward on ourselves, and *learned*, perhaps, *Something of what we are*" (my italics).

resemblances are perceived by the Imagination, which "delights" in its own activities (149.20).[25] The pleasure derived from such perception is, indeed, so powerful that it outweighs the pain of an emotion *per se* painful.[26] In this mood, the poet is, as it were, at once "under the ... pressure of" (49.17–18) his emotion and in the position of that generalized observer whose sympathy, even with pain, is "produced and carried on by subtle combinations with pleasure" (51.13); he is "pleased with his own passions and volitions, ... delighting to contemplate similar volitions and passions as manifested in the goings-on of the Universe, and habitually impelled to create them where he does not find them" (48.33–49.1): that is, he perceives the general significance of his emotion by recognizing its conformity to the norm, and finds pleasure in this perception.[27] Such a process seems to be analogous to, or an amplification of, that achievement of the *mot juste*, with resulting pleasure, to which Wordsworth devoted the sonnet cited above: that knowledge which enables him to embody his thought in words is similar to, indeed part of, the knowledge which he eventually achieves of the significance of his subject: a knowledge which makes him "clear of sight" and enables him "By instinct to enjoy because he sees And see by reason that he can enjoy" (*Prel.*, p. 621).

The time-lag between the original emotion and the recollection of it has been sufficiently noticed by the critics. Nothing that Wordsworth says in the Preface, however, implies that the interval is neces-

25/Cf. *M.Y.*, i.149: "My mind wantons with grateful joy in the exercise of its own powers."

26/The generalizing phrases "of whatever kind" and "any passions whatsoever" (27.34–36) are meant to indicate that painful emotions are not excluded. Cf. *Prel.*, XII.244–47.

27/Cf. *H.C.R.*, p. 89: "The poet first conceives the essential nature of his object and strips it of all its casualties and accidental individual dress, and in this he is a philosopher; ... [then] he reclothes his idea in an individual dress which expresses the essential quality, and has also the spirit and life of a sensual object, and this transmutes the philosophic into a poetic exhibition"; p. 191: "imagination is the faculty by which the poet conceives and produces – that is, images – individual forms in which are *embodied universal ideas* or *abstractions*." Robinson's notion of consecutive stages in the first passage is probably an over-simplification.

sarily a long one.[28] Indeed, he wrote a good many poems as soon, or almost as soon, as the subject attracted his attention: consider, for instance, among the "Poems of the Imagination," the Fenwick notes to *A Night-Piece, Written in March*, perhaps *The Thorn*,[29] *Tintern Abbey*, "It is no spirit," *The Wishing-Gate Destroyed, To the Clouds*;[30] elsewhere, the first three lines of *Address to Kilchurn Castle*. Yet it is noteworthy that the last of these was completed "many years after," when the significance of the scene, and of the contrast indicated in the three lines "thrown off at the moment I first caught sight of the ruin," had been more clearly perceived. Of the other poems, most involve recollection: *A Night-Piece*, in a sense to be indicated shortly; *The Thorn*, of a ballad; *Tintern Abbey*, of a previous visit to the scene; "It is no spirit," probably of admired lines of Milton, and a psychological principle illustrated by them which Wordsworth thought important (*Paradise Lost*, iv.604–9; cf. M.Y., i.148); *The Wishing-Gate Destroyed*, of an earlier poem; *To the Clouds*, of a similar scene and similar meditations some years before.[31] In such cases, an emotion presently felt triggered the urge to composition, but the poems serve rather to give significance to other (though indeed related) emotions recollected, perhaps, during the progress of composition. This is hardly the process described in the Preface, but is no doubt an approximation to it.

Such poems are perhaps to be connected with the "shy spirit" of *The Waggoner* when it leaps "From hiding-places ten years deep." More complex are the occasions when it "haunts me with familiar face, Returning, like a ghost unlaid, Until the debt I owe be paid"

28/The "long and deep" thought of 19.20 applies to feelings in general, not only to any particular emotion which might give rise to a poem.

29/In so far as the thorn itself is the "subject" of the poem.

30/It is worth noting that, of these seven poems, four are in blank verse and are based on direct observation of natural scenery: the poet records what he sees in the most "natural" medium available to him.

31/Cf. lines 87–94 with *Misc. Son.*, ii.xi–xii. But as the connection was not made till about 1842 (*P.W.*, ii.320, textual n.), we may debate whether the sentiments of *To the Clouds* really sprang from the occasion, or whether they are an inorganic addition the real origin of which lies in the occasion of the two sonnets.

(*The Waggoner*, IV.209–15). We are sometimes able to trace such hauntings and Wordsworth's successive attempts to lay the ghost. A comparatively simple instance is his effort to deal adequately with the feelings aroused by the scenery of the Simplon Pass. He stated them baldly in prose at the time: "Among the more awful scenes of the Alps, I had not a thought of man, or a single created being; my whole soul was turned to him who produced the terrible majesty before me" (*E.Y.*, p. 34). In *Descriptive Sketches* he made no attempt even to describe the scene.[32] In 1799 he produced the remarkable version of it which appears in *The Prelude*, VI.556–72, and he made many later attempts to improve it.

The images in this passage are concerned with the perpetual release of energy from an infinite source: the woods decay but are "never to be decay'd"; the blast of the waterfall is so continuous that it may be synaesthetically regarded as "stationary"; the winds do continuous battle; the source of the "torrents" appears to be the infinity of the sky;[33] the sound of the stream, continuous itself, spreads its energy to the crags.[34] To this unified perception Wordsworth returns, in spite of numerous attempts to revise: the "fragments of primeval mountain spread In powerless ruin" are rejected,

[32]/He borrowed *Prel.*, VI.561, 563–64 from *D.S.* (1793), 130, 249–50, but in *D.S.* the lines are applied to different scenes.

[33]/The epithets "clear blue" expand the visual image of the sky.

[34]/The notion is clearer in reading B³ (*Prel.*, p. 211). The whole passage is possibly connected with a description of Atlas in Shaftesbury's *Moralists* (*Characteristicks* [n.p., 1738], ii.389): "See! with what trembling Steps poor Mankind tread the narrow Brink of the deep Precipices! From whence with *giddy* [565] Horrour they look down, mistrusting even the Ground which bears 'em; whilst they hear the *hollow* [559] Sound of *Torrents* [561] underneath, and see the *Ruin* [562, textual n.] of the *impending* [562, textual n.] *Rock* [562; cf. *blocks*, 562, textual n.]; with falling *Trees* [557] which hang with their Roots upwards, and seem to draw more Ruin after 'em" (italics mine). To Shaftesbury, this scene symbolizes "the Revolutions of past Ages, the fleeting Forms of Things, and the Decay even of this our *Globe*"; he found symbols of deity rather in the forest which the rhapsodist next describes (pp. 390–91). Similar phrases occur in John Dennis's letter of 25 October 1688, in Dennis, ii.380–81: "the unusual heighth ... the impending Rock ... the Torrent ... craggy Clifts ... Clouds ... craggy Rocks ... black Clouds ... the noise of the Cascades, or the down fall of Waters ... Ruins upon Ruins in monstrous Heaps ... the frightful view of

probably because they signify energy finally expended; the "blocks ... Impending, nor permitted yet to fall," because their energy is only potential. The final version agrees almost exactly with that of MS. A, where almost every image contributes to the poet's realization of a sense of infinite continuity: in 1799 he knew why, in 1790, his "soul was turned to him who produced the terrible majesty."

A more complex instance is the description of the scene at the top of Snowdon which appears at the beginning of Book XIII of *The Prelude*. Wordsworth saw this scene in 1791 (*Prel.*, p. 622); he wrote the description, perhaps, in 1799 (Havens, p. 610). Meanwhile it exercised a continual fascination on him. What is clearly the same scene appears in *Descriptive Sketches* (1793), 495–509, here placed in the Alps and ascribed to dawn.[35] It is described in terms which derive largely from Beattie's *Minstrel*;[36] the basic image of a sea of mist persists from Beattie through *Descriptive Sketches* up to the final version in *The Prelude*; verbal parallels are numerous, and a detail from Beattie omitted from *Descriptive Sketches* finds its way into *The Prelude*.[37]

the Precipices, and the foaming Waters that threw themselves headlong down them. ..." The similarity between Shaftesbury and Dennis is pointed out by Marjorie Hope Nicolson, *Mountain Gloom and Mountain Glory* (Norton Library ed., New York, 1963), p. 289. Wordsworth is probably improving upon what had become, by the end of the century, a conventionally "sublime" treatment of a comparatively familiar scene. He might have known either passage cited above, or both, by 1799: he certainly knew both authors later (Zall, 133.14, 171.17).

35/Wordsworth presumably saw a scene of this kind in the Alps. But it seems most improbable that he saw two scenes so closely resembling each other in two places and on two occasions, and we must therefore assume either that he transferred details of the Snowdon scene to what he saw in the Alps, or vice versa. Either assumption implies a falsification of factual record, in one or other poem; but falsification seems less likely in *The Prelude*. The characteristic feature, the blue gulf (*D.S.*, 1793, 498; *Prel.*, XIII.56), seems more likely to occur on a moonlit night than at dawn.

36/Book I, st.21, cited in *P.W.*, i.328. From here, probably, arises the ascription of the scene to dawn: cf. st.20, cited by Dorothy Wordsworth in a letter of 1793 (*E.Y.*, p. 101); the stanza which she thought a good description of her brother (*E.Y.*, p. 100) is st.22.

37/*Prel.*, XIII.45: "A hundred hills their dusky backs upheaved"; Beattie's "with mountains now embossed." Wordsworth also remembers *Paradise Lost*, VII.285–86: "the Mountains ... thir broad bare backs upheave."

In 1798 Wordsworth "composed on the road ... extempore" the lines called *A Night-Piece*. The central situation of this poem exactly parallels the beginning of the "vision" of *The Prelude*: the sudden appearance of a clear moon to a traveller intent merely on making his way:

> "At length a pleasant instantaneous gleam
> Startles the pensive traveller while he treads
> His lonesome path, with unobserving eye
> Bent earthwards; he looks up – the clouds are split
> Asunder, – and above his head he sees
> The clear Moon, and the glory of the heavens."[38]

The passages converge verbally as Wordsworth revises, as if the experiences merged into each other as they rested in Wordsworth's mind.[39]

But it is not till he comes to write the passage in *The Prelude* that Wordsworth records the significance of this scene. The "pastoral Swiss" of *Descriptive Sketches* receives from it "Joys only given to uncorrupted hearts" (491), and the reader is enjoined not to think that "He looks below with undelighted eye" (511). From the related scene in *A Night-Piece* Wordsworth received "delight" or "deep joy" (l.24 and textual n., *P.W.*, ii.209), and he "mused" upon it; but the outcome of his musings is not recorded. We may, indeed, doubt whether the subsequent "meditation" in *The Prelude* on this analogue of the Imagination did, in fact, arise in him "that night" as he asserts. Rather, we may conjecture, he perceived it and, probably, the scene of *A Night-Piece* with

38/An earlier version can be reconstructed from *P.W.*, ii.208.
39/Note the adaptation of the opening of *A Night-Piece* to *Prel.*, XIII. 10 ff.: close (*N.-P.*, 2; *Prel.*, 10); wan (*N.-P.*, 3; *Prel.*, 11); indistinctly seen (*N.-P.*, 4; Little could we see, *Prel.*, 15); dull (*N.-P.*, 5; *Prel.*, 11); pensive (*N.-P.*, 9; *Prel.* [B²], 18); dark abyss (*N.-P.*, 16; *Prel.* [1850], 72); Startles (*N.-P.*, 9; a startling gleam, *Prel.* [A²], 40). The situation is one of those in which an unusual aspect of nature is perceived with added force by a mind previously occupied with something else; see Chapter VII, sec. iv, below.

"a feeling and a love,
That had no need of a remoter charm,
By thought supplied, nor any interest
Unborrowed from the eye." (*Tintern Abbey*, 80–83)

So much, indeed, he says of this, the period of *An Evening Walk* and *Descriptive Sketches*, in the Preface of 1815, citing the lines just quoted to emphasize his point.[40] The meditation, then, is more likely to have arisen in 1799, out of emotion recollected many times, but, perhaps with the assistance of Coleridge,[41] finally seen in its full and generalized significance, and known to be roused by "The perfect image of a mighty Mind, Of one that feeds upon infinity." At the pleasure which Wordsworth derived from this knowledge we can only guess, in terms of the suggestions made above; but of its importance to him the Preface of 1815 leaves no doubt.

III *Validity*

How wide or general may be the validity of the theory discussed in the last two sections is a question much too large to be answered fully here. But a study of some modern attempts to describe the poetic process reveals that elements of Wordsworth's account have been widely accepted.[42]

To one writer it is evident that "art proper" is the expression of

40/The extracts from *An Evening Walk* and *Descriptive Sketches* given in the edition of 1815 "represent implicitly some of the features of a youthful mind, at a time when images of nature supplied to it the place of thought, sentiment, and almost of action" (144.5–17).

41/Coleridge compares "the power of giving the interest of novelty by the modifying colors of imagination" to "The sudden charm, which accidents of light and shade, which moon-light or sun-set diffused over a known and familiar landscape" (*Biog. Lit.*, ii.5). The landscape in this case was not "familiar" to Wordsworth, but he knew many like it.

42/In 1957 (*P.L.B.*, p. 108), I wrote as if Wordsworth had originated the concept of "emotion recollected in tranquillity." It is now clear to me that, though he may well have drawn on his own experience in formulating the concept, Wordsworth was anticipated in the eighteenth century. The most remarkable

emotion; to another, that unless the artist *"feels* profoundly what he perceives – unless it is significant to him – it is of no use to him as a matter of art"; to a third, that "certain images" which he has used in his own verse "recur, charged with emotion, rather than others"; to a fourth, that "It is the energetic charge of feeling upon the contents of memory ... which distinguish[es] the poet's images from the images of the 'ordinary man.'"[43] Such statements are congruous with Wordsworth's claim for the generally emotional basis of poetry.

"The poet's mind," says one of our theorists, "is ... a receptacle for seizing and storing up numberless feelings, phrases, images, which remain there until the particles which can unite to form a new compound are present together." Another affirms that "a man may live for years with the memory of an experience burning in him, may even desire ... to perpetuate it, yet never go about to do so until some day 'a voice says "Write" ' "; that "The poet ... will usually allow a pause between the inspiring impulse and the actual work." "Between an event of reality and the embodiment of that event in a poem there lies an act of distancing, a period of gestation, sometimes short,

statement I know before 1800 is in Diderot's *Paradoxe sur le Comédien,* in *Œuvres,* ed. Billy, Bibliothèque de la Pléiade, xxv (Paris, 1951), 1055: "Est-ce au moment où vous venez de perdre votre ami ou votre maîtresse que vous composerez un poème sur sa mort? Non ... C'est lorsque la grande douleur est passée, quand l'extrême sensibilité est amortie, lorsqu'on est loin de la catastrophe, que l'âme est calme, qu'on se rappelle son bonheur éclipsé, qu'on est capable d'apprécier la perte qu'on a faite, que la mémoire se réunit à l'imagination, l'une pour retracer, l'autre pour exagérer la douceur d'un temps passé; qu'on se possède et qu'on parle bien. On dit qu'on pleure, mais on ne pleure pas lorsqu'on poursuit une épithète énergique qui se refuse; on dit qu'on pleure, mais on ne pleure pas lorsqu'on s'occupe à rendre son vers harmonieux: ou si les larmes coulent, la plume tombe des mains, on se livre à son sentiment et l'on cesse de composer." As the *Paradoxe* was not published until 1830, though written in 1773, it is unlikely that Wordsworth knew it. It has been claimed that Wordsworth knew, through Coleridge, a passage of similar drift in Schiller's "Ueber Bürgers Gedichte": see L. A. Willoughby, "Wordsworth and Germany," in *German Studies presented to H. G. Fiedler* (Oxford, 1938), pp. 443–45; and for a seemingly related passage of uncertain date in Coleridge's note-books, see C.N.B., i.787, and n.

43/Collingwood, p. 109; Mackenzie, p. 38; T. S. Eliot, *The Use of Poetry and the Use of Criticism* (London, 1933), p. 148; Whalley, p. 76.

sometimes long."[44] These passages are not inconsistent with Wordsworth's "hiding-places ten years deep."

The evaluation of emotion, the possibly latent knowledge, brought to light by the poetic process, that the emotion is important because of its connection with general truth, may be illustrated by such statements as the following: "Until a man has expressed his emotion, he does not yet know what emotion it is. The act of expressing it is therefore an exploration of his own emotions. He is trying to find out what these emotions are." "A man comes in contact with a certain object which causes in him a state of consciousness whose quality as a means to life is to him so high that he is compelled to perpetuate it in itself. ... Before his experience can be of use as a theme, ... he must know the experience. ... But ... he [may be] aware of it only as some deep emotional disturbance ... whose cause is out of reach of his conscious cognition." In the artistic experience "there seemed to operate ... a kind of knowing ... the form or archetype of human experience is to be found in paradeigmatic experience and not in the experience of everyday man in a workaday world; and ... this order of experience is its own argument, carries its own proof within itself, is at once an event of value and of knowing. ... The poet carries in his head no prefigured model of his completed poem: he must discover his poem in making it."[45]

A connected account of the poetic process by a modern poet presents parallels even more striking. Stephen Spender informs us that "perhaps ... memory is the faculty of poetry, because the imagination itself is an exercise of memory." Of his poem *Seascape*, he tells us further that "The idea of this poem is a vision of the sea. The faith of the poet is that if this vision is clearly stated, it will be significant." This seems to be a version of Wordsworth's "feelings connected with important subjects" (19.25); Spender's "faith" in the "significance" of his vision seems analogous to Wordsworth's conviction that the powerful feelings which overflow as poetry are connected, however

44/T. S. Eliot, *Selected Essays* (London, 1934), p. 19; Mackenzie, p. 66; Rosamond E. M. Harding, *An Anatomy of Inspiration* (3rd ed., Cambridge, 1948), p. 60; Whalley, p. 78.

45/Collingwood, p. 111; Mackenzie, pp. 22–27, 85, 94; Whalley, pp. xv, 31, 84.

latently, with "important subjects," even though he did not always begin to write "with a distinct purpose formally conceived" (19.11). Finally, Spender's observation that "our ability to imagine is our ability to remember what we have already once experienced and to apply it to some different situation" seems clearly parallel to Wordsworth's discovery, in his remembered emotions, of wider significance, of general truth.[46]

The weight of this evidence for the wide validity of Wordsworth's theory is impressive but not wholly conclusive. Some poems, such as Wordsworth's *Written in March* and (probably) Keats's *Ode to Autumn*, seem to have been written on the spur of the moment. In others, such as Wordsworth's *Tintern Abbey*, an immediate emotional stimulus initiates composition, but is not the poem's emotional centre, which is rather to be found in recollected emotion. So in Shelley's *Adonais*, the death of Keats prompted a poem the emotional centre of which is Shelley's anger at his own treatment by the reviewers as much as, or rather than, at the death of Keats.[47] Keats's *Ode to a Nightingale* seems to be a case in which a remembered stimulus (the bird's song) prompted a poem whose emotional centre lies in other memories again, of the death of his brother or in thoughts of mortality in general.

Such poems differ from the two passages of *The Prelude* discussed above in section ii in that, as far as the internal or external evidence goes, no immediate emotional stimulus urged Wordsworth to the description of the Simplon Pass and the vision seen from Snowdon.[48] These are better described in other terms: in terms of Eliot's "objec-

46/*The Making of a Poem* (London, 1955), pp. 50, 57. Mr. Spender's "idea which exists clearly enough on some level of the mind where it yet eludes the attempt to state it" (p. 50) seems to resemble Wordsworth's account of beginning a poem with no "distinct purpose formally conceived," or his "thought" before it achieves the "incarnation" of language.

47/This is clear from the cancelled passages of Shelley's Preface, in *Works*, ed. Ingpen and Peck (London, 1926–30), ii.406–9. It was recognized by Mrs. Shelley (*Works*, iv.122); cf. N. I. White, *Shelley* (New York, 1940), ii.293.

48/He might have been stimulated to write about the Simplon Pass by reading Shaftesbury or Dennis, and about Snowdon by conversation with Coleridge; see sec. ii, nn. 34 and 41, above. In neither case is the stimulus likely to have been "emotional."

tive correlative" or Coleridge's "reconciliation of opposites." John Keats and his death are an objective correlative to Shelley's anger against reviewers; Keats's physical death and his poetic immortality are reconciled as a victory against the reviewers. The song of the nightingale is, perhaps, the objective correlative of Keats's desire to escape from thoughts of mortality; the seeming immortality of the bird is the opposite of human mortality (the poem hardly achieves a reconciliation).

It seems probable, then, that Wordsworth's theory is widely but not generally applicable: some poems are written in the way Wordsworth describes; others, including some of Wordsworth's, are written in a similar way, but need the stimulus of an emotion immediately felt before composition can begin; others, again, are written under the stimulus of immediate feeling and draw on no particular recollected emotion. Wordsworth's description of the poetic process, then, seems valid for himself and for some poets; it is not wholly valid for some of his own poems and for some other poets. Even though it thus lacks the general validity which the tone of Wordsworth's language claims for it, it remains a valuable record of a psychological process by which some poetry, and certainly much of Wordsworth's most important poetry, may be produced.[49]

49/Except in cases where direct borrowing from the Preface is obvious (as in Shelley's *Defence of Poetry*), the criticism of Wordsworth's contemporaries and juniors does not seem to make much use of the elements of his theory indicated above. For a notable example of agreement, however, see Landor's "Remonstrance and Reply," in *Works*, ed. Welby and Wheeler, xv (London, 1935), 225–26.

Four ✳ The Additions of 1802

1 *The Argument*

Thus far we have followed Wordsworth's argument mainly as it is presented in material common to the texts of 1800 and 1802. The drift of it is tolerably clear. Wordsworth has based his language on that of rustics because that language is "plain," "forcible," "philosophical" (that is, adequate to the ideas it expresses), and, most important, "permanent." He has rejected conventional poeticisms because they do not occur in this language: they do not contribute to the characteristics just mentioned. The language thus arrived at is claimed to be essentially identical with that of prose. In the text of 1800, Wordsworth proceeds, with an obvious connection of ideas, to justify his use of metre.

In the text of 1802, this justification is deferred by the insertion of a long passage (47.18–54.35) best known for some eloquent paragraphs (48.27 ff.) which purport mainly to discuss the question, "What is a Poet?" (48.28).[1] But Wordsworth begins to make significant alterations to the text of 1800 at an earlier point (47.18); and the drift of his argument from this point cannot well be understood unless it is realized that, while he ranges widely over the general aesthetics of poetry, he is still engaged, fundamentally, in demonstrating that poetry does not require "artificial distinctions" of

---

1/Possibly the matter derives from the essay proposed for the second volume of *Lyrical Ballads, 1800; see Journals,* i.63, and E.Y., pp. 307–9.

language (47.17, 50.8–10, 53.35). The demonstration takes the form of answering a series of hypothetical objections to his views.

The first of these objections is based on the presence in poetry of rhyme and metre (47.14 ff.). It is answered on grounds which, in the text of 1802, do not seem wholly satisfactory,[2] but which lead Wordsworth to glance at the question of what we may, for the moment, call dramatic realism in poetry (48.3 ff.).[3] After a paragraph introducing wider aspects of the subject, he reverts to the matter of dramatic realism (48.29 ff.), and concludes, seemingly, that complete dramatic realism is neither attainable in practice by the poet (49.14 ff.), nor desirable, since it may be "painful or disgusting" (49.29–32; cf. 47.23: "the vulgarity and meanness of ordinary life"). He returns to this matter in 53.23 ff., where he asserts, in spite of the considerations just mentioned, that "the dramatic parts of composition are defective, in proportion as they deviate from the real language of nature," and, more significantly for the present discussion, "are coloured by [an individual or traditional poetic] diction."

The second hypothetical objection is based on the concession that the poet fails, at least from time to time, to achieve dramatic realism; that is, fails to "produce upon all occasions language as exquisitely

2/The objection urges that since rhyme and metre demonstrate by their mere presence that poetry is not prose, it cannot logically be asserted that the languages of the two mediums should be identical (47.14–18). In 1800 (25.3 ff.), Wordsworth answers that, because rhyme and metre contribute to the total effect of poetry an element which is *constant* ("regular and uniform") in its effect, we can ignore this element when we are concerned to discuss a possibly variable element such as language: the effect of rhyme and metre will be the same whether the language is "artificial" or "natural," and their presence does not dictate which it shall be. In 1802 Wordsworth concedes that a "distinction" is made between two kinds of language, but it is made, not between the language of prose and the language of poetry, but, by virtue of the process called "selection" (47.18–23), between the language of poetry and "the language really spoken by men ... the vulgarity and meanness of ordinary life"; and this latter term has no particular relevance to the objection proposed in 47.14–18. See further *P.L.B.*, Commentary, n. on 277 ff.

3/The term is not wholly appropriate since it suggests a theory of poetry as imitation, a theory with which, as we shall see, Wordsworth is not here concerned. See Stephen M. Parrish, "The Wordsworth-Coleridge Controversy," *PMLA*, lxxiii (1958), 367–74.

fitted for the passion as that which the real passion itself suggests" (50.4–12). Wordsworth answers the objection mainly by shifting his ground and asserting the importance of poetry and its subject-matter. The poet is concerned with (what Wordsworth calls) general truth, that is, the "knowledge which all men carry about with them" (52.1), "the general passions and thoughts and feelings of men" (54.9), to which his attention is directed by "the grand elementary principle of pleasure" (51.9, cf. 52.7). With a subject-matter of such importance, "transitory and accidental ornaments" (53.19–20) are incongruous; for the poet's use of them can be justified only by "the assumed meanness of his subject" (53.21–22).[4] The attempt to answer an aesthetic problem by an argument verging on the ethical may have seemed less strange to Wordsworth than it does to the modern reader, in view of Wordsworth's frequent association of aesthetic and moral judgments (*P.L.B.*, Commentary, n. on 302).

The third hypothetical objection of the series is, as it were, a corollary to the second: conceding that Wordsworth has proved his point with respect to "the dramatic parts of composition," the imaginary objector proposes that a "distinction of language ... may be proper and necessary where the Poet speaks to us in his own person and character" (53.34–37). Similarly, Wordsworth's answer is given mainly in terms of a corollary to his second reply. The stress shifts from the importance of the poet's subject to its generality. What is general knowledge is best expressed in the language of those whose property it is, in the language of "all other men who feel vividly and see clearly" (54.20). Moreover, on grounds merely of intelligibility, the poet's audience is such that "he must express himself as other men express themselves"; any other language is that of intellectual snobbery (54.25–29).

At this point the argument begins to shift back to the discussion of metre with which we have already dealt; and Wordsworth proceeds

---

4/"Transitory and accidental ornaments" are required only to impart grandeur to a "mean" subject. But poetry does not deal with mean subjects, but with "general truth." Therefore such ornaments should not appear in poetry.

to answer the question: "Why, professing these opinions, have I written in verse?" (55.10). The question is now somewhat remote, since the phrase "these opinions" is now forced to refer not so much to the possible identity of the language of poetry with the language of prose as to Wordsworth's concern lest a justification should be found for "artificial distinctions" of style between the language of poetry and – not prose (47.16), but – whatever language "the passion naturally suggests" (48.6), "nature" (49.33), "language as exquisitely fitted for the passion as that which the real passion itself suggests," or an approximation to it (50.6–7), "the real language of nature" (53.28–29), the language of "all other men who feel vividly and see clearly" (54.20), or the language in which "other men express themselves" (54.29). Unless the language variously defined in the phrases just cited is to be identified with that of prose,[5] it is clear that Wordsworth fails to answer the objection originally proposed in 47.14 ff., and that his return to the subject of prose in 55.9 ff. is not prompted by the immediately foregoing "opinions."

II *The Language of Men*

The truth is that, in the passage inserted in the text of 1802, and in the Appendix on poetic diction, Wordsworth is not concerned with "the language of prose," but with material almost entirely new, and with a new emphasis on the virtues of "the real language of nature." The ideas now introduced have scarcely been touched on in the Preface of 1800, except in so far as they are to be connected with the two references to poetry as "the spontaneous overflow of powerful feelings" (19.16, 27.27–28; in 1802, 42.8, 57.36–37), which are *obiter dicta* embedded, the first in an account of the moral purpose of Wordsworth's poems, and the second in Wordsworth's theory of metre.

5/This identification is not feasible since "the language of prose, when prose is well written" (46.6) is incompatible with "the vulgarity and meanness of ordinary life" (47.23), which is, or may be, characteristic of "the real language of nature."

The ideas are, in the order in which Wordsworth introduces them, these: that the language which expresses passion is "naturally" figurative (47.30–48.3); and that "real" feeling inspires in "men" a language which is, in some sense, notably eloquent, or powerful, or expressive, or peculiarly authentic (49.15–19, 49.21–23, 50.5–7).

The two ideas of the figurative language of passion and of the eloquence of "men in real life" fall together in the figure of the Primitive Poet of the Appendix. Wordsworth is concerned to define his conception of poetic diction: he reaches the conclusion that poetic diction is that sort of language which uses figures of speech when they are not justified by passion. "The earliest Poets of all nations" (63.9–10) are conceived as the reporters of their own or others' passionate utterances, "the language of extraordinary occasions" (64.12–13), which, possibly in fact but certainly in eighteenth-century rhetorical theory, are characterized by figures of speech. Poetic diction arises when later poets employ the same sort of language – in particular, when they "set themselves to a mechanical adoption of those figures of speech" – "without having the same animating passion" (63.14–16).

We are, however, less concerned here with the notion of poetic diction than with certain affinities between the Primitive Poet and the "men" of the Preface. For "the earliest Poets ... wrote from passion excited by real events; they wrote naturally, and as men" (63.9–11); and their language, though "daring, and figurative [and] felt to differ materially from ordinary language" (63.12, 64.11–12), "was really spoken by men," by the poet or by others. Thus "the earliest Poets" were, when they composed, "men in a state of vivid sensation" (38.4–5), or the reporters of such men, "men in real life, under the actual pressure of ... passions" (49.17–18). It appears to follow that the "language of men in a state of vivid sensation" of the Preface will be daring, figurative, and generally eloquent. This is not the argument of 1800, but by the time he came to write the version of 1802 Wordsworth seems to have held this view. Thus at 47.19–20 he claims that the language of his poetry is "a selection of the language really spoken by men," and shortly he observes that "if the Poet's subject be judiciously chosen, it will naturally, and upon fit occasion, lead him to passions the language of which, if selected truly and judiciously, must necessarily be dignified and variegated, and alive with metaphors and figures"; that is, "the language really spoken by men," when it deals with passion, contains metaphors and figures.[6] In a revised version of an earlier passage which says nothing about passion and figures, he grants that personification is "a figure of speech occasionally prompted by passion" (44.35, cf. 22.15 ff.). He says little more about figures, but he has something to say about passion and the eloquence it inspires in "men in real life."

In the Preface, these ideas are conveyed in a passage (48.30 ff., and especially 49.14–50.12) which describes the activity of the poet when he attempts dramatic poetry. This passage we shall analyse later; here it is worth noting that, in so far as it implies the ultimate authenticity of the language of real life as the expression of passion, its ideas are repeated in Book XII of *The Prelude*, and that here, moreover, the identification of eloquent "men" with "men of low and rustic life," which is not made except by implication in the Preface, is boldly affirmed. The book purports to record, *inter alia*, Wordsworth's observation of "men as they are men within themselves" (*Prel.*, XII.225) between 1795 and 1797; but it seems not to have been written before 1805, and the interval is obviously sufficient for the ideas of the Preface and Appendix of 1802 to have attached themselves to Wordsworth's memories of ten years before. Three passages concern us. On "the lonely roads" of the Southwest, Wordsworth heard "From mouths of lowly men and of obscure A tale of honour" (*Prel.*, XII.182–83). He heard it told, according to a line occurring in MS. Y and subsequently deleted,[7] "in the tongue of truest eloquence." His discovery of the dignity of "men as they are men within themselves," as typified by the men he saw during these years, "and see daily now [in 1805] Before me in my rural neighbourhood," by "the best of those who live ... In Nature's presence," – this discovery

6/A commonplace of eighteenth-century theory: see *P.L.B.*, Commentary, n. on 290 ff.

7/It was probably deleted because Wordsworth found it not invariably true: the men described in lines 264–74 are not, in fact, eloquent.

was the inspiration of his future verse (*Prel.*, XII.220–48). Such verse, he prophesied, would not please certain shallow-minded readers, who are contrasted with "men ... of other mold[8] ..., Expressing liveliest thoughts in lively words As native passion dictates" (*Prel.*, XII.260–64), and with others who are inarticulate poets. The correspondence (verbal in the case of the passage just cited) with the 1802 addition to the Preface is clear; and it is also clear that those who use "the tongue of truest eloquence" and who express "liveliest thoughts in lively words As native passion dictates" are men of "low and rustic life." The third passage in the poem repeats Wordsworth's ideas about "selection":

> "thence [from 'the very heart of man'] may I select
> Sorrow that is not sorrow, but delight,
> And miserable love that is not pain
> To hear of." (*Prel.*, XII.244–47)

Here "select" repeats, not the idea of "selection" of language, but the judicious choosing of subject-matter of the Preface, 47.30; the remainder of the passage reflects the removal by "selection" (of language) of "what would otherwise be painful ... in the passion," for the purpose of giving "pleasure" (49.29 ff.).

These ideas are hardly compatible with the ideas on language advanced in the text of 1800. There we are told that the language of "men" uses "simple and unelaborated expressions" to convey feelings (18.23); yet the language of men in the addition of 1802 is, as we saw earlier, dignified, variegated, and figurative when it expresses passion. Simplicity and lack of elaboration may be compatible with dignity; it is not obvious that they are compatible with a variegated and figurative language, and it is thus difficult to see how, in terms of the whole text of 1802, the poet's language may derive from the rustic's. Again, the language of the Primitive Poet is "daring, and

---

8/MS. Y: "of better make." That these men are rustics is indicated by l.265: the "men" of 260 and the "others" of 264 are two sorts of men who are found "among the walks of homely life."

figurative"; moreover, such a language is the "natural" expression by "men" of "powerful feelings" (63.11–12); "it was really spoken by men" (64.13 ff.), by the poet himself or by others whose speech he reported. Yet, according to the text of 1800, as we have just seen, "men" "convey their feelings ... in simple and unelaborated expressions" – perhaps in "ordinary language"? (64.12) – certainly not in a "daring and figurative" language.

In brief, the stress in the text of 1800 (and in *The Excursion*, 1.341 ff.) lies on the ideas of simplicity, lack of elaboration, and a (mere) adequacy of language to thought; in the additions of 1802 (and in *The Prelude*, Book XII), the stress lies rather on the figurative nature of "the language of men" and on its abundant adequacy to the passion it expresses. The shift in emphasis may be illustrated by the 1800 note to *The Thorn*: "Poetry is passion: it is the history or science of feelings: now every man must know that an attempt is rarely made to communicate impassioned feelings without something of an accompanying consciousness of the inadequateness of our own powers, or the deficiencies of language. During such efforts there will be a craving in the mind, and as long as it is unsatisfied the Speaker will cling to the same words, or words of the same character" (13.26–33).[9] It is hard to see how a "consciousness of the inadequate-

9/The passage attempts to justify the use of "repetition and apparent tauto-logy"; they are said to be "frequently beauties of the highest kind." How this follows, from the passage quoted or from the idea that "the mind luxuriates in the repetition of words which appear successfully to communicate its feelings," is not clear, unless Wordsworth means merely that they give a realistic impression of an attempt to "communicate impassioned feelings." This may be his intention, in view of his concern with dramatic realism in the addition of 1802, and in view of similar observations by other critics: Gerard, *Genius*, p. 151: "When a person is under the influence of any passion, the difficulty is not to recollect the objects closely connected with it, but to prevent their haunting him continually. An angry man, for example, can scarce avoid thinking of the person who has offended him, and of the injury [&c., &c.,] and in a word dwelling on the conception of every thing immediately relating to his anger"; Adam Smith, *Works*, ed. Stewart (London, 1811), v.274–75: the man feeling passion "repeat[s] to himself ... sometimes even aloud, and almost always in the same words, the particular thought which either delights or distresses him. ... Neither Prose nor Poetry can venture to imitate those almost endless repetitions of passion ... they would become almost insufferably tiresome if they did." Wordsworth's defence of repetition almost sounds like a retort to this passage.

ness of our own powers, or the deficiencies of language," accompanying "an attempt ... to communicate impassioned feelings," is to be reconciled with "the freedom and power of real and substantial action and suffering" (49.22–23).

Wordsworth's new ideas are commonplaces of certain eighteenth- and nineteenth-century poetics which are based, in particular, on primitivistic theories of language and literature. The notion that passion is expressed in figures occurs frequently in eighteenth-century criticism (see *P.L.B.*, Commentary, n. on 290 ff.), and is especially common in primitivistic theories, which link it with theories of the eloquence of "the earliest Poets of all nations," considered by Wordsworth in the Appendix. The view that "real" passion inspires eloquence, and that the dramatic poet must, for reasons at which we shall glance shortly, achieve an imaginative identification of himself with his characters (49.23–27), is again characteristic of primitivistic critics, though Wordsworth's immediate source for this notion, if we may judge from verbal parallels, seems to be Quintilian.[10]

More generally, Wordsworth's views are based on what have been defined as "expressive" theories of poetry, in terms of which "Poetry is the overflow, utterance, or projection of the thought and feelings of the poet. ... A work of art is essentially the internal made external, resulting from a creative process operating under the impulse of feeling, and embodying the combined product of the poet's perceptions, thoughts, and feelings. The primary source and subject matter of a poem, therefore, are the attributes and actions of the poet's own mind; or if aspects of the external world, then these only as they are converted from fact to poetry by the feelings and operations of the poet's mind" (Abrams, pp. 21–22). For Wordsworth's new ideas imply that, whether the poet writes subjective lyric or dramatic speech, he will, in some sense, write poetry by expressing himself rather than by imitating the utterance of others.

The appearance of the new ideas in the text of 1802 coincides, and

---

10/See *P.L.B.*, Commentary, nn. on 325 ff., 337–41, 345–49. The reference in Zall, 49.fns.3 and 4, is incorrect. See also *P.L.B.*, Introductory Note to Appendix, pp. 192–93.

appears to be linked, with an amplification of Wordsworth's notion of the process called "selection": a concept which will be considered later. Neither of the ideas occurs with any emphasis, except in the phrase "the spontaneous overflow of powerful feelings," and the related "Poetry is passion," in anything that Wordsworth wrote before 1802. He is, of course, concerned, at any rate nominally, with the expression of "passion" in the Preface of 1800: with the expression of "a state of vivid sensation" (16.1–2), of "the essential passions of the heart ... elementary feelings" (18.6–12), of a "state of excitement" (19.37), of the "great and simple affections" (20.2), and the like. But he has said nothing of the virtues of figurative language in the expression of passion,[11] and he has made no higher claim for the language of rustics than that it is more permanent and more "philosophical" than the objectionable language of poets of a certain kind – than poetic diction.

In terms of this new emphasis, Wordsworth attempts in 1802 an account of the activity of the poet, in particular, when he "speaks through the mouths of his characters" (47.27–28); when, that is, he is not recording his own personal emotions, but dealing with imaginary situations and writing dramatic poetry. This activity is vaguely adumbrated at 47.28 ff., in a passage the main purport of which is to show that any "elevation of style" in the shape of figures must have its justification in passion: "if the Poet's subject be judiciously chosen, it will naturally, and upon fit occasion, lead him to passions the language of which, if selected truly and judiciously, must necessarily be dignified and variegated, and alive with metaphors and figures."

Apart from the scantily glossed phrase "spontaneous overflow of powerful feelings," it is clear that the text of 1800 contains no such description of the poet in activity. Thus the word *selection*, denoting, apparently, a major part of the poet's activity, occurs only once in the text of 1800. In 1802 it creeps into a slightly amplified passage (40.31) near the beginning of the discussion of the language of rus-

11/The remark on personification (44.35) was added in 1802.

tics, but it is not till the passage now under consideration that it begins to make its presence felt (47.19–20, 48.2, 49.31, 54.30–32). In 1802 Wordsworth calls it "the principle on which I have so much insisted" (49.30), though in fact he has only just begun to "insist" on it, and though this is the last important reference to it.

The rarity of the word in the text of 1800 makes it difficult to define the sense in which Wordsworth there intends it. But the reader who had only that text before him would, perhaps, most naturally assume that the process of selection was the same as, or closely similar to, the "purification" of the language of rustics (18.17–18). Here, as we saw in Chapter I, "the real language of men," or the language of rustics, seems to be conceived as a large stock of linguistic elements marked by certain characteristics, from which the poet may select" whatever elements suit his particular purpose. These elements will be retained, and there will, of course, be a corresponding rejection of the "real defects" of this stock of language, as well as of what may be irrelevant to the poet's immediate purpose.

Such a view, congruous with a mimetic theory of poetry,[12] approaches the notion of the poem as an artefact, and of the poet as a "maker" who constructs his poem from just so much and just such of his raw material (the language of men) as will constitute the poem he wishes to construct. Just so, a sculptor might be said to "select" that part of his material which is his statue, rejecting the rest of the mass because it may have "real defects," or, in any case, because it is not relevant to his present purpose whether or not it is inherently defective.[13]

This view is not very different, and might indeed have been derived, from Johnson's account of the language of Shakespearean comedy, which seems "to have been gathered by diligent selection out of common conversation, and common occurrences"; and again: "If there be ... a stile which never becomes obsolete, a certain mode

12/See introductory remarks to Chapter III, above.
13/So René Wellek and Austin Warren, *Theory of Literature* (London, 1949), p. 177.

of phraseology so consonant and congenial to the analogy and principles of its respective language as to remain settled and unaltered;[14] this style is probably to be sought in the common intercourse of life, among those who speak only to be understood, without ambition of elegance. ... [From such a language Shakespeare] seems to have gathered his comick dialogue."[15] So, too, Wordsworth's defence of repetition in the note of 1800 to *The Thorn* is not inconsistent with such a view: repetition in moments of emotional stress is one element of the many in "the common intercourse of life" from which the poet may select a quasi-realistic language.[16] From this scanty evidence, we may perhaps conclude that in 1800 Wordsworth, as far as the notion of selection defines the activity of the poet, conceived it as a purposive and conscious working on the large mass of "the real language of men," undertaken with a view to imitating that language.

This is not the viewpoint of the phrase of 1800, "the spontaneous overflow of powerful feelings," and the account of the poet in activity which is now supplied by the text of 1802. For the notion of selection is now relegated to the place of a secondary activity, and it appears that the poet's utterance comes to him, in the first instance, not by his conscious selection of words, phrases, idioms, and the like from a large mass of linguistic elements broadly defined as "the real language of men," but rather by an automatic process which is initiated by the poet's passion: a "spontaneous overflow [in language] of powerful feelings" which have been aroused in the poet by a "subject ... judiciously chosen."

Two aspects of this account require consideration: the automatism of the process, and the difficulty of relating passions so aroused in

14/Note the emphasis on permanence. So Johnson's *Dictionary* (4th ed., London, 1773), i. sig. H⁴: "the familiar and colloquial part of our language, being diffused among those classes who had no ambition of refinement, or affectation of novelty, has suffered very little change."

15/Raleigh, pp. 13, 19–20. Johnson's remarks on the permanent value of Shakespeare's comic characters show affinity with Wordsworth's on the permanence of the rustic's characteristics; both sorts of character are said to be "durable" (Raleigh, p. 19; Zall, 18.14 and 41.10).

16/Johnson obviously thinks of the dialogue of Shakespeare's comedies as more realistic than that of the tragedies.

the poet to those of his dramatic characters through whose mouths the poet is said to speak. The first aspect we shall consider briefly now, the second, in more detail, in the next section.

Automatism is implied by the adjective *spontaneous* of 1800 and, in the passage now under examination, by the phrase "passions the language of which," suggesting the genitival relation of language to passion, the inevitable and automatic verbal response to the stimulus of passion, and the inevitable and automatic linking of particular passion to particular (authentic and adequate) utterance. These ideas are emphasized by the adverbs *naturally* and *necessarily*; they are repeated later. Thus at 48.5–6—"should the Poet interweave any foreign splendour of his own with that [unusual language] which the passion naturally suggests"—we have again the idea of automatic utterance ("naturally suggests"), coupled with the notion that it is aesthetically reprehensible for the poet consciously to interfere with the automatism, at any rate by addition. The phrasing indeed hints that only unwarranted "foreign splendour" can be regarded by the poet as "his own": the authentic part of the utterance has, as it were, a life of its own, and uses the poet only as a mouthpiece, like the priest acting only as an audible medium for a divine oracle.[17] The

17/Similar is the attack on rhyme in Dennis, i.376: "the Expression, which Nature dictates at first, and which is powerful, sounding, significant, and in short the true one, is very often alter'd upon the Account of the Rhime. And a Word or two are chang'd, which destroys its Beauty, and the greater part of its Force; makes it less strong, less sounding, less significant, and weakens the Spirit, and sets the Sentiment in a false Light: From whence it follows that Rime in the greater Poetry running counter to Nature must be against Art. But as every Sentiment has but one particular Expression which of Right belongs to it, so that Expression has but one particular Harmony which is adapted to that peculiar Degree of Spirit which naturally attends on the Sentiment. Now Nature ... very often in the greater Poetry dictates that Harmony together with the Expression." A constant theme in Wordsworth's *Guide to the Lakes* is the undesirability of tampering with the *natural* appearance of the district, or with such man-made structures as manage to conform to it. See especially Knight, ii.81: "much as these scenes have been injured by what has been taken from them – buildings, trees, and woods, either through negligence, necessity, avarice, or caprice – it is not the removals, but the harsh *additions* that have been made, which are the worst grievance – a standing and unavoidable annoyance." The affinity of these ideas with those under consideration is obvious.

poet must utter the truth and nothing but the truth, though not necessarily, as we shall see, the whole truth, of his emotional experience. Again, at 49.23 ff. we are informed that the language which the poet utters, when he "confound[s] and identif[ies] his own feelings" with those of his dramatic characters, is *suggested to him* (by the feelings); and again, "that there is no necessity to trick out or to elevate nature," and so again at 50.7, 53.16–33; and, to some extent, at 55.1–8, where it is implied that poetic diction "interfer[es] ... with the passion," that is, prevents its authentic presentation to the reader, whereas metre does not.

III *"The Dramatic Parts of Composition"*

The activity of the poet when he "speaks through the mouths of his characters" is more specifically defined in 48.27 ff., where the rather imprecise statements of 47.27 ff. are clarified and amplified. The poet is more successful than other men at "conjuring up passions" without external stimulus (49.3–8), and he is, similarly, more successful at expressing these passions (49.9–13). But the language which he uses is less effective, in some sense (inferior in "liveliness and truth"), than that used by "men" who, from external stimulus, are under the influence of "real" passion (49.14–19). Therefore the poet, when he deals with dramatic characters, must "confound and identify his own feelings" with those of his characters (49.23–27).[18] In such an emotional state, it is implied, the poet will be able, "for short spaces of time" (49.25), to utter a language which is authentic and adequate to the passion; but since such identification cannot be consistently maintained, "it is impossible for the Poet to produce upon all occasions language as exquisitely fitted for the passion as that which the real passion itself suggests" (50.5–7).

18/Thus the vague phrase of 48.1, "lead him to passions," evidently means, not "lead him to deal with passions," but "induce passions in him, cause him to feel passions."

Clearly, this account is based squarely, not on the mimetic theory of 1800, but on an expressive poetic, of which the characteristic poetic form is not drama but subjective lyric. Wordsworth is attempting to show how, on the basis of such a theory, dramatic poetry manages to be written at all. For it is clear that, if poetry is "the spontaneous overflow of [the poet's own] powerful feelings," the poet is incompetent to express the feelings of other (albeit imaginary) persons unless he can, by some psychological process, make the feelings of such persons his own. Wordsworth admits the incompetence, with the qualification that, by means of sympathetic identification, the characters' feelings may, "for short spaces of time perhaps," be made the poet's own. The poet may, indeed must, if he is to write such poetry, make himself as far as possible like a man really feeling the passion; the "shadows" of passions which he can "conjure up" must, for the moment, become real; and the language resulting from this process will be authentic, or adequate to the passion, or "truthful," because the poet *is*, for longer or shorter periods, a man feeling the passion with which the poet deals. He puts himself in such a position that he is able to use the language of real life. He is, although he deals with what began as a "shadow" of real passion, in the position of, first, "men in real life, under the actual pressure of ... passions," and, secondly, of the Primitive Poets, who "wrote naturally, and as men," and who "felt powerfully" (63.11). Yet, inevitably, his success can usually be only partial: "it is impossible for the Poet to produce upon all occasions language as exquisitely fitted for the passion as that which the real passion itself suggests" (50.5–7). To the imaginary interjector who seizes upon this failure in order to press his case for "artificial distinctions" of style, Wordsworth replies with new arguments which we shall consider later.

Difficulties in this account arise in Wordsworth's application of the theory of poetry as "expression" to the particular problem of dramatic poetry, and especially in 50.5–7 quoted above. For such a statement suggests at first glance a theory of poetry, not as expression from within, but as imitation, and hence a value judgment based upon poetry as an image or reflection of the external world: in this case, a judgment upon the poet's success or failure in imitating the language prompted by "the real passion."[19] But, since passion "really" exists only in particular cases, it is clear that the only standard of value available is a real-life incident of passion fully reported to the judging audience. Hence follow two corollaries: the poet deals with a real-life situation, dramatic poetry is a phonographic report of real-life utterance, and, if the audience is to judge of the poet's success, it does so merely by checking, against an available exemplar, the accuracy of the poet's report; or: the poet deals with a fictitious situation, yet there is a real-life exemplar of this fictitious situation available to the judging audience for purposes of comparison.[20]

The first of these corollaries is, except in rare instances, unacceptable; the second is nonsensical. Yet the analogy which follows (50.7–12) seems to support them: for, as there are in fact two versions of a translated work, the original and the translation, the one of which does not achieve the authenticity of the other, so, according to this interpretation of Wordsworth's words, there would seem to be two versions of the expression of passion, the one based on "the real passion" and therefore entirely authentic, the other based on intermittent sympathetic identification and therefore only partially authentic.

19/The remarks in the note on *The Thorn* on repetition, cited above, are consistent with a poetic based on imitation: they are generalized observation of the speech habits of men which the poet may imitate to achieve realism; and such a poetic is, again, consistent with the impression conveyed by the Preface of 1800 of the poet as "maker." Cicero, says Sidney, "inflamed with a well-grounded rage, ... would haue his words (as it were) double out of his mouth, and so doe that artificially which we see men doe in choller naturally" (*Apologie*, in *Elizabethan Critical Essays*, ed. Gregory Smith [Oxford, 1904], i.202).

20/The implication of the preceding account (49.1 ff.) is that the poet generally deals with fictitious situations, or with situations which he knows at second hand. This is confirmed by several of the characteristic ballads of 1798: *The Thorn* and *The Idiot Boy*, the "plots" of which were largely invented by Wordsworth, and *Goody Blake*, the "plot" of which came from his reading, though he believed it to be based on fact. This implication seems to be ignored by Mr. Sharrock when he claims that Wordsworth's theory demands "the words of the original participants in the action" (Sharrock, p. 401); where the action is fictitious, the notion of "original participants" has no meaning.

In spite of the analogy,[21] this interpretation cannot agree with Wordsworth's intention. We must interpret his phrase "that [language] which the real passion itself suggests" to mean: "that [language] which is suggested by the passion [with which the poet has to deal] when it actually occurs in similar situations in real life"; or: "that [language] which would be suggested by the passion [with which the poet has to deal] if the situation [now dealt with by the poet] actually occurred in real life."[22] The language defined by these glosses has no immediate relevance to a poetic based on the concept of imitation: for in the first case the poem would necessarily be a distorted image of the postulated exemplar, and in the second case the postulated exemplar has no existence, and the accuracy of the image cannot be assessed. We must seek a standard of value other than successful imitation.

Such a standard lies in the basic theory of "expression" itself. In terms of this theory, a truly poetical language is in the first instance prompted by, and prompted only by, passion;[23] on those occasions when the poet is not prompted by passion (either "really" felt, or felt by means of sympathetic identification) his utterance will, *ipso facto*, fail as poetry.[24] His success or failure in imitation is not in question; for his successful utterance is *of the same kind* as real-life utterance prompted by passion, and not a reflection of it.

Wordsworth's account, thus interpreted, differs from earlier and later accounts based on expressive poetics in two respects: his con-

21/Wordsworth does not make it clear whether he thinks the primary analogy between translator and poet true or false, though he rejects its implication (50.12–13). See *P.L.B.*, Commentary, n. on 363–67.

22/Cf. Gerard, *Genius*, p. 357: "it is the fancy, excited by the lively conception of the passion, running into the same thoughts which the passion, if really working, would suggest, and placing the artist in the situation in which he would then be, that puts it in his power to imagine, and consequently to represent, its causes and its objects in a way proper for infusing it into others."

23/Even when the style is, with propriety, "subdued and temperate" (nonfigurative, or less figurative than elsewhere?), it is prompted by passions, albeit "of a milder character" (48.7–11).

24/Bad poets produced poetic diction by imitating the figures of Primitive Poets "without having the same animating passion" as had produced the exemplars (63.14–15).

cession of the intermittent nature of the poet's success, and his insistence on the principle of "selection" for the purpose of affording "pleasure."

Failure of sympathetic identification, and hence of the dramatic poetry which depends on it, is, of course, envisaged by other critics. But it is usually envisaged as complete failure opposed to complete success, or as typical of a merely unsuccessful poet or poetic method. Thus the accounts given by Alexander Gerard and William Duff take it more or less for granted that, *ex hypothesi*, anyone who has a just claim to the title of poet will be successful in this respect: Gerard's "person whose sensibility of heart enables him to conceive the passion with vivacity, to catch it as by infection"; or Duff's "person ... endued with a vivacity and vigour of Imagination, as well as an exquisite sensibility of every emotion," who "has nothing else to do, in order to move the passions of others, but to represent his own feelings in a strong and lively manner." In such accounts, a poet is, by definition, one whose sympathetic identifications are successful and sustained; indeed, it would appear, sustained with ease. Gerard and others place in separate categories the successful products of sympathetic identification and mere "descriptions" of passion, but do not concede the possibility of partial failure and a resulting mixed genre; for it is the "indifferent poet" who "feels not the passion, [who] has not force of genius or sensibility of heart sufficient for conceiving how it would affect a person who felt it"; who consequently "gives not a natural *representation* of the passion, but a laboured *description* of it."[25]

Wordsworth, who presumably writes with the caution of experience, is more modest in his claims. But his concession of partial failure ought not to be interpreted, as it has been (see Sharrock, *passim*), as a rejection of poetry in favour of real life. For an expressive poetic does not deny the possibility of an accurate report of real life in poetry: it affirms rather that poetry will not result when real

25/Gerard, *Genius*, p. 357; Duff, p. 153; Gerard, *Genius*, pp. 172, 169. For further details, see *P.L.B.*, Commentary, n. on 345–49.

life, and, in particular, passion really felt, is not directly or indirectly
at the basis of the poet's utterance; that the utterances (though not
necessarily, or even usually, the situations) of the poet and of real
life are essentially of the same kind, and prompted by the same kind
of stimulus: the one is not a mere mirror of the other, "a matter of
amusement and idle pleasure" (50.15). On the basis of such a theory,
the phenomenon of dramatic poetry clearly demands particular consideration, in order that it may be brought within the category of
"expression." Wordsworth is concerned to show that the psychological process by which this may be achieved is not likely to be infallible, but this is the only kind of failure which he is at the moment
conceding: in other genres, such as subjective lyric ("where the Poet
speaks to us in his own person and character," 53.36–37), the fallible
element, sympathetic identification, does not enter into the poetic
process.

IV *Selection*

The process called "selection" might, as we have seen, be regarded,
in terms of the text of 1800, as the primary activity of the poet in the
making of a poem: a discarding of such of his material (the language
of men) as is irrelevant to his purpose, and a retention of what he
needs – the poem itself, apart from the metrical form to which the
language is "fitted."

Whether or not this interpretation is justified, it is clear that, in the
addition of 1802, selection is regarded as only a secondary activity.
It is now conceived to operate, not upon the total mass of "the language of men," but upon a portion of it, already limited by virtue of
its originating passion. From this point of view, much of the process
of selection as it is perhaps to be understood from the text of 1800 is,
in terms of the text of 1802, already performed when the selection of
1802 is required to work upon the language of passion. Expressed
somewhat differently: the selection of 1802 works upon the language

of one man (the poet) rather than upon the language of men; and, while it is implied throughout, and later stated, that the poet's language does not "differ in any material degree from that of all other men who feel vividly and see clearly" (54.19–20), yet this virtual identification of the poet's language with the language of men is here merely implicit, and secondary in emphasis to the notion of language as the individual's inevitable response to passion. To such an individual language the involved definition, in the early part of the Preface, of the language of men, given as objectively as Wordsworth's clumsy apparatus will allow, is not primarily relevant; it tends, indeed, towards a mimetic theory of poetry. For the language so defined might, in theory, be used by the poet even if it were not his "natural" language: as poetry may be written by an Englishman in French or Latin, the "natural" languages of others, or even in Basic English, a variety of his "natural" language so severely restricted by definition and rule that it is "unnatural." In such cases the poet may be said to imitate the utterance of those to whom such languages are "natural," rather than to "express his feelings naturally." This fairly objective and "mimetic" approach to language which is the primary approach of the Preface of 1800,[26] and which is retained without significant alteration in the early part of the full text, clashes inevitably with the almost purely "expressive" approach of 1802.

The later view is more in accordance with Wordsworth's conception of language as "an incarnation of the thought" and not as "only a clothing for it" (125.27–28). For the interpretation of the version of 1800 which has been suggested hints at thought already existing, in some sense, before it is given verbal expression, or even existing in some verbal form from which it may be translated, when necessary, into a rather strictly defined "language of men"; the version of 1802, on the other hand, hints at thought (or "passion") immediately, in-

---

26/So Wordsworth says specifically, in a passage descending from 1800: "I have proposed to myself to *imitate*, and, as far as is possible, to adopt the very language of men" (44.31–33). Cf. sec.iii, n.19, above, on similar ideas in the note of 1800 to *The Thorn*. In 1801 Wordsworth called *The Brothers* and *Michael* "faithful *copies* from Nature" (36.28).

evitably, and automatically embodied in language, and without intelligible existence unless so embodied.

The language which is thus automatically prompted by passion, real or sympathetic, is the supremely authentic expression of it. Wordsworth's general argument at this point proposes to demonstrate that this authentic utterance cannot be tampered with, by addition, without loss of authenticity: for "no faults have such a killing power as those which prove that [the poet] is not in earnest, that he is acting a part, has leisure for affectation, and feels that without it he could do nothing" (107.16–19). The poet who has "leisure" to "trick out or to elevate nature" (49.33), to think up "excellences of another kind" (50.9), or to devise "transitory and accidental ornaments" (53.19–20), is, clearly, not so deeply in the throes of "powerful feelings" that he is in an emotional condition appropriate to the production of poetry. *Lycidas*, observed Johnson, in phrases which Wordsworth perhaps remembered, "is not to be considered as the effusion of real passion; for passion runs not after remote allusions and obscure opinions. ... Where there is leisure for fiction there is little grief."[27]

Yet Wordsworth allows one major concession to the theory of poetry as artefact not effusion. The "real language of nature," however achieved by the poet, is, according to the emphasis of 1802, not merely authentic but abundantly so in the expression of passion. For the purpose of poetry, which is to provide "pleasure" (49.29),[28] it may, indeed, be excessively authentic, because it may convey, as well as passion, "the painful feeling which will always be found intermingled with powerful descriptions of the deeper passions" (58.23–24), or even "the vulgarity and meanness of ordinary life" (47.23); in short, "what would ... be painful or disgusting in the passion" (49.31–32). The poet uses metre, according to Wordsworth's views

27/*Lives*, i.163; cf. i.37: "when [Cowley] wishes to make us weep, he forgets to weep himself."
28/One of Wordsworth's most firmly held tenets in documents connected with *Lyrical Ballads*: 10.8, 16, 20; 38.5–7, 10, 13–14; 49.29; 50.29–30; 51.3–31; 52.6–21; 55.24; 56.11–12; 57.2–5, 19, 32; 58.6–24.

on that element of poetry, in order to add "a complex feeling of delight" (58.22) which will, in a measure, cancel out the "painful feeling." Selection works in the same sense, not by adding "delight," but by subtracting, in a measure, the "painful feeling," by "removing what would otherwise be painful or disgusting." Selection is thus an attenuating process, a pruning of the over-abundant eloquence of real life; it is a *writing-down* of the excessive vehemence, of the intolerable, or at least painful, authenticity of "the real language of men."[29] If the addition of metre is a sugaring of the bitter pill of passion, selection is an extraction of the more bitter elements which leaves the pleasurable ones available and palatable to the reader.

It is impossible to estimate with certainty the extent to which the application of this principle affected Wordsworth's poetry. His account is so imprecise that we cannot even gather whether the process is approximately contemporaneous with the main act of composition, or whether, on the other hand, it is the same as, or similar to, his well-known habits of revision, which in many cases altered early specimens of "natural" language in the direction of a more "literary" idiom.[30] Is it, in either case, essentially different from that search for precision which every writer makes: for the right word, the more athletic idiom, the more logically ordered sentence, or the more illuminating figure?

From Wordsworth's account we might judge that selection does in fact differ from this process. For the search for precision is a search

29/This account is congruous with the associationist view that a sensation which in moderation is pleasant becomes painful when in excess: see Hartley, pp. xvi, 156; Priestley, *Oratory*, p. 264 (cited above, Chapter II, n.7).

30/The Preface gives no positive support to Garrod's view that "It is not that [the poet] first uses *real* language, mechanically selected and refined, and that he then tempers this, and the passions which it embodies, by the unreality of metre; but, far rather, by imaginative processes which are contemporaneous – and indeed, a unity – he uses, naturally, spontaneously, necessarily, both a 'selected' real language and the metrical forms which help to transmute real passions" (p. 167). The opposite interpretation is suggested by the possible analogy of Wordsworth's recorded revisions, by his remarks on the "adventitious" nature of metre (see above, pp. 27–28, and *P.L.B.*, Commentary, n. on 277 ff.), and by his use of the already uttered language of others in poems such as *Repentance*, discussed below.

for authenticity, and for Wordsworth authenticity is already guaranteed by the pressure of passion. The search for authenticity may proceed by means of amplification, whereas selection proceeds by attenuation, and amplification which is not warranted by passion is expressly frowned upon by Wordsworth.

The question arises: what happens when (if ever) the attenuation of selection proceeds so far that the language of nature disappears? It is difficult to answer because, where no verbal source appears to exist for a particular poem, we cannot be certain that Wordsworth's primary, "unselected" utterance has been recorded, and because, where verbal sources for poems of this period do exist, they are rarely in a language which could reasonably be called passionate. The line from *Simon Lee*, "He dearly loves their voices," is too short to be significant, and shows no attenuation. Reports by Dorothy Wordsworth which gave rise to such poems as *Beggars* and *Resolution and Independence* record the language of men, but not the language of passion (*Journals*, i.47, 63). A semi-literary source such as Dorothy's account of daffodils upon which Wordsworth worked for "I wandered lonely as a cloud" is, in a sense, a record of emotion, but hardly "the spontaneous overflow of powerful feelings"; Wordsworth rejects some of her ideas and words, but what he rejects could hardly be described as "painful or disgusting."[31]

The account of his method which Wordsworth gave to J. T. Coleridge in 1836 is more immediately useful: "he said his principle had been to give the oral part as nearly as he could in the very words of the speakers, where he narrated a real story, dropping, of course, all vulgarisms or provincialisms, and borrowing sometimes a Bible turn

---

31/*Journals*, i.131. For a good account of Wordsworth's method in this poem, in a somewhat different terminology from that employed here, see Frederick A. Pottle, "The Eye and the Object in the Poetry of Wordsworth," in *Wordsworth: Centenary Studies*, ed. Dunklin (Princeton, 1951), pp. 23–42. That the account in the *Journal* might owe something to Wordsworth's own response to the scene at the time, later recollected with the aid of the *Journal*, is a possibility worth consideration, but not mentioned by Professor Pottle. See also Z. S. Fink, *The Early Wordsworthian Milieu* (Oxford, 1958), p. 66. Cf. *P.W.*, ii.503 and iii.427, for instances of borrowing from Wordsworth's verse by the *Journal*.

of expression: these former were mere accidents, not essential to the
truth in representing how the human heart and passions worked;
and to give these last faithfully was his object."[32] Here selection (or
the "purification" of 41.12–14?) is represented by "dropping ... all
vulgarisms or provincialisms"; but "borrowing ... a Bible turn of
expression" does not seem to fall within the scope of such a process,
but to be rather a substitution or amplification. The result of such a
process might, no doubt, be dramatically appropriate to a person of
"low and rustic life," but rather in terms of a mimetic than of an
expressive poetic: an interpretation which finds a little support in the
phrase *"representing* how the human heart and passions worked."

Similar considerations apply to an apparently unique instance
where Wordsworth based a poem directly upon a recorded, extended
utterance in "the real language of nature," reported by Dorothy
from the lips of one of "low and rustic life": the poem *Repentance.*[33]
We shall set out the parallel passages and observe Wordsworth's
operations:

(i)

J[34]   I said many a time he's not come fra London ...

MS.1   When the fine Man came to us from London, said I

MS.2   When the bribe of the Tempter came to us, said I

1820   When the troublesome Tempter beset us, said I   [5]

(ii)

J   ... to buy our land, however.

MSS., 1820   ... we'll die   [7]

Before he shall go with an inch of the land!   [8]

32/*Prose Works*, ed. Grosart (London, 1876), iii.426.

33/Dated 1804 by Wordsworth, but since it occurs in the note-book of Sara
Hutchinson described by Miss Darbishire in *P.W.*, ii (2nd ed., Oxford, 1952),
535 ff., it is much more probable that it belongs, with the other poems in this
MS., to the first half of 1802, and is thus approximately contemporary with the
additions to the Preface. Cf. for a similarly probable misdating, ed. cit., p. 538,
n.1.

34/J = *Journals*, i.83; MSS. = the manuscripts cited in *P.W.*, ii.46–47.

(iii)

J	... and when I had been a bit poorly ...
MSS.	When my sick crazy body had lain without sleep
1820	And in sickness, if night had been sparing of sleep [29]

(iv)

J	O how pleased I used to be ... I would gang out upon a hill ...
MSS.	What a comfort did sunrise bestow when I stood
Corr.MS.3	How cheering the sunshiny hill when I stood
1820	How cheerful, at sunrise, the hill where I stood [30]

(v)

J	... and look ower't fields and see them ...
MSS.	And looked down on the fields and the kine and the sheep From the top of the hill
Corr.MS.3	And looked [Looking] down on the kine, and our treasure of sheep [31]
and 1820	That besprinkled the field [32]

(vi)

J	... and it used to do me so much good you cannot think.
MSS., 1820	... 'twas like youth in my blood! [32]

On the assumption that Dorothy's report is accurate,[35] the most noticeable feature of Wordsworth's version is not the attenuation of the language of passion, but the amplification of it. Only in passage v does Wordsworth's version come very near the report, and even here the final version inserts the notions of "treasure" and "besprinkled." Elsewhere, Wordsworth adds and poeticises. In passages i and ii the report uses that studied spareness of statement which we noted

35/The Fenwick n. on *Misc. Son.*, II.x (*P.W.*, iii.427), states that "no inconsiderable part of [*Repentance*] was taken verbatim from the language of the speaker herself." As Wordsworth himself apparently did not hear Margaret Ashburner, we may reasonably assume that he had no more accurate report than Dorothy's (as far as it goes) to work on; though he may have had a fuller version than the *Journal* gives.

earlier as characteristic of Wordsworth's "language of prose" (p. 22, above). From this reticence Wordsworth moves further in successive versions: the pregnant "London" disappears early, evaporating and expanding into "the bribe of the Tempter" and "the troublesome Tempter," "with his bags [purse] proudly grasped in his hand." The dialectal intensive "however"[36] makes way for the conventionally rhetorical "we'll die before." In passage iii Wordsworth refines the colloquialism and adds, apparently, the notion of lack of sleep. "Sunrise" creeps into passage iv without obvious warrant except for the unauthentic "sparing of sleep" just preceding. The process is epitomized in passage vi where Margaret Ashburner's presumably "vulgar and mean" phrase is utterly rejected by the process of selection, and replaced by a poeticism which would have been more appropriate had she suffered from senile decay rather than consumption.

In drawing conclusions from Wordsworth's procedure in this poem, we must assume that he thought it as justifiable to work upon another's utterance prompted by "the actual pressure of ... passions" (49.17–18) as upon his own utterance prompted by "real" or sympathetic passion. This assumption, though it turns the poet for the time being into a reporter, may be supported on several grounds. First, it puts the poet in the position of that Primitive Poet who used "language ... which he had heard uttered by those around him" (64.14–16), and who, in spite of or because of this, is, in Wordsworth's view, no less a poet. Secondly, the language is still "the spontaneous overflow of powerful feelings," though not the poet's, except in the sense that the feelings may have been made his own by sympathetic identification, even if their "overflow" was known to him in advance by hearsay.[37] Thirdly, as we saw earlier, the poet's utterances are of the same kind as those prompted by "real" passion (p. 73, above).

36/See *E.D.D.*, *s.v.*, sense II.1: "Used as an emphatic expletive: indeed, in fact, truly. *Gen.* used to end a sentence." Cf. *O.E.D.*, *s.v.*, sense 4: "In any way whatsoever; at all."

37/On another occasion, Wordsworth "could not escape from those very words [in the *Journal*], and so he could not write the poem [*Beggars*]" (*Journals*, i.123; cf. i.47). But Dorothy's account of the beggars is not "the spontaneous overflow of powerful feelings."

And, lastly, the assumption is in accord with the report of J. T. Coleridge cited above.

With these points in mind, it would seem reasonable to conclude that, in Wordsworth's view, poetry may emerge from an accurate report of another's passionate utterances, and that selection may, therefore, operate upon this raw material as well as upon that which may emerge from the poet's report of his own emotional experience. If this is so, we apparently have a specimen of its operations in the parallel passages cited above; and we must conclude that selection (the only modifier of the language of passion which has Wordsworth's countenance) not only rejects and retains, but also replaces what it rejects and amplifies what it retains: a process which might not seem to differ *toto caelo* from "trick[ing] out or ... elevat[ing] nature." And if we think it worth while to observe that a common-sense view of the procedure of many poets would lead us to suppose that some or all of these processes are involved in the production of many poems, yet we must observe at the same time that the sum of the processes is not aptly defined as "selection."

v *"Language Exquisitely Fitted for the Passion"*

The imaginary objector who presses the case for "artificial distinctions" of language finds a flaw in Wordsworth's argument in the admission that the sympathetic identification so desirable for the production of authentic utterance in dramatic poetry cannot be consistently maintained: since the excellence of "language as exquisitely fitted for the passion as that which the real passion itself suggests" (50.6–7) can be achieved only intermittently, the deficiencies at this level of excellence might be filled by "excellences of another kind."

To this objection Wordsworth offers no direct retort, except that it implies an encouragement to "idleness" (in striving for authenticity of utterance?) "and unmanly despair" (of reaching it as often as possible?). The effort towards authenticity must be made: for "the dramatic parts of composition are defective, in proportion as they deviate from the real language of nature, and are coloured by a diction of the Poet's own" (53.27–29). Granted the theory of poetry on which Wordsworth here relies, and the source of the failure, no other retort seems possible: where there is no passion, real, or simulated to an adequate degree and attributable to the poet's dramatic characters, no poetry overflows.

Sensing, presumably, the inevitable limitation of this line of argument, Wordsworth shifts his ground to an exposition of poetry as concerned with general truth, in an attempt to show that poetry so conceived cannot tolerate "artificial distinctions" of language. The argument, perhaps the most eloquent passage in the Preface, is nevertheless full of obscurities, and, in particular, has been found difficult to connect logically with the account of the poet given in the preceding three paragraphs (48.27–50.3).

The difficulty may be epitomized in some such manner as the following. If it is admitted that "it is impossible for the Poet to produce upon all occasions language as exquisitely fitted for the passion as that which the real passion itself suggests" (50.5–7), with what logic can it be said that "Poetry is the image of man and nature" (50.24–25) since the image of man presumably involves a representation of his passionate speech? Or how can it be said that "there is no object standing between the Poet and the image of things" (50.33–51.1) except the "necessity of giving immediate pleasure" (50.29–30), when another, and much more formidable, "object" appears to have been described in the at least intermittent failure of the poet to "produce ... language ... exquisitely fitted for the passion"?

We may profitably clear away certain misconceptions before attempting to resolve this difficulty. Wordsworth in these passages makes no criticism of language as a medium of expression or communication (Sharrock, *passim*, esp. pp. 398–401). The failure which he concedes is a failure, not of language, but of the state of the poet's mind in which poetic language has its origin, namely, "passion," "emotion," or "powerful feelings." Once the appropriate state of mind is achieved, then, if nothing extraneous intervenes, authentic utterance is assured; but the difficulty, to Wordsworth, lies in the achieving of that state of mind.

"The appropriate state of mind" appears to vary with poetic mode. In the dramatic mode, the requirement is clear: it is a sympathetic identification of poet with dramatic characters in which, "for short spaces of time," the poet must "confound and identify his own feelings with theirs" (49.25–27). This procedure will produce, by suggestion (49.28), a language which is the basis of authentic dramatic utterance and which does not require "tricking out" or "elevating" (49.33), though it may require "selection" (49.31) before it is actually suitable for poetry. The authenticity of this language appears to be contrasted favourably with a comparatively unauthentic language which might be "suggested," not by sympathetic passion, but by the poet's "fancy or imagination."[38] For some reason which Wordsworth does not explain, he regards sympathetic identification as a state which can be maintained only "for short spaces of time" (49.25), so that, as the following paragraph puts it, "it is impossible for the Poet to produce *upon all occasions* language as exquisitely fitted for the passion as that which the real passion itself suggests" (50.5–7). Thus the poet's success in the dramatic mode is likely to be, at best, intermittent; and it is upon this that the imaginary objector seizes as the ground for his plea for "excellences of another kind" (50.9).

The non-dramatic mode is discussed later, in a passage (53.34 ff.) which refers to that immediately preceding the lines we have just discussed (48.29–49.13). We are now informed that the "passions

38/This seems to be the intention of the sentence "Here, then, ... and truth" (49.29–50.3): a distinction between the languages "suggested" by two procedures, or from two sources – sympathetic identification, and "fancy or imagination." The first is equivalent, or approximately equivalent, to "the emanations of reality and truth"; the second falls short of that standard. It would be possible to read the sentence as meaning that the "emanations of reality and truth" stand higher in authenticity than the promptings of sympathetic feeling, which are suggested by the poet's "fancy or imagination"; or that the "emanations of reality and truth" stand higher than the promptings of sympathetic feelings, which in turn stand higher than the promptings of the poet's "fancy and imagination."

and thoughts and feelings" (54.8) which the poet may "conjure up" (49.3) "without immediate external excitement" (49.12–13, 54.6) "are the general passions and thoughts and feelings of men" (54.8–9). They are concerned with general truth (54.10–15): "How, then, can [the Poet's] language differ in any material degree from that of all other men who feel vividly and see clearly? ... he must express himself as other men express themselves" (54.19–29).

We have, therefore, definitions of the emotional bases (and corresponding "languages") of two broadly defined poetic modes: the dramatic and the non-dramatic. Success in either mode depends upon the poet's assumption of the appropriate emotional stance; and, of the two, the stance appropriate to the dramatic mode is, in Wordsworth's view, the more difficult to achieve or, at any rate, to maintain. A poetry written consistently in terms of one or other (or both, on occasion) of these requirements would be, in fact, an "image of man and nature." From the terms of this last proposition, some light may be cast on our problem. For what is discussed in the passages just considered is not so much poetry *per se* as inherent difficulties in producing it. It is upon poetry *per se*, "real" poetry, "consistently successful" poetry, poetry "worthy of the name" (or whatever gloss of this kind may seem acceptable) – it is upon such an ideal poetry, surely, and not upon individual metrical compositions which may or may not achieve consistently that authenticity of utterance which poetry demands for its perfection, that Wordsworth lavishes his praise. Towards this ideal the poet, setting aside "idleness and unmanly despair," strives, though he does not, in practice, achieve it invariably, or even frequently. But when he does, he produces an "image of man and nature," and nothing then stands between him and "the image of things" except the need to give pleasure. "The dramatic parts of composition are *defective*, in proportion as they deviate from the real language of nature" (53.27–29); such defective parts are, indeed, not poetry, not "the image of man and nature," but merely unsuccessful attempts towards that end. The poet's words will "frequently" be "incommensurate with the passion" (57.6–7);

when they are, he may approximate more closely to the idea of poetry by a judicious choice of metre; but the pessimism here revealed, and the acknowledged need for a means of compensating for such defects, do not imply any depreciation of poetry as such, but only of the poet's efforts towards it in particular compositions. The ideal is not damaged by deviations from it: that a sinner purports or strives to follow a moral code does not justify the conclusion that the code is meaningless or impossible. So Wordsworth draws attention to the extraordinary value of poetry, while remaining fully aware that some, perhaps many, compositions, or parts of compositions, written by men who call themselves poets, including William Wordsworth,[39] are not poetry. They would resemble poetry even less, he argues, if the poet gave up the attempt to "bring [his] language near to the real language of men" (59.11–12), and used instead a jargon "peculiar to him as an individual Poet, or belonging simply to Poets in general" (53.30–31). For "all good poetry is the spontaneous overflow of powerful feelings," and feelings do not overflow in poetic diction; "good" poetry will not tolerate "transitory and accidental ornaments ... the necessity of which must manifestly depend upon the assumed meanness of [the poet's] subject" (53.19–22). The justification of such a "sublime notion of Poetry" we shall consider in the next section.

VI *General Truth*

Wordsworth's most urgently argued counter to his imaginary objector is that the poet, since he deals with general truth, ought not to "break in upon the sanctity and truth of his pictures by transitory and accidental ornaments, and endeavour to excite admiration of himself by arts, the necessity of which must manifestly depend upon

39/See 59.16–28. Sidney says: "if the Philosophers haue more rightly shewed themselues Philosophers then the Poets haue obtained to the high top of their profession, ... it is, I say againe, not the fault of the Art, but that by fewe men that Arte can bee accomplished" (*Apologie*, in *Elizabethan Critical Essays*, ed. Gregory Smith [Oxford, 1904], i.166).

the assumed meanness of his subject" (53.18–22). We shall consider Wordsworth's conception of general truth from two viewpoints: in this section, the nature of general truth; in the next, the mode by which it is perceived.

Wordsworth's account is nominally based on a well-known passage in Aristotle (*Poetics*, 1451.b.5–7); but the ominous phrase "I have been told," and the misquotation "Poetry is the most philosophic of all writing" (50.18–19), do not inspire confidence in Wordsworth's understanding of his authority.[40] The terms of the contrast between poet and historian (50.25–51.2) are Aristotle's; but the nature of it, that the poet's is the easier task, is not mentioned in the *Poetics*. Wordsworth's stress on the notion of pleasure is much more marked than is Aristotle's, and the idea is linked with the conception of general truth in a manner not to be found in the *Poetics* (see 1448.b.5–9). More generally, it is probably true that Wordsworth's idea of general truth differs, radically perhaps, from Aristotle's, but certainly in the much wider scope of Wordsworth's view.

Wordsworth's argument runs somewhat as follows: [i] Poetry deals with general truth (50.18–25). [ii] It is easier for the poet to represent accurately general truth than for the historian to represent particular truth (50.25–51.2). [iii] The only restriction which prevents the poet from representing general truth with complete fidelity is the need to give pleasure to the average man (50.28–33). [iv] This need to give pleasure to the average man, far from being a degradation of poetry, is consonant with the general scheme of things (51.3–11). [v] For upon the principle of pleasure depends sympathy, even with pain (51.11–13); [vi] and upon it depends knowledge, even of unpleasant subjects (51.13–21). [vii] Just so, and more generally, the mental make-up of man, with which he contemplates the world, is such that, when he contemplates it, the feelings excited are, on balance, pleasurable (51.21–31). [viii] The poet deals with this common mental make-up and with the feelings thus excited (52.1–9); [ix] his

40/He should have said that poetry is more philosophical than history. See *P.L.B.*, Commentary, n. on 373.

approach to it is comparable with that of the scientist to particular, and obscure, aspects of nature (52.9–35). [x] Within his scope will come any knowledge, even that of the scientist, which may become common intellectual property (52.36–53.16). [xi] Poetry thus deals with a subject so important that it will not tolerate ornaments (53.16–22). Of the sections indicated above, [ii] will best be discussed later; the remainder will be considered now as casting light on Wordsworth's conception of general truth.

Sections iii–vii are in the nature of a digression upon the element of pleasure in poetry which might be "considered as a degradation of the Poet's art" (51.3–4). The length of the digression perhaps arises from fear of a charge of inconsistency between 50.28–51.2 and 50.13–15, where the view of poetry as "a matter of amusement and idle pleasure" is deplored: Wordsworth is concerned to show that poetry does indeed impart pleasure, but not "idle pleasure." "Poetry," he observes, "is the image of man and nature"; but the image may be a distorted, or, much rather, an incomplete image, if a wholly faithful image would fail to give pleasure, presumably by conveying what might be "painful or disgusting in the passion" with which the poet deals. Indeed, in the particular case of the epitaph, the result of the selective process "*is* truth, and of the highest order! for, though doubtless things are not apparent which did exist, yet, the object being looked at through [a tender haze or a luminous mist], parts and proportions are brought into distinct view which before had been only imperfectly or unconsciously seen: it is truth hallowed by love" (101.35–102.2). What is represented by "love" in the case of an epitaph is evidently generalized as "pleasure" in the case of poetry in general. And if someone should ask why the need to give pleasure overrides the desirability of an absolutely faithful image of man and nature, Wordsworth would reply that it is consonant with "nature," with the scheme of things, with general truth itself. For it is generally true that man's reactions to the world about him are, on balance, pleasurable; whence it appears to follow that a reader's reactions to that image of things with which the poet presents him should be, on balance, pleasurable also. Just so, the omission from the epitaph of what was actually unpleasant in the character of the deceased corresponds to an actual change in the attitude of the once hostile observer: "Enmity melts away; and, as it disappears, unsightliness, disproportion, and deformity, vanish; and, through the influence of commiseration, a harmony of love and beauty succeeds" (102.7–10).

The passage represented by sections viii–x of our summary sets out, in terms which seemed even to contemporary readers somewhat too ecstatic for expository prose,[41] Wordsworth's conception of general truth. He stated it rather more simply at the beginning of the Advertisement of 1798: "every subject which can interest the human mind" (10.2). With more precise detail, he tells us in the Preface that "the sensations and objects which the Poet describes" are "our moral sentiments and animal sensations, and ... the causes which excite these; ... the operations of the elements and the appearances of the visible universe; ... storm and sun-shine, ... the revolutions of the seasons, ... cold and heat, ... loss of friends and kindred, ... injuries and resentments, gratitude and hope, ... fear and sorrow" (54.10–17). Here, indeed, is God's plenty, but hardly Aristotle's general truth, a notion concerned with a much more technical matter, the logic of dramatic fable and the audience's perception of that logic.[42] Wordsworth's conception of general truth seems to be that it comprises all human knowledge which is not specifically technical and therefore restricted in its appeal to experts in the techniques concerned. Thus the poet need not write to appeal to "a lawyer, a physician, a mariner, an astronomer, or a natural philosopher" (50.31–32); Man *qua* Man is both his subject and his audience. General truth, says the second *Essay upon Epitaphs*, is *"the universal intellectual property of man; – sensations which all men have felt and feel in some degree daily and hourly; – truths whose very interest and importance have

41/Coleridge to Southey, 29 July 1802 (*C.L.*, ii.830).
42/Wordsworth's notion is less akin to Aristotle's than to Juvenal's "Quicquid agunt homines, votum, timor, ira, voluptas, Gaudia, discursus, nostri est farrago libelli" (*Sat.*, I.85–86).

caused them to be unattended to, as things which could take care of themselves." Such truths are to be *"uttered in such connection as shall make it felt that they are not adopted – not spoken by rote, but perceived in their whole compass with the freshness and clearness of an original intuition" (117.33–118.6); or, as the Preface puts it, general truth is "carried alive into the heart by passion; truth which is its own testimony" (50.21–22).

To such descriptions of general truth it is likely that Aristotle's conception of dramatic probability does indeed conform. That which is dramatically probable commends itself as such by the test of our own experience, of ourselves or of others. That ambition seeks to remove obstacles in its path, as in the case of Macbeth; that jealousy has an ambivalent attitude towards its object, and is abnormally susceptible to hints of sexual infidelity, as is Othello's: these are general truths confirmed by the experience of most of us or by our observation of others; we should not recognize Shakespeare's plots as credible if they were not. The story of Michael appeals because it is our common experience that fathers love their sons and that a sufficient number of sons betray their fathers' trust. Yet many of Wordsworth's less successful poems which might be similarly justified in terms of this conception of general truth lack a similar appeal. We shall consider some examples.

In an earlier chapter, it was observed that many readers find in *The Thorn* a divided aim: the portrayal of "the maternal passion" obscured by an attempt to portray a superstitious mind. Wordsworth, in the note to the poem, is at pains to point out that the second object is his major one, and there seems to be no reason why we should not take him at his word. Let it be clearly recognized, then, that the object of *The Thorn* is not to portray the maternal passion except incidentally, but to present "some of the general laws by which superstition acts upon the mind" (12.15–16). The laws by which superstition acts on the mind are, to Wordsworth's thinking, part of general truth; they could not otherwise be described as *laws*. The protest of the reader, that this presentation obscures the story of the betrayed

mother, is nothing to Wordsworth's point; but it is a tacit acknowl-
edgement that some parts of general truth are more interesting than
others. The reader, sensing this, feels that the interesting part is
inadequately treated, and unwarrantably obscured by the verbosity
of Wordsworth engaged in an investigation of the laws of superstition.[43]

Goody Blake is, on the surface, a plain tale of human brutality
aptly rewarded by supernatural intervention. In the Preface, the
supernatural is carefully explained away as "the truth, that the
power of the human imagination is sufficient to produce such
changes even in our physical nature as might almost appear miraculous" (59.1–4). That the "many hundreds of people who would never
have heard of" this "important truth" might fail to recognize it as
such, or if necessary might prefer to assume a "willing suspension
of disbelief" to the effect that a curse uttered is effective, merely *qua*
curse, are points which do not seem to have occurred to Wordsworth.
That is, it seems probable that belief in curses, genuine or assumed
for the enjoyment of poetry, Aristotle's probable impossibility
(*Poetics*, 1460.a.26–27; cf. 1454.b.6–8), is more likely to be part of
the "universal intellectual property of man" than Wordsworth's
proposition about the imagination, more in accordance with psycho-

43/Thus Mr. Sharrock (pp. 402–3) claims that "the real subject of the poem, of
course, is the woman's tragedy, not the sea-captain's superstitious nature. ... The
sea-captain with his banality and repetitions was chosen because they provide
the most fitting medium for an experience which defies language in its tragic
poignancy." We shall understand the poem better if we regard it rather as an
attempt to portray a superstitious nature moved by the woman's tragedy, as
Wordsworth's note and treatment indeed suggest. His use of the theme of the
deserted woman is too frequent, and too frequently direct, to allow us to suppose that here he adopts an oblique mode because he thinks that the woman's
tragedy "defies language." We may note that *The Thorn* is not classified with
The Idiot Boy and *The Mad Mother* as an illustration of "the maternal passion"
(42.33), and that in Wordsworth's classification of 1815 and later years it appears
among the "Poems of the Imagination," whereas the other two are among the
"Poems Founded on the Affections." See the detailed exposition of a closely
similar view of the poem in Stephen M. Parrish, " 'The Thorn': Wordsworth's
Dramatic Monologue," *ELH*, xxiv (1957), 153–63. I do not think that the poem
provides definite evidence for (or, indeed, against) Mr. Parrish's view that "its
central 'event' has no existence outside of the narrator's imagination" (p. 155);
but the reference to the poem in *Prel.*, xiii.402–3, might perhaps be cited against
Mr. Parrish.

logical science though that may be. Indeed, the very proposition that "many hundreds of people ... would never have heard of" this important truth, "had it not been narrated as a Ballad" (59.6–7), seems sufficient evidence for this conclusion. Wordsworth's similar attempts to show, in *Peter Bell*, that a "natural" Brutus will start a spirit as well as a supernatural Caesar are well known.[44]

Another curious instance is the sonnet "With Ships the sea was sprinkled."[45] At least one woman, if not "many hundreds of people," failed to perceive in this poem the truth of the proposition that "There is scarcely one of my Poems which does not aim to direct the attention to some moral sentiment, or to some general principle, or law of thought, or of our intellectual constitution"; in this case, "that the mind can have no rest among a multitude of objects, of which it either cannot make one whole, or from which it cannot single out one individual, whereupon may be concentrated the attention divided among or distracted by a multitude" (81.4–11). The connection of the sonnet with this principle Wordsworth proceeds to demonstrate with some labour for the benefit of Mrs. Fermor, who may, for anything we know, have received the exposition with gratitude. Wordsworth evidently considered the principle which he expounds an important one; and indeed it has obvious affinities with the workings of the Imagination which he describes in the Preface of 1815.[46] But we may be permitted to doubt whether every operation of an "important" faculty is in itself important: sight and hearing are important faculties of the human make-up, but not everything seen or heard is therefore important, and in not every exercise of the faculties does the "mind wanton with grateful joy in the exercise of its own powers" (82.10).[47]

44/See especially Lascelles Abercrombie, *The Art of Wordsworth* (London, 1952), pp. 134–54.

45/*Misc. Son.*, I.xxxii; *P.W.*, iii.18; cited in Zall, p. 80.

46/"the Imagination also shapes and *creates*; and how? By innumerable processes; and in none does it more delight than in that of consolidating numbers into unity, and dissolving and separating unity into number" (149.18–21).

47/Florence Marsh, *Wordsworth's Imagery* (New Haven, 1952), p. 126, goes so far as to claim that "Anything related to the action of the mind Wordsworth regarded as poetic."

In brief, some of Wordsworth's poems, as he feared, deal with "unworthy subjects," in that he has "given to things a false importance" (59.18–20). Yet the importance he attributed to the subjects may, in a sense, be justified if a sufficiently wide sense is given to the notion of general truth. For, if all aspects of general truth are regarded as equally important (and nothing in the passage we are considering prevents us from believing that this was Wordsworth's view), then the poet may write, confident of success, on (so to speak) almost anything which affects man and is not of an obscurely technical nature. Wordsworth was on safer ground, we may think, when he wrote in 1800 of the need to "discover what is really important to men" (19.23–24), and defined the poet's task as "to follow the fluxes and refluxes of the mind when agitated by the great and simple affections of our nature" (20.1–2). Thus in *The Idiot Boy* and *The Mad Mother* he traces, as he says, "the maternal passion"; but in *The Thorn* he portrays, not the mind agitated by maternal passion, but a particular sort of mind agitated by the spectacle of another mind agitated by the maternal passion. If superstition were one of "the great and simple affections," the poem would, at best, have a divided aim; but most people would probably regard superstition as an evil or a folly: it has other names when it is not so regarded. Thus the reader who pays due attention to Wordsworth's purpose and method in this poem is oppressed with a sense that the more important has been wilfully subordinated to the less in the scale of things,[48] a scale of which Wordsworth sometimes seems to have lost sight in his enthusiasm for general truth.

Goody Blake may similarly be regarded as a study in cruelty, and a resultant hatred so powerful that it appears to affect its object physically without recourse to physical means. We question the means by which this result is achieved no more than we question the machinery of epic or the sense of fate in Greek tragedy: that a curse

48/Whence it follows that critics have been prompt to commend those stanzas of *The Thorn* which present the maternal passion rather than the superstitious sea-captain; e.g., *Biog. Lit.*, ii.36–38; Sharrock, p. 402.

works has been believed by more people than those who are read in Wordsworthian psychology. And when Wordsworth presses the point that a curse works by reason of a subjective reaction in the mind of the cursed, we may retort that this is the view of the scientist, as Wordsworth described him in 1815, who treats of "things ... as they *are* ... as they exist in themselves," and not of the poet, who deals with things "as they *appear* ... as they *seem* to exist to the senses and to the *passions*" (160.5–6).[49] Another interpretation of the facts which the poem presents is as consistent with "the universal intellectual property of man" as, if not more consistent than, Wordsworth's interpretation of them in the Preface.

With these and similar poems in mind, we may question whether Wordsworth's conception of general truth as he presents it in the additions of 1802 is as valuable a guide for the poet as his stress on the importance of selected aspects of it in the text of 1800. It seems probable, indeed, that his view of the proper material for verse was, over these crucial years, widening to a degree dangerous to the success of his poetry. Such a process was detected by Coleridge in 1802: "He has written lately a number of Poems (32 in all) some of them of considerable Length (the longest 160 Lines) the greater number of these to my feelings very excellent Compositions but here & there a daring Humbleness of Language & Versification, and a strict adherence to matter of fact, even to prolixity, that startled me."[50] The wider the conception of general truth, the more *recherché* will be

---

49/The poem itself, of course, presents "things ... as they *appear*"; the criticism above is directed against Wordsworth's unpoetical explanation and the frame of mind which it reveals. Stephen M. Parrish, "Dramatic Technique in the *Lyrical Ballads*," *PMLA*, lxxiv (1959), 88–97, suggests that Wordsworth intends the reader to infer a naïve narrator who accepts the validity of the curse and is unable to recognize the "truth" as the Preface presents it.

50/*C.L.*, ii.830. It is difficult to account for thirty-two poems written "lately" with respect to 29 July 1802; but for the titles of twenty-eight or twenty-nine written between March and the date of Coleridge's letter, see F. W. Bateson, *Wordsworth: A Re-interpretation* (London, 1954), pp. 215–16. The longest of 160 lines is evidently *Resolution and Independence* (140 lines in the standard text, plus three stanzas [21 lines] which Wordsworth never published; see *P.W.*, ii [2nd ed., Oxford, 1952], 237, 238, 541).

the particular instances by which the poet seeks to illustrate it. Even in 1800, "the maternal passion" was to be traced "through many of its more subtle windings" (20.4–5), rather than in its more obvious exhibitions such as we find, for instance, in Shakespeare's Lady Macduff. The culmination of such an extension of the conception appears in the inclusion in general truth of what is factually true, merely because it is true: for that which is factually true is obviously part of that large conglomerate of things which are true – a part of general truth. At such a stage in his thinking the poet will lean more and more on the matter of fact, which is by Wordsworth identified, ironically enough, with science, the antithesis of poetry (47.fn.2). We may regard *Goody Blake* as a tale of anger and hatred, or as a quasi-scientific, if oblique, exposition of the subjective workings of the imagination; but only in the latter case will we be concerned to know that the episode "is a *fact.*" Aristotle, indeed, permits the poet to deal with fact, but only on the ground that "nothing forbids some of the things that actually have happened to be such as are likely to happen";[51] and that which "might almost appear miraculous" is, we may think, unlikely to happen, though it may be recorded (as Erasmus Darwin recorded it) as an isolated fact worthy of the scientist's attention.

Such an extension of the notion of general truth was criticized by John Wilson, and defended by Wordsworth, in their correspondence of 1802. Wilson observes that "no description can please where the sympathies of our soul are not excited, and no narration interest where we do not enter into the feelings of some of the parties concerned. On this principle, many feelings which are undoubtedly natural, are improper subjects for poetry. ... There are a thousand occurrences happening every day which do not in the least interest an unconcerned spectator, though they no doubt occasion various emotions in the breast of those to whom they immediately relate. To describe these in poetry would be improper" (Smith, p. 56). These notions Wilson applies in particular to *The Idiot Boy.*

51/*Poetics*, 1451.b.29–32. Translation of A. H. Gilbert, *Literary Criticism: Plato to Dryden* (New York, 1940), p. 82.

Wordsworth retorts by pointing to the deficiencies in "human nature, as it has been and ever will be," and to the literary prejudices, of a sophisticated upper- and middle-class audience – the despised "Public" of later utterances (see 187.14 ff.; *M.Y.*, i.145, 150, 194– 5): "These persons are, it is true, a part of human nature, but we err lamentably if we suppose them to be fair representatives of the vast mass of human existence." He aims, he affirms, to correct such deficiencies: "a great Poet ... ought, to a certain degree, to rectify men's feelings, to give them new compositions of feeling, to render their feelings more sane, pure, and permanent, in short, more consonant to nature, that is, to eternal nature, and the great moving spirit of things. He ought to travel before men occasionally as well as at their sides." Some have appreciated *The Idiot Boy*: "This proves that the feelings there delineated are such as men *may* sympathise with. This is enough for my purpose. It is not enough for me as a Poet, to delineate merely such feelings as all men *do* sympathise with; but it is also highly desirable to add to these others, such as all men *may* sympathise with, and such as there is reason to believe they would be better and more moral beings if they did sympathise with" (71.19–75.4).[52] "It is not enough"; "it is highly desirable to add"; "He ought to travel before men"; "Of genius ... the only infallible sign is the widening the sphere of human sensibility. ... Genius is the introduction of a new element into the intellectual universe" (184.19–23);[53] these and similar phrases are symptomatic of Wordsworth's urge to expand the conception of general truth. His application of the principle is responsible for some of his most remarkable poetic discoveries; when uncritical, it is equally responsible for his most astonishing failures. The same mind that by subtle probing discovered in itself "the hiding-places of man's power" (*Prel.* [1850],

52/In 1812 Wordsworth "is convinced that if men are to become better and wiser, the poems will sooner or later find their admirers" (*H.C.R.*, p. 73).

53/Cf. *Prel.*, xii.301–5; *M.Y.*, ii.178; *H.C.R.*, p. 89. Arnold, on the contrary, considered that "there are ... few actions which unite in themselves, in the highest degree, the conditions of excellence," that is, "which most powerfully appeal to the great primary human affections; to those elementary feelings which subsist permanently in the race, and which are independent of time" (*Poetical Works*, ed. Tinker and Lowry [London, 1950], pp. xxi, xix-xx).

XII.279), in the finest parts of *The Prelude*, also thought it defensible to record, in the sonnet discussed above, one of its most trivial operations.

In so far as general truth, in Wordsworth's sense, is that which actually exists or happens, rather than an abstraction, that factor which is common to what actually exists or happens in various instances, it is clear that its language is, appropriately, the real language of men; in so far as it approaches the matter of fact, its language is, appropriately, the language of prose. More pertinently to the present discussion, Wordsworth's profound concern over the language of dramatic poetry is explicable in terms of this view of general truth. For, in terms of this view and of an expressive poetic, the authenticity of the language of subjective lyric is guaranteed, since it records what actually goes on in the mind of the poet; but how can language record what actually goes on in the mind of a dramatic character who has no real existence? This problem, as we saw earlier, Wordsworth solves, in his own fashion, not completely to his own satisfaction; but what concerns us here is that the demand for complete authenticity in language is parallel to the notion that general truth is a conglomerate of authenticated facts, a body of real events rather than an abstracted norm. That men speak so and not thus is one of these verifiable facts, which it is part of the poet's task to preserve free from distortion. "Transitory and accidental ornaments" are therefore to be rejected, we may think, not so much because Wordsworth has been successful in conveying a "sublime notion" of poetry, or of its subject-matter which is general truth, as because it is part of general truth that the speech of "men" does not use "transitory and accidental ornaments." Poets and critics who have held a somewhat different view of general truth have been less concerned with this particular sort of authenticity in language, and have thought, perhaps, that "freedom and power" belong rather to the poet than to the man who feels passion; and to the poet precisely because he is *not* "under the actual pressure of ... passions,"[54] not oppressed by a "consciousness of the inadequateness of [his] powers, or the defi-

54/See *Biog. Lit.*, ii.15, cited above, Chapter III, sec. ii, n.17.

ciencies of language," not concerned to reproduce such deficiencies, but rather, with the aid of his freedom, to transcend the limitations of "the real language of men."

VII *The Perception of General Truth*

Wordsworth's mode of perceiving general truth is a version of that eighteenth-century mode of thinking which Arthur O. Lovejoy called "Uniformitarianism," whereby "The reason, it is assumed to be evident, is identical in all men; and the life of reason therefore, it is tacitly or explicitly inferred, must admit of no diversity. Differences in opinion or in taste are evidences of error, and universality of appeal or of acceptance tends to be taken, not merely as an effect, but as in itself a mark or criterion, of truth" (Lovejoy, pp. 79–80). This conception needs qualification by modifiers proposed by Lovejoy himself: first, and most important, that " 'reason' ... is not chiefly synonymous with intellect and antithetic to feeling – which, indeed, it may include – but is a name for that which is fundamental and constant in the generic constitution of man" (p. 89). Secondly: "the belief that – precisely because all individuals, *quâ* rational, are fundamentally alike, and because this uniform element in them is the only important element – truth is to be attained by every individual for himself, by the exercise of his private judgment uninfluenced by tradition or external authority; in other words, by 'the pure light of nature' which shines in all alike." This characteristic Lovejoy called "Rationalistic individualism."[55] We shall examine Wordsworth's view of general truth in the light of this major notion and its modifications.

The mere introduction by Wordsworth of the notion of general truth is sufficient evidence that he had a strong sense of the uniformity of mankind; and his very turns of phrase show that his argument in the passage concerned is based squarely upon it: "Poetry is

55/Lovejoy, p. 82. In his appeal to "the consent of all nations" to justify his use of metre (55.21–22), Wordsworth uses what Lovejoy (p. 83) calls "The appeal to the 'consensus gentium.'"

the image of man and nature" (50.24–25); "general principles drawn from the contemplation of particular facts" (51.14–15); "man in his own nature and in his ordinary life" (51.24–25); "this knowledge which all men carry about with them, and ... these sympathies in which without any other discipline than that of our daily life we are fitted to take delight" (52.1–3); "general nature" (52.8–9); "the knowledge of the [poet] cleaves to us as a necessary part of our existence, our natural and unalienable inheritance" (52.13–15); the poet's "song in which all human beings join with him" (52.19–20); "In spite of difference of soil and climate, of language and manners, of laws and customs ... the Poet binds together ... the vast empire of human society, as it is spread over the whole earth, and over all time" (52.27–31).[56] The generalizing we and its forms, -ever, and man or men, are in constant use.[57] The point is made, with less emphasis though still as a basic assumption, in the Advertisement of 1798: "every subject which can interest the human mind" (10.2); "a natural delineation of human passions, human characters, and human incidents" (10.18–19); and in the text of 1800: "the primary laws of our nature" (18.3–4); "repeated experience and regular feelings" (18.24–25); "the great and simple affections of our nature" (20.2); "elements ... belonging ... to nature" (20.20); "the great and universal passions of men, the most general and interesting of their occupations" (25.18–20).

Outside the Preface, Wordsworth is, more characteristically, concerned to draw a contrast between his own and other modes of thought which he admires, on the one hand, and, on the other, those of men who deal rather with the points of difference between individuals than with points of resemblance. This contrast appears in his correspondence both early and late: the Lyrical Ballads "may ... enlarge our feelings of reverence for our species, and our knowledge of human nature, by shewing that our best qualities are possessed by

---

56/"Cosmopolitanism" (Lovejoy, pp. 83–84).
57/See 50.24, 33; 51.8, 10–16, 22, 24, 29; 52.1, 3, 4, 5, 16, 17, 20, 32, 33; 53.1–2, 9, 11, 13, 16.

men whom we are too apt to consider, not with reference to the points in which they resemble us, but to those in which they manifestly differ from us" (36.31–37.3); "some cannot bear to see delicate and refined feelings ascribed to men in low conditions of society, because their vanity and self-love tell them that these belong only to themselves and men like themselves in dress, station, and way of life. ... [The poet is to please] human nature, as it has been and ever will be" (71.4–20); "I have endeavoured to dwell with truth upon those points of human nature in which all men resemble each other, rather than on those accidents of manners and character produced by times and circumstances" (*L.Y.*, p. 127); "in my treatment of the intellectual instincts affections & passions of mankind, I am nobly distinguished by having drawn out into notice the points in which they resemble each other, in preference to dwelling, as dramatic Authors must do,[58] upon those in which they differ. If my writings are to last, it will ... be mainly owing to this characteristic. They will please for the single cause, 'That we have all of us one human heart!'"[59]

This contrast, and the antithetical manner which an attempt to discriminate between man and man encourages, become major themes in the three *Essays upon Epitaphs.* The epitaph does and should draw upon commonplaces: for

"We shrink from the thought of placing [the] merits and defects [of deceased persons] to be weighed against each other in the nice balance of pure intellect; nor do we find much temptation to detect the shades by which a good quality or virtue is discriminated in them from an excellence known by the same general name as it exists in

58/Note again the concern over dramatic poetry; cf. sec. iii above.
59/*C.R.*, p. 273. The line of verse is from *The Old Cumberland Beggar,* a poem designed mainly to illustrate this proposition. Cf. also *H.C.R.*, p. 535: Wordsworth "did not expect or desire from posterity any other fame than that which would be given him for the way in which his poems exhibit man in his essentially human character and relations – as child, parent, husband, the qualities which are common to all men as opposed to those which distinguish one man from another." The contrast, its terms implicitly or explicitly related to the Imagination and the Reason, is common in *The Prelude* and in other poems: see Havens, pp. 317–18, 319–20, nn. to *Prel.* (1850), II.203–32, 221.

the mind of another; and least of all do we incline to these refinements when under the pressure of Sorrow, Admiration, or Regret, or when actuated by any of those feelings which incite men to prolong the memory of their Friends and Kindred, by records placed in the bosom of the all-uniting and equalizing Receptacle of the Dead." (100.15–25)

Individualization is indeed permissible; but universality and individualization should "temper, restrain, and exalt each other" (101.17–18).

"It suffices ... that the Trunk and the main Branches of the Worth of the Deceased be boldly and unaffectedly represented. Any further detail, minutely and scrupulously pursued, especially if this be done with laborious and antithetic discriminations, must inevitably frustrate it's own purpose; ... for, the Understanding having been so busy in it's petty occupation, how could the heart of the Mourner be other than cold? ... in no place are we so much disposed to dwell upon those points, of nature and condition, wherein all Men resemble each other, as in [the church or by the grave] ... Let an Epitaph then, contain at least these acknowledgments to our common nature; nor let the sense of their importance be sacrificed to a balance of opposite qualities or minute distinctions in individual character." (102.24–103.15)

On such considerations Wordsworth bases his attack on the epitaphs of Pope.[60]

For such a knowledge of general truth the poet might, presumably, rely on one or both of two sources indicated in our preceding section: on observation of himself as a typical man, or on his generalized experience of other men.[61] In practice, Wordsworth must have relied

---

60/Cf. also: "the pride that induces [the reader] to dwell upon those points wherein Men differ from each other, to the exclusion of those in which all Men are alike, or the same" (182.33–35).

61/Which might include, presumably, his experience of literature, though Wordsworth pays no attention to this in the Preface. Whatever Wordsworth's theme of the deserted mother (for instance) may owe to his experiences in France, it also has obvious affinities with a common theme of popular and

on both. Presumably a man cannot represent with authenticity the emotions of a woman and a mother,[62] or a sane man the passions of an idiot, by observing himself. We are obliged to guess at the scope of Wordsworth's observation of mothers, mad, foolish, or even normal, before 1798. But the latter part of his letter to John Wilson of 1802 is full of information about idiots which is implicitly supported by Wordsworth's observation, direct or indirect, of idiots "in the lower classes of society" and "Among the Alps, where they are numerous" (73.15, 30). He seems to have had an actual individual in mind when he wrote *The Idiot Boy*; moreover, "I have known several with imperfect faculties who are handsome in their persons and features. There is one, at present, within a mile of my own house, remarkably so" (74.16–20). The figure of Michael derives, in some sense, from the character of Thomas Poole; further, "from the comparative infrequency of small landed properties in [Poole's] neighbourhood, [his] situation has not been altogether as favourable as mine,"[63] presumably for the observation of such characters.

It seems significant that these remarks are concerned with poems

quasi-popular ballads of the time. On the conventionality of the themes and forms in *Lyrical Ballads*, see Robert Mayo, "The Contemporaneity of the *Lyrical Ballads*," PMLA, lxix (1954), 486–522.

62/Cf. F. C. Prescott, *The Poetic Mind* (New York, 1922), pp. 207–8, on "the heroines of the masculine novelists." Note, on the other hand, the passage from Balzac cited by Prescott, p. 209: "Hearing these people, I was able to adopt their life; I felt their rags on my back, I walked along with my feet in their worn-out shoes; their desires, their wants, all passed into my soul, and my soul passed into theirs." This seems to be a case of sympathetic identification following observation. More strikingly, Flaubert is reputed to have affirmed, "Mme. Bovary, c'est moi!" (Albert Thibaudet, *Gustave Flaubert* [Paris, 1922], p. 93).

63/E.Y., p. 322. The Fenwick note to *The Excursion* provides much information on Wordsworth's methods of creating characters. Margaret came from observation (*P.W.*, v.373, 376), and so did the Solitary (p. 374; but see Edward E. Bostetter, "Wordsworth's Dim and Perilous Way," PMLA, lxxi [1956], 433–50); the Pedlar is partly Wordsworth, partly one James Patrick (pp. 373–74); but the Pastor is wholly invented (p. 375). See also p. 417, n. to 738–826; p. 442, n. to 671; and many other references throughout the Fenwick note to the use of observation, hearsay, and the like. For transfer of Wordsworth's own feelings to his characters, see pp. 418–19, introductory n. to Book III. This information is moderately consistent with the view expressed below in the text, that Wordsworth tended to rely on observation up to the end of 1800 or thereabouts.

written by the end of 1800. They are consistent with the views of a poet who, though not himself of "Low and rustic life," yet chose to draw his subject-matter from that class, and to use a language belonging to it which was not, strictly speaking, his own. They are consistent, in fact, with those several traces of a mimetic theory of poetry which we have previously observed in the Preface of 1800 but not in the additions of 1802.[64] The rustic, from this point of view, is mankind's epitome, and general truth may be presented in an imitation of his actions and passions and language, made by a poet who is, for the purposes of this theory, *spectator ab extra*, and who might be, as far as the process and its results are concerned, indifferently a man or a Martian.

This is not the viewpoint of the additions of 1802. Observation, though not excluded by an expressive poetic, and to some extent implicit in any theory of uniformitarianism, is in 1802 markedly lacking in emphasis. If the poet can now be said to write while looking steadily at his subject (45.16), it must be understood that the subject thus steadily observed, even when dramatic poetry is in question, is now mainly his own mind. In terms of this poetic, the poet, rather than the rustic, is mankind's epitome; and in expressing himself he expresses all men. For the poet "is a man speaking to men" (48.29–30); among his characteristic qualities "is implied nothing differing in kind from other men, but only in degree" (54.2–4); the "passions and thoughts and feelings" which he con-

64/Similarly, they are consistent with good neo-classical theory in Wordsworth's predecessors: see the passages from Johnson's Preface to Shakespeare, cited in sec. ii above; or Richard Hurd, "Notes on [Horace's] Art of Poetry," in *Works* (London, 1811), i.260: "What way then of determining the precise bounds and limits of [a passion]? Only by observing in numerous instances, *i.e.* from a large extensive knowledge of practical life, how it usually, in such characters, and under such circumstances, prevails"; p. 261: "Whether this representation of Sophocles be not more agreeable to *truth*, as collected from wide observation, *i.e.* from human nature at large, than that of Euripides, the capable reader will judge. If it be, the reason I suppose to have been, *that Sophocles painted his characters, such, as, from attending to numerous instances of the same kind, he would conclude they ought to be; Euripides, such, as a narrower sphere of observation had persuaded him they were."*

jures up "are the general passions and thoughts and feelings of men" (54.8–9). Various great commonplaces "are the sensations and objects which the Poet describes, as they are the sensations of other men, and the objects which interest them. The Poet thinks and feels in the spirit of the passions of men" (54.16–19). So Coleridge puts upon the notions of observation, and mimesis based upon it, a low value in the poetic scale of things: "By what *rule* that does not leave the reader at the poet's mercy, and the poet at his own, is the latter to distinguish between the language suitable to *suppressed*, and the language, which is characteristic of *indulged* anger? Or between that of rage and that of jealousy? Is it obtained by wandering about in search of angry or jealous people in uncultivated society, in order to copy their words? Or not far rather by the power of imagination proceeding upon the *all in each* of human nature? By *meditation*, rather than by *observation*? And by the latter in consequence only of the former?"[65]

Yet the viewpoint cannot be utterly subjective. That the poet can recognize the generality of his "passions and thoughts and feelings" indicates that he has some objective conception of "the general passions and thoughts and feelings of men" as a standard of comparison. We are to find "the best measure" of "human nature, as it has been and ever will be," "from within; by stripping our own hearts

[65]/*Biog. Lit.*, ii.64. The contrast with Hurd's views just cited is striking. Cf. *S.C.*, i.122, 201, 206; ii.14, 85, 98 ff.; and note the admission (ii.101) that characters may emerge from observation (Fielding's minor characters cited). An intermediate position in Sir Joshua Reynolds, *Discourses* (London, 1907), pp. 107–8: "A knowledge of the disposition and character of the human mind can be acquired only by experience; a great deal will be learned, I admit, by a habit of examining what passes in our bosoms, what are our own motives of action, and of what kind of sentiments we are conscious on any occasion. We may suppose an uniformity, and conclude that the same effect will be produced by the same cause in the mind of others ... but we can never be sure that our own sentiments are true and right, till they are confirmed by more extensive observation ... as he who does not know himself, does not know others, so it may be said ... that he who does not know others, knows himself but very imperfectly." By "true and right" Reynolds means, obviously, "in accordance with general experience." Johnson writes of descriptions of "the human passions ... of which every man carries the archetype within him" (*Adventurer*, No. 138); but "*Othello* is the ... offspring of observation impregnated by genius" (Raleigh, p. 33).

naked"; but also by "looking out of ourselves towards men who lead the simplest lives, and those most according to nature" (71.19–23). In 1800 Wordsworth recognized that such a control could not be infallible: "I am sensible that my associations must have sometimes been particular instead of general, and that, consequently, giving to things a false importance, sometimes from diseased impulses I may have written upon unworthy subjects" (29.5–9): an aesthetic crime parallel to the use of "a diction of the Poet's own, ... peculiar to him as an individual Poet" (53.29–30).

In spite of such modifications explicit and implicit, the most marked emphasis of the addition of 1802 remains on the poet as his own subject, as representative man: an emphasis which looks forward to that significant general heading in the *Poems* of 1807, "Moods of My Own Mind," and, even more significantly, to *The Prelude*.[66]

It is probably to this emphasis that we should look for the reason why, to Wordsworth, the poet's task is much easier than the historian's (50.25–51.2). Such a view might, indeed, be consistent with a poetic of imitation based on observation, in that what generally happens is more open to observation and imitation than what has happened, perhaps contrary to probability, in particular cases. This seems less likely to be Wordsworth's intention than that the poet's task is the easier because the poet is a man; because he is, by definition as it were, one familiar with general truth. He is necessarily unfamiliar with the abstruse details of particular historical situations, the authenticity of which stands "upon external testimony" (50.21); but he is not unfamiliar with the things which men commonly do, feel, or think; for, being a man, he must do, feel, or think them himself. Such truth is "its own testimony" (50.22) because the poet knows it to be true in himself.

The title of Lovejoy's paper is "The Parallel of Deism and Classicism." No one need suppose, from the preceding discussion, that

66/The generalizing subtitle, "The Growth of *a Poet's* Mind," is Mrs. Wordsworth's. To Wordsworth, *The Prelude* was "a Poem on my own earlier life" (E.Y., pp. 436, 447, 454, 470, 513, 518, 586, 605).

Wordsworth ought to be considered a neo-classic poet. Emphases have, clearly, been shifted: Wordsworth's reliance on the notion of "rationalistic individualism" is, from the neo-classic point of view, excessive. It is, indeed, the justification for that widening of the conception of general truth which was discussed in the preceding section. The doctrine as the eighteenth century understood it, that man *qua* man is right because he agrees with all men, and that deviation from this norm of rectitude is merely error, becomes, in Wordsworth's hands, the argument that agreement between the poet and some men is sufficient proof that he has attained general truth, and that those who agree with him are, obviously, the pure in heart, whereas those who do not are, as obviously, the sophisticated Public, prejudiced, lacking in true taste, and aberrant from "nature." *The Idiot Boy* "has, I know, frequently produced the same effect as it did upon you and your friends; but there are many also to whom it affords exquisite delight, and who, indeed, prefer it to any other of my poems. This proves that the feelings there delineated are such as men *may* sympathise with. *This is enough for my purpose*" (74.29–33; my italics in the last sentence). This, no doubt the battle-cry of all *avant-garde* artists, becomes an obsessing theme in Wordsworth's correspondence relating to the unfavourable reception of the *Poems* of 1807, refuses to be kept out of the Preface of 1815 (151.13–24), and is fully developed, in the *Essay, Supplementary to the Preface*, to the position that poetry (such as Wordsworth's) unpopular in its own day is likely, if not certain, to achieve immortality. We are concerned here less to inquire into the truth of this argument than to see its fairly inevitable emergence from positions taken up by Wordsworth as early as 1802.

Wordsworth diverges from neo-classic practice in his relation to general truth in another sense. The characteristic mode of eighteenth-century neo-classicism is, in Wordsworth's eyes, antithetical; the characteristic genre is satire. The mode is, in Wordsworth's view, decorous with the genre. For *"vice and folly are in contradiction with the moral principle which can never be extinguished in the mind: and, therefore, wanting this controul, are irregular, capricious,

and inconsistent with themselves. ... It is reasonable, then, that ...
Dryden and Pope [in their satirical portraits] should represent qualities and actions at war with each other and with themselves: and that
the page should be suitably crowded with antithetical expressions"
(120.12–121.5). Such a mode, however, is inappropriate "where virtue ought to be described in the language of affectionate admiration"
(121.6–8), and in this respect Pope in his epitaphs erred grossly. In
other terms: the satirist accepts as a norm which is universally held,
and which does not require special exposition, a uniform moral and
social outlook; he concentrates his attention upon deviations from
the norm. To this emphasis Wordsworth's theory and practice stand
opposed: he is concerned to expound the norm, which is sometimes
in danger of being obscured,[67] and, further, to demonstrate that the

67/Cf. "the universal intellectual property of man ... truths whose very interest and importance have caused them to be unattended to, as things which could
take care of themselves" (117.33–118.1); and 40.28 ff., on "The principal object"
of *Lyrical Ballads*: "ordinary things ... presented to the mind in an unusual way
... tracing ... the primary laws of our nature"; and the whole of the following
passage, 41.1–12. See my edition of *Lyrical Ballads*, 1798 (London, 1967), pp.
xxxi–xxxv. Wordsworth thought his own industrializing age peculiarly unfavourable to the perception of the norm: see 43.29–44.24, and note especially the
stress on the current taste for the abnormal in: "gross and violent stimulants ...
savage torpor ... craving for extraordinary incident ... frantic ... sickly and stupid
... idle and extravagant [literature] ... outrageous stimulation." These ideas
appear, in another context, as early as 1796 or 1797, in the Preface to *The
Borderers*: *"good actions being for the most part ... silent and regularly pro-
gressive, they do not present those sudden results which can afford a sufficient
stimulus to a troubled mind. In processes of vice the effects are more frequently
immediate, palpable and extensive ... [Oswald] has rebelled against the world
and the laws of the world ... he cannot exist without occupation, he requires
constant provocatives ... whenever ... he finds such contrarieties as seem to affect
the principles of *morals*, he exults over his discovery ... to such a mind those
enterprizes which are the most extraordinary will in time appear the most
inviting. His appetite from being exhausted becomes unnatural ... he finds his
temptation in strangeness ... his thirst after the extraordinary buoys him up ...
his creed is ... made and not adopted" (4.20–6.31). Oswald, in his rejection of the
normal in feelings, morals, and beliefs, thus presents, on an heroic scale, the
state of the average English mind as Wordsworth saw it in his generation: he
achieves in his actions that "outrageous stimulation" which Englishmen of
1800 sought, according to our text, vicariously in their literature. By a different
antithesis, James Scoggins arrives at an essentially similar conclusion: "Wordsworth ... refused to accept the universally unquestioned assumption that the

norm may be observed where superficial deviations might be thought symptomatic of its absence. For this purpose, no doubt, the poet, though "a man speaking to men," must be "endued with more lively sensibility, more enthusiasm and tenderness, ... a greater knowledge of human nature, and a more comprehensive soul, than are supposed to be common among mankind" (48.29–33). Thus equipped, he is prepared to trace "the maternal passion through many of its *more subtle windings*" (42.33–34); to carry *"every where* with him relationship and love" (52.26); "to follow the steps of the Man of Science ... carrying sensation into the midst of the objects of the Science itself" (53.3–6); to observe "affinities In objects where no brotherhood exists To common minds" (*Prel.*, II.403–5). By such changes of emphasis, perhaps, rather than by utter rejection and opposition, is the change from classic to romantic accomplished.

province of poetry is the world of fictions. His revolt ... was not against literature exactly, but against literature conceived of as exclusively fictional. ... The argument is ... for a rediscovery of the meaning of objects and man's passions, both of which men had ceased to know fully" ("The Preface to *Lyrical Ballads*: A Revolution in Dispute," in *Studies in Criticism and Aesthetics 1660–1800*, ed. Howard Anderson and John S. Shea [Minneapolis, 1967], pp. 390–92). Wordsworth's own reasons for the neglect include not only Mr. Scoggins', that "false poets had substituted their arbitrary and fictional worlds for the real one" (p. 392), i.e., the "frantic ... sickly and stupid ... idle and extravagant" literature of his age, but also all the other reasons cited earlier in this note.

From the preceding chapters we may gather the materials for a brief account of the agreements and disagreements between the two texts of the Preface.

The Subject

Both texts show Wordsworth concerned primarily with man as his subject-matter. He is concerned to illustrate "general truth," the norm of human behaviour, "nature" in the sense of human nature rather than of external nature. And he is concerned to illustrate it positively, to show its existence where its absence might have been suspected. He is concerned also to assert its value, to show that behaviour which coincides with the norm is morally valuable, rather than to emphasize, as did the great satirists of a preceding generation, that deviation from the norm is morally reprehensible. He seeks the norm rather than deviations from it, and finds it where deviations might be expected on a superficial view, in the simple, the foolish, and even the insane, in "Souls that appear to have no depth at all To vulgar eyes."[1] "I look," he wrote in 1800,

> "for Man,
> The common Creature of the Brotherhood,
> Differing but little from the Man elsewhere."
>
> (*Recl.*, I. i.352–54)

1/*Prel.*, XII.167–68. "To careless eyes" (text of 1850) is probably nearer Wordsworth's intention.

He thought his own time peculiarly in need of such a search, his own generation peculiarly insensitive to the norm and its moral value.

The text of 1802 shows a marked development in Wordsworth's conception of the general truth of human behaviour. Such an extension is inherent in his earlier approach: the poet who begins with the postulate that *"Even* in obscure places the norm may be found" is liable to forget the force of the adverb in his widening search for the norm. Having found it in some odd corners of humanity, he is likely to find it wherever he looks. There is, indeed, an excellent chance that he will find it where no one thought to look before; but he may also tend to think he finds it in places which have rightly been ignored by other poets. Hence arises, as we have seen, an increased reliance on the matter of fact, on that which is regarded as part of general truth merely because it is factually true; or on that which may indeed be generally true, but which is of small significance, and which the poet nevertheless values because it is generally true. The poet, who may find himself, at best, a member of a group which sympathizes with his explorations of new poetic fields, now tends to rely more and more upon a subjective judgment of the truth of his perception and the consequent value of his poetry.[2]

The Mode

The text of 1800, as we have seen, is primarily a definition and defence of a particular rhetoric. The rhetoric is defined in roundabout terms, presumably because Wordsworth knows no others; it is defended on the grounds that it has widespread and permanent appeal. It is generally used and generally understood; it is consonant with

2/Wordsworth's sensitiveness to criticism of his work, implicit in 29.17–24, begins to make itself felt in 1802, when the Public is first attacked (70.35 ff.). His irritation at the objections of friends first appears at the same time (*E.Y.*, pp. 364–67), when a potential revolt among some of his usually admiring circle had to be crushed with stern discipline administered both by himself and by Dorothy. The sensitiveness increases as a result of the reception of the *Poems* of 1807, and comes to a head, as we shall see later, in the critical writings of 1815, stimulated, no doubt, by the reception of *The Excursion*.

"nature," and therefore likely to persist. And as the attention of the age is perversely directed to various unnatural and impermanent interests, so the poetical language of Wordsworth's age has been perverted by the use of an unnatural and impermanent rhetoric.

The defence of Wordsworth's rhetoric is continued in the text of 1802, but with a new emphasis. The notion of permanence, while still implied, is now emphasized much less than the notion of "nature." Wordsworth's rhetoric comes to be seen as part of general truth, one fact of the many which go to make up that large conglomerate which it is the poet's task to report.

The Theory

Except in those brief and obscure passages which deal with poetry as "the spontaneous overflow of powerful feelings," the text of 1800 presents a theory of poetry mainly mimetic. The poet sets out to represent the characters and actions of rustics, and to imitate, subject to certain restrictions, their language as accurately as possible. He conceives the norm of human conduct as already embodied, entirely or approximately, in the rustic; the norm of human speech, in the speech of the rustic. With such a model ready to his hand, the poet's own character and feelings are indifferent in the making of his poetry, so long as his poem mirrors with more or less accuracy the actions and speech of the rustic.[3] The poet, from this point of view, is an artificer, and his poem is an artefact, constructed from materials gathered by his observation of others, and shaped and assembled to the lines of a given model.

The text of 1802 presents a poetic almost entirely expressive: the

3/The view of Professor Abrams, that "the relation between the language of 'Tintern Abbey' and the speech of a Lake Country shepherd is not primarily one of lexical or of grammatical, but of genetic equivalence. Both forms of discourse ... are instances of language really spoken by men under the stress of genuine feeling" (Abrams, p. 110), is tenable with regard to the poem mentioned, but not generally. A writer does not say that he proposes "to imitate, and, as far as is possible, to adopt" a particular language (44.32–33) when he means merely that he proposes to write in whatever language has already been made his own.

rustic and his language largely disappear as the poet's norms, the poet himself becomes the representative of general humanity, and his own speech becomes the norm of expression. He expresses his feelings because they are the representative feelings of humanity; and, because his speech is the expression of feeling, its authenticity is assured. Should he have occasion to attribute his speech to persons other than himself, his primary procedure is to identify his feelings with those of such persons. The expressive procedure and the resulting authenticity of language are thus maintained in dramatic poetry.

These characteristics, and the development in Wordsworth's thinking which they show, are interrelated. The widening of Wordsworth's conception of general truth is congruous with the defence of his rhetoric on the grounds of general truth rather than of permanence, though the two standards are mutually consistent. Since the widening is achieved and authenticated by the poet's perception of general truth, rather than by an acceptance of the consensus of general opinion on generally observed phenomena, it is clear that the widening also involves the replacement of the rustic by the poet as the norm of human behaviour; and with this replacement, the substitution of an expressive theory of poetry for a mimetic theory is obviously congruous.

To account for this drift in Wordsworth's thinking is, except in very general terms, difficult. The Appendix of 1802, indeed, shows an interest in academic historical primitivism and an associated expressive poetic which is lacking in 1800. In the critic and poet of 1800 whose ideas include marked signs of cultural primitivism based, apparently, on his own observation, and an obscurely stated version of an expressive poetic based, probably, on Wordsworth's own experience – in such a poet and critic the opinions expressed in such accounts as Enfield's *Enquirer* paper in the *Monthly Magazine* would no doubt find fertile soil. A plausible sequence of events which might help to explain the development in Wordsworth's views would be: a reading of the *Monthly Magazine* which gave rise to the identification in 1800 of the language of poetry with that of prose; a re-reading, with a view to clarifying his ideas on the nature of poetic diction, which produced the Appendix of 1802; and a transfer into the Preface of 1802 of the expressive poetic which is implied in Enfield's paper.

Such a conjecture, however, is not meant to imply that Enfield's ideas were more than a fertilizing influence. They were commonplaces of the age, and Wordsworth's mind was prepared to receive them and to develop them in the light of his own experience. His concern over the difficulties of producing dramatic poetry on the basis of an expressive poetic indicates that he did not merely take such commonplaces on trust.[4] Moreover, we have pointers earlier than 1802 which indicate a probable course of Wordsworth's development. *The Prelude,* as distinct from the wider project of *The Recluse,* seems to have been conceived in 1799. And it is significant that, while in these two (actual and potential) major works Wordsworth recalls or announces his intention to write about man and general truth, the subject of the works themselves is William Wordsworth. Again, the assumption inherent in the text of 1800, that general truth may be perceived by observation of the behaviour of a particular social class, deviations from which are in the nature of sophistications, might easily be modified towards the view that the perception may be achieved by observation of one man, namely the poet. Thus, observation of the all in the representative minority of rustics, modified to observation of the all in each,[5] in the representative minority of one, demands a corresponding change from mimetic to expressive poetic.

4/He takes them on trust when they do not directly concern his own practice: the account of the Primitive Poet, the comparatively late emergence of metrical form, and the like.

5/There seems to be no direct evidence of Coleridge's influence in such a direction at this time. But he criticizes the text of 1800 rather than that of 1802, and deplores the mimetic theory implied by reliance on the rustic as the epitome of mankind (*Biog. Lit.,* ii.64, cited above, p. 105). On the other hand, he was unfavourably "startled" by Wordsworth's practice as early as 1802 (*C.L.,* ii.830, cited above, p. 95); in 1803 he noted with concern instances of "Self-involution in Wordsworth ... & I trembled, lest a Film should arise, and thicken on his moral Eye" (*C.L.,* ii.1013).

Six ✳ Essays upon Epitaphs

1 *The Background*

In the *Essays upon Epitaphs* of 1810, we find reiterated certain principles of poetics which can be extracted from the tangled arguments of the Preface. There is the idea of the desirability of a poetic language permanently effective; as effective to subsequent generations as to the poet and his immediate audience, and uninfluenced by transitory fashions in poetic diction (Chapter I above). The poem is seen as "the spontaneous overflow of powerful feelings," as the expression of what lies within the poet's mind rather than as the imitation of what he may observe without (Chapters III, IV). But it is seen as the expression, not of emotion raw and uncontrolled, but tempered and modified, by the habitual meditative processes of the poet's mind; by the process called "selection," which is used to ensure that the reader receives pleasure, and not pain or disgust, from the expression of passion; and by the disciplinary effect of the metrical form, which ensures that the reader does not mistake the poet's passionate utterance for an uncensored report of real life (Chapters II; IV, sec. iv). Lastly, the poem is the expression, not only of the poet's feelings, but also, and because of the essential humanity of the poet, of a widely defined concept which Wordsworth calls "general truth."

To these ideas the Essays add new concepts, some implicit in the Preface, which point forward to the partially Coleridgean discussion of the Fancy and the Imagination which occupies the major part of

Wordsworth's Preface of 1815. But the essays reveal a much firmer grasp of the principles first stated in the Preface to *Lyrical Ballads*; and this for several reasons.

The Preface, as we have seen, is at odds with itself in its general theory of poetics. Its basis remains the argument of the version of 1800, that poetry arises, or may arise, from an imitation (Coleridge would have called it a copy) of the "real language of men" (16.1), arrived at, we must assume, by empirical observation, by "looking steadily at my subject" (22.30). Upon this basis is imposed, inorganically, an account of poetry as arising from "powerful feelings," a concept by no means implicit in the basic argument of 1800. In the text of 1802 and subsequent versions, the expressive poetic adumbrated in two paragraphs of the text of 1800 is expanded, to take account of the psychological process (sympathetic identification of poet with dramatic character) which enables the poet to write dramatic poetry while yet venting "the spontaneous overflow of powerful feelings." The whole text of 1802 is thus an inorganic composite which wavers between mutually exclusive poetics and which reveals a state of flux in Wordsworth's theories about the year 1800 (see Chapters III–V).

From this defect the *Essays upon Epitaphs* are free; and their freedom arises from Wordsworth's peculiarly apt choice of a particular poetic form upon which to base his argument. For, whereas the Preface to *Lyrical Ballads* in its basic argument made of the poet *spectator ab extra*, observing, without necessary emotional involvement, the behaviour and language of a particular social class of which he was himself not a member, the epitaph is such that (in Wordsworth's view) it cannot effectively be written at all if emotional involvement with the subject is lacking. Moreover, the subject of the epitaph is such that, eventually, it is within the scope of every man: every man, eventually, is faced with the situation which makes him, actually or potentially, the writer of an epitaph. "To be born and to die are the two points in which all men feel themselves to be in absolute coincidence ... *the course of life has placed all men, at some time or other, in" the condition of being stricken in soul at the death of an intimate (100.29–101.1, 124.14–16). By narrowing the scope of his enquiry to a particular poetic form, then, Wordsworth has succeeded, paradoxically, in widening his argument so that by implication it covers all poetry which arises in the manner described in the inorganic portions of the Preface to *Lyrical Ballads*: from the controlled expression of "powerful feelings." The epitaph is thus seen to be a kind of poetic epitome: the virtues of a good epitaph are characteristic of all or most good poetry, and the faults of a bad are characteristic of all or most bad poetry (sec. vii, below).

To such an argument, certain embarrassing features of the Preface are irrelevant, and they are therefore absent from the Essays. The involved sociological argument whereby Wordsworth seeks to justify the use of "Low and rustic life" as his subject-matter, and of its language, is no longer required; for Wordsworth is no longer concerned with the rustic as the epitome of mankind, or with his language as peculiarly "philosophical" (18.5–31). The subject of the epitaph is such that no epitome of this kind is needed: death and immortality are concepts so near men's bosoms that all, not merely the pure in heart who were earlier typified by the rustic, must be emotionally involved. True, the town and the country are still opposed: the country churchyard shares with the wayside burial ground of the Greeks and Romans virtues which can be perceived only with difficulty in the city (96.18 ff.); yet this is remote from the poetic theory of the epitaph. True also, townsmen like Pope and Lord Lyttleton wrote bad epitaphs, and to write such epitaphs is the mark of the not wholly moral man (113.19 ff.); but the faults of their writings are not connected with their social background.

In the epitaph, too, there is little need for the far-ranging pursuit of general truth which is recommended in the Preface and to some extent exemplified in the characteristic *Lyrical Ballads* (Chapter IV, secs. vi, vii). For it is the most widely received of all general truths that men are born, and die, and in some sense hope for immortality; that the dead are mourned and their hope of immortality recorded.

The feelings of men towards these matters need not, then, be sought in their "more subtle windings" (20.4–5). The feelings are widely known and respected; their occasion is indeed a matter of fact, but it needs no seeking; therefore in the epitaph we shall need no mad mothers or idiot boys or retired sea-captains. The epitaph deals, not with that general truth which may be found in obscure corners, but with commonplaces, as it is the purport of the first Essay to point out with emphasis; it deals with "truths whose very interest and importance have caused them to be unattended to, as things which could take care of themselves" (117.35–118.1).

These difficulties of the Preface removed, the Essays offer a more firmly grounded treatment of the major themes of the Preface.

II *Permanence*

By its very nature, the epitaph calls urgently for a language of permanent poetic appeal: a language such as the Preface to *Lyrical Ballads* attempts to define. For the purpose of the monument on which the epitaph is engraved is, "first, to guard the remains of the deceased from irreverent approach or from savage violation; and, secondly, to preserve their memory" (92.3–5). These two motives "do in fact resolve themselves into one," to wit, "the consciousness of a principle of Immortality in the human soul" (92.16, 25–26). That which is designed to commemorate the immortality of the human soul must, from the nature of the case, approach as nearly as possible to a permanent record: the permanence of the human spirit must be matched by the permanence of that which records it.

On the means whereby poetic permanence is to be achieved in the epitaph, Wordsworth does not commit himself except in comparatively general terms. This is to be expected in view of the shift from mimetic to expressive theory which was outlined above. For it is only on the basis of a mimetic theory that the language of a particular social class can be singled out as that upon which the poet should base the language of his poetry, especially when the poet himself is not a member of that class. Where emotional involvement is essential to the production of poetry, we shall expect that no voice other than the poet's shall be heard: the language of rustics, or of any other comparatively strictly defined class, is, to this theory, an irrelevance. Even the slight fiction involved when the epitaph speaks in the person of the deceased, though it presents certain advantages, is not to be preferred to the more straightforward manner of the epitaph which adopts the true voice of the mourner (104.16–37). No "language," therefore, is defined by the Essays as peculiarly appropriate to the epitaph. Certain sorts of language are, indeed, deplored as peculiarly inappropriate; in general, those dictated by the fashions of the age:

*"a man called to a task in which he is not practised may have his expression thoroughly defiled and clogged by the style prevalent in his age, yet still through the force of circumstances that have roused him, his under feeling may remain strong and pure. Yet this may be wholly concealed from common view. Indeed, the favourite style of different ages is so different and wanders so far from propriety that if it were not that first rate writers in all nations and tongues are governed by common principles, we might suppose that truth and nature were things not to be looked for in books." (114.13–22)

*"The far-searching influence of the power, which, for want of a better name, we will denominate, Taste, is in nothing more evinced than in the changeful character and complexion of [the epitaph]." (124.18–22)

In particular, the characteristic antithetical line of Pope and his school, in which *"one half of the process is mechanical, words doing their own work, and one half of the line manufacturing the rest" (118.21–22), is not to be tolerated.

These, however, are negative recommendations. Rather than "style" or "language," the total emotional approach of the poet to his subject, his "thoughts" rather than his "language," are what determine the value and the permanence of the epitaph. But since the poet's thoughts should "have the infinitude of truth"; and since, moreover, he should use "those expressions which are not what the garb is to the body but what the body is to the soul, themselves a constituent part and power or function in the thought ... an incarna-́ tion of the thought" (125.8–27) – for these reasons, the sharp distinction just made between "thoughts" and "language" is not a valid one for Wordsworth in the context of the Essays. The one concept necessarily involves the other, and the poet's "thoughts" will not achieve intelligible form, either for himself or for his audience, unless and until they have been embodied in "language."

Hence Wordsworth is much more concerned to describe the poet's emotional attitude towards his subject than to define, in sociological or any other terms, the language suited to the epitaph. In so far as the permanence of the poetry is in question, his major recommendation is towards what we may call *reticence*. The "thoughts and feelings expressed" in an epitaph should be "liberated from that weakness and anguish of sorrow which is in nature transitory" (103.35–104.1). A line of Mason's "flows nobly from the heart and the imagination; but perhaps it is not one of those impassioned thoughts which should be fixed in language upon a sepulchral stone. It is in its nature too poignant and transitory" (123.24–27).[1] A phrase of Gray's is similarly characterized (Knight, ii.180). A line of Pope's in many contexts *"would be natural and becoming; but in a permanent Inscription things only should be admitted that have an enduring place in the mind" (Knight, ii.181). A vivid phrase attributed to the Duke of Ormonde *"has the infinitude of truth! But, though in this there is no momentary illusion, nothing fugitive, it would still have been unbecoming, had it been placed in open view over the Son's grave; inasmuch as such expression of it would have had an ostentatious air" (Knight, ii.181). The very physical form of the record is in accord with these recommendations: "to raise a

---

1/The poem discussed is William Mason, *Epitaph on Mrs. Mason, in the Cathedral at Bristol.*

Monument is a sober and a reflective act ... the inscription which it bears is intended to be permanent and for universal perusal; and ... , for this reason, the thoughts and feelings expressed should be permanent also. ... The very form and substance of the monument which has received the inscription, and the appearance of the letters, testifying with what a slow and laborious hand they must have been engraven, might seem to reproach the Author who had given way upon this occasion to transports of mind, or to quick turns of conflicting passion" (103.32–104.14). Some names are, from this point of view, their own epitaphs, and ensure the permanence of the record: "The mighty Benefactors of mankind, as they are not only known by the immediate Survivors, but will continue to be known familiarly to latest Posterity, do not stand in need of biographic sketches. ... This is already done by their actions, in the Memories of Men" (105.28–33). "Their naked names" are almost a sufficient memorial. And the most impressive epitaph that Wordsworth ever discovered was also his supreme example of reticence: *"a very small Stone laid upon the ground, bearing nothing more than the name of the Deceased with the date of birth and death, importing that it was an Infant which had been born one day and died the following. ... more awful thoughts of rights conferred, of hopes awakened, of remembrances stealing away or vanishing were imparted to my mind by that Inscription there before my eyes than by any other that it has ever been my lot to meet with upon a Tombstone" (Knight, ii.186–7).

III *Powerful Feelings*

That the epitaph records, in some sense, an "overflow of powerful feelings" (19.16, 27.27–28) goes almost without saying. Wordsworth is, indeed, concerned to show that, at basis, the form arises from the sense of man's immortality, without which "Man could never have had awakened in him the desire to live in the remembrance of his fellows" (92.26–27); but since the deceased does not usually write his own epitaph, we must look for the immediate source in the survivors. This is to be found in what Wordsworth regards as a derivative of the sense of immortality: "a wish to preserve for future times vestiges of the departed" (Knight, ii.129). For from the sense of immortality and from reason "conjoined, and under their countenance, the human affections are gradually formed and opened out ... it is to me inconceivable, that the sympathies of love towards each other, which grow with our growth, could ever attain any new strength, or even preserve the old, after we had received from the outward senses the impression of Death ... if the same were not counteracted by [the sense of immortality]" (94.14–24).

On the simplest level, the writer of an epitaph is a mourner, who records his love for the deceased and his sorrow at his death: "the Writer who would excite sympathy is bound in this case more than in any other, to give proof that he himself has been moved" (103.30–32). If, however, he adopts a certain style, this proof will be obscured: "the Understanding having been so busy in it's petty occupation [of seeking out excessive and antithetical detail], how could the heart of the Mourner be other than cold?" (102.34–35). This basis granted and the need to give proof of it acknowledged, Wordsworth is ready, in the second Essay, to propose an overriding criterion whereby the value of an epitaph is to be judged. He discusses (Knight, ii.153) an epitaph of the quality of which he is doubtful; for it savours, in the quasi-pun on "Sir George" and "Saint George," of the "quaint or out-of-the-way thoughts" of the Metaphysical poets. Yet, considering the accepted social structure of the age which produced the epitaph, Wordsworth is inclined to re-assess: *"I should rather conclude the whole to be a work of honest simplicity; and that the sense of worldly dignity associated with the title, in a degree habitual to our ancestors but which at this time we can but feebly sympathize with, and the imaginative feeling involved, viz. the saintly and chivalrous Name of the Champion of England, were unaffectedly linked together" (Knight, ii.153). So the pun is found to be "natural" when seen against the social decencies of its time.

From this and more especially from other examples, Wordsworth hopes that he has placed "in a clear view the power and majesty of impassioned faith, whatever be its object. ... And this I have done ... with a wish to bring the ingenuous into still closer communion with those primary sensations of the human heart, which are the vital springs of sublime and pathetic composition, in this and in every other kind ... from these primary sensations such composition speaks" (107.1–10). Hence is established *"a criterion of sincerity, by which a Writer may be judged; and this is of high import. For, when a Man is treating an interesting subject, or one which he ought not to treat at all unless he be interested, no faults have such a killing power as those which prove that he is not in earnest, that he is acting a part, has leisure for affectation, and feels that without it he could do nothing" (107.13–19).

We have arrived at a concept which has survived as a major critical canon almost to our own time, if it does not still persist; I know of no earlier extended statement of it.[2] It dominates the rest of the second Essay. Lack of sincerity "is worse in a sepulchral inscription, precisely in the same degree as that mode of composition calls for sincerity more urgently than any other" (107.20–22). It will compensate, "in some degree," for "errors in style or manner" of any kind (107.25–26), provided that the reader's "reflection" is deep enough to penetrate to the sincerity through the verbiage. Montrose's epitaph on Charles I is unsuitable for a tombstone, *"but who can doubt that the writer was transported to the height of the occasion? ... His soul labours ... all modes of existence that forward his purpose are to be pressed into the service. The whole is instinct with spirit. ... Hyperbole in the language of Montrose is a mean instrument made mighty because wielded by an afflicted Soul" (108.12–21, 110.13–14).

Camden's tribute to Sidney[3] is a "simple effusion of the moment,"

2/For a general discussion, see David Perkins, *Wordsworth and the Poetry of Sincerity* (Cambridge, Mass., 1964), *passim*.
3/Wordsworth attributes this to "Weever," i.e., John Weever, *Ancient Funerall Monuments within the United Monarchie of Great Britaine, Ireland, and the Islands Adiacent ...* (London, 1631), the source of many of the epitaphs

contrasted with the "laboured composition" which once served as Sidney's epitaph in St. Paul's (109.35–110.2). An "extravagant" epitaph from Westmorland can be "translated into a natural style," and its sincerity will then be clear: *"this man, notwithstanding his extravagant expression was a sincere mourner, and ... his heart, during the very act of composition was moved" (110.37–111.14). On the other hand, Lord Lyttleton's epitaph on his wife *"would derive little advantage from being translated into another style ... for there is no under current, no skeleton or stamina, of thought and feeling"; yet "Lord Lyttleton dearly loved his wife," and in his epitaph we have an instance of "a feeling heart, not merely misled, but wholly laid asleep by" false taste (112.15–20, 113.9–10).

It is characteristic of the Essays that the elements of their critical theory which are here analysed separately are so closely woven in the texture of the whole that one merges with the other; we are left with the impression of a firm grasp moulding the elements into a new and complex whole. Hence it is that sincerity turns out to be the hallmark not of poetic merit alone. It is a characteristic of the whole man, of that total personal approach to the occasion of the epitaph (or any other poem) which we noted earlier as the major element in Wordsworth's conception of the epitaph as permanent in its appeal. For the sincerity of the epitaph is a mark of the moral stature of the poet.

Of this matter Wordsworth had cast out some obscure hints in the Preface to *Lyrical Ballads*. He hoped that he might produce "a class of Poetry ... well adapted to interest mankind permanently, and not unimportant in the multiplicity and in the quality of its moral relations" (16.23–25). The purpose which he attributed to his work in *Lyrical Ballads* he may have considered as primarily moral; he thought the "affections" of his reader might well be "ameliorated" ("strengthened and purified" in later texts) (19.32–33). An accurate judgment on style "is in itself of the highest importance to our taste and moral feelings" (48.14–15). If his "conclusions are admitted ... our moral feelings influencing and influenced by [our] judgments

---

quoted in the Essays and of other matter; but Weever (as he acknowledges) is here quoting Camden's *Britannia*.

[on literature] will ... be corrected and purified" (48.21–26). On "the accuracy with which similitude in dissimilitude, and dissimilitude in similitude are perceived, depend our taste and our moral feelings" (27.18–20).[4]

These obscurities are illuminated by the second Essay. Insincerity, in the epitaph especially, "shocks the moral sense" (107.20). More boldly, Wordsworth affirms that, in the case of the epitaph, *"Literature is ... so far identified with morals, the quality of the act so far determined by our notion of the aim and purpose of the agent, that nothing can please us ... if we are persuaded that the primary virtues of sincerity, earnestness, and a real interest in the main object are wanting" (113.22–27). In the case of an author who writes a certain type of bad epitaph, "we cannot refrain from attributing no small part of his intellectual to a moral demerit" (113.31–32). As with the poet, so with the reader: the "moral notions and dispositions" of a man who gives attention to the arts *"must either be purified and strengthened, or corrupted and impaired. How can it be otherwise when his ability to enter into the spirit of works in literature must depend upon his feelings, his imagination, and his understanding ... in fine upon all that makes up the moral and intellectual Man?" (114.5–12). Thus we move from the basic principle of emotional involvement, through the concept of sincerity, to the view that art and morals are intimately related; that a right attitude to both is the mark of the full man who is at once the good poet and the good reader.

A corollary to the concept of sincerity concerns the use of metrical form in the epitaph. In the Preface to *Lyrical Ballads*, Wordsworth had proposed the use of metre as pleasurable in itself and also as a control, less upon the poet's language than upon the reader's reaction to that language. Its artificiality, like the process of selection, tempers the language of passion, by imparting an aesthetic distance to the whole poem. The reader is to perceive the "natural," and sometimes painful, language of passion in a frame of artifice which is metre, and he is therefore assured that he deals with an imitation

4/See Chapter III, sec. i.

(in the Coleridgean sense) of real life, not with the utterances of real life in the raw (see Chapter II).

Of this function of metre as a tempering agent, subtly argued in the Preface, or as (in certain circumstances) a stimulating agent, Wordsworth in the Essays says nothing. Rather, he reverts to a position suggested by such phrases in the Preface as these: "fitting to metrical arrangement a selection of the real language of men" (15.3–16.1); "if metre be superadded [to a selection of the language of men]" (47.24); "to such description I have endeavoured to super-add the charm which ... is acknowledged to exist in metrical lan-guage" (25.24–26). Such utterances suggest a concept of metre as mere ornament, imposed upon a verbal structure already poetically valuable in its own right and not essentially modified by the addition of metre. This view, from which Wordsworth moves away as the argument of the Preface (especially in the text of 1802) proceeds, seems to be also that of the Essays; indeed, so indifferent a matter is it to the epitaph that Wordsworth does not even trouble to refer to the "charm" of metrical language with which he began his argument in favour of it in the Preface: "the basis must remain the same in either [prose or verse]; and ... the difference can only lie in the super-structure" (115.6–8). The tempering of the language of passion he evidently considers, as we shall see in the next section, already per-formed by the characteristic approach of the writer of good epitaphs.

The case is altered when Wordsworth turns to consider what he regards as bad epitaphs. For, in such cases, metre is a risk, a tempta-tion towards "phrases of fancy, or ... the more remote regions of illustrative imagery" (115.10–11); towards the "arbitrary and capri-cious habits of expression," the "artificial distinctions," the "pecu-liar" or "particular" language which, according to the Preface, is demanded by metre in the view of some poets and theorists (18.29–30; 47.17; 53.30–33). This is a temptation to which a "judicious man" will not succumb when he writes an epitaph, for "the occasion of writing an epitaph is matter-of-fact in its intensity, and forbids more authoritatively than any other species of composition all modes of fiction, except those which the very strength of passion has created" (115.8–15). Pope has fallen into this temptation, for he wrote epitaphs not *"as a plain Man" but "as a metrical Wit" (115.23–24). Wordsworth sees that Pope's characteristic metrical form suits, if indeed it does not dictate, a rhetoric basically unfulfilling of the needs of the epitaph. His shrewd observations on the consequent vices of the Augustan manner, and his equally shrewd characterization of the virtues of Pope's style, we shall consider more fully in another context.

IV *Selection*

In a passage added in 1802 to the Preface to *Lyrical Ballads*, Wordsworth proposed, in the interests of poetic pleasure, a conscious control on the language suggested to the poet by the process of sympathetic identification with dramatic character. He called this process "selection," whereby the poet sets about "modifying only the language which is thus suggested to him by a consideration that he describes for a particular purpose, that of giving pleasure." This seems to mean no more than that if the poet has "suggested" to him what is commonly called "violent language" as being peculiarly authentic in the presentation of his imagined character, he ought to take care that the language is not so violent as to be "painful or disgusting" (49.27–32).

In the *Essays upon Epitaphs*, a different sort of selection is proposed as especially appropriate to the epitaph. For the poet's "delineation [of the deceased] is performed by the side of the Grave; and, what is more, the grave of one whom he loves and admires" (101.24–26). Therefore,

"The character of a deceased Friend or beloved Kinsman is not seen, no – nor ought to be seen, otherwise than as a Tree through a tender haze or a luminous mist, that spiritualizes and beautifies it; that takes away indeed, but only to the end that the parts which are not abstracted may appear more dignified and lovely, may impress and affect the more. Shall we say then that this is not truth, not a faithful image; and that accordingly the purposes of commemoration cannot be answered? – It *is* truth, and of the highest order! for, though doubtless things are not apparent which did exist, yet, the object being looked at through this medium, parts and proportions are brought into distinct view which before had been only imperfectly or unconsciously seen: it is truth hallowed by love – the joint offspring of the worth of the Dead and the affections of the Living!" (101.28–102.3)

Here, we should say, is selection of "subject-matter" rather than of "language," if we did not remember that to Wordsworth language is now the "incarnation of the thought." We are confronted, again, with the totality of the poet's approach; the epitaph, so handled, becomes an image, or rather an expression, of the whole man's sincere recollection of the deceased. Even a once hostile observer would agree to the truth of the expression (102.4 ff.).[5]

Moreover, selection thus conceived does not, as it seemed to do in the account given in the Preface, *attenuate* the emotional potential of the poem. There, a possible authentic eloquence seemed to require discipline, lest its utter authenticity should pain the reader (49.27–32);[6] here, on the contrary, the selective process raises the potential to its maximum, and at the same time expresses with authenticity the feelings of the poet at the time of composition, "by the side of the Grave" (102.24–25).

5/Cf. Tennyson's juvenile *On a Dead Enemy*, in *Poetic and Dramatic Works*, ed. Rolfe (Boston and New York, 1898), p. 772:

> I came in haste with cursing breath,
>   And heart of hardest steel;
> But when I saw thee cold in death,
>   I felt as man should feel.
> For when I look upon that face,
>   That cold, unheeding, frigid brow,
> Where neither rage nor fear has place,
>   By Heaven! I cannot hate thee now!

The poem has the Ciceronian motto "Non odi mortuum."

6/See Chapter IV, sec. iv.

At the beginning of the second Essay, it is admitted that the process is, indeed, common: having seen all the records of virtue in a country churchyard, the visitor *"will be tempted to exclaim ... , 'Where are all the *bad* People buried?' " (Knight, ii.145). Yet the total reaction of the visitor may be one of serenity; for there is reason to believe that, as with the more subtly defined selective process discussed above, *"the encomiastic language of rural Tombstones does not so far exceed reality as might lightly be supposed" (Knight, ii.148). Such language is too common to be dismissed as mere fiction; and, though the unsympathetic observer could find much in rural life contrary to the sense of the epitaphs, yet they are true in the sense not only that there is much virtue in rustics, but also that they record honestly *"the strength and sanctity of these feelings which persons in humble stations of society connect with their departed Friends & Kindred" (Knight, ii.148). The record is true in the only sense in which an epitaph need, or can, be true: as a record of the feelings of the survivors towards the deceased. "An experienced and well-regulated mind will not, therefore, be insensible to this monotonous language of sorrow and affectionate admiration; but will find under that veil a substance of individual truth" (Knight, ii.149).

v Reticence

In spite of the operations of this variety of selection, a kind of attenuating control is nevertheless seen to be necessary, lest the epitaph should be the mere outpouring of undisciplined emotion. We have already met with the demand for reticence in our discussion of the permanence of the epitaph; we shall need to expand our view of it. Reticence is desirable, as we saw, because the "weakness and anguish of sorrow ... is in nature transitory" (103.36–104.1), and therefore incompatible with the permanence of the record.

More than this: "though the Writer who would excite sympathy is bound in this case more than in any other, to give proof that he himself has been moved, it is to be remembered, that to raise a Monument is a sober and a reflective act" (103.30–33). Here we may recognize something like a re-statement of the Preface's doctrine of "emotion recollected in tranquillity" (27.28).[7] For the time-lag between original emotion and completed poem is, in the case of the epitaph, as it were physically enforced on the poet, since "an Epitaph presupposes a Monument upon which it is to be engraven" (91.32–33). Of this, as well as of the permanence of the record, the physical symbol is "The very form and substance of the monument ... and the appearance of the letters, testifying with what a slow and laborious hand they must have been engraven" (104.9–12). Again, as the monument itself betokens permanence, reflection, and restraint, serving, as an artefact, a purpose similar to that attributed to metrical form in the Preface, so the grave itself, in its physical nature, is a persuasive to temperate utterance: "a Grave is a tranquillizing object: resignation, in course of time, springs up from it as naturally as the wild flowers, besprinkling the turf with which it may be covered, or gathering round the monument by which it is defended" (104.5–9). Not that the resignation and tranquillity indicate a failure of emotion, any more than, in the Preface (27.27–34), the state of the poet during composition is conceived to be the tranquillity in which the original emotion is recollected: "The passions should be subdued, the emotions controlled; strong indeed, but nothing ungovernable or wholly involuntary. Seemliness requires this, and truth requires it also: for how can the Narrator otherwise be trusted?" (104.2–5).

A means of tempering the passion is the quasi-dramatic form in which "Epitaphs ... personate the Deceased, and represent him as speaking from his own Tomb-stone" (104.17–19); and this for two reasons, or a two-fold reason. It forces the poet, as we say, "out of himself," and therefore out of the mere emotion which primarily prompts utterance; and it forces him into the imagined mould of the deceased conceived in a particular way: as one "telling you him-

7/See Chapter III, sec. ii.

self that his pains are gone; that a state of rest is come; and he conjures you to weep for him no longer. He [performs] the office of a Judge, who has no temptations to mislead him, and whose decisions cannot but be dispassionate" (104.19–25). The imaginative effort involved, and the particular *persona* towards which the sympathetic imagination strives, combine to temper the primary passion: "Thus is Death disarmed of its sting, and affliction unsubstantialized. By this tender fiction the Survivors bind themselves to a sedater sorrow, and employ the intervention of the imagination in order that the reason may speak her own language earlier than she would otherwise have been enabled to do" (104.25–30). But if such a tempering can be achieved without the aid of the fiction, so much the better: the result will be nearer the truth.

Restraints appropriate to the epitaph are not necessarily required in some other forms. A line of Mason's, as we have seen, is "too poignant and transitory" for the form; but *"A Husband meditating by his Wife's grave would throw off such a feeling, and would give voice to it; and it would be in its place in a Monody to her Memory" (123.27–30). Similar considerations apply to a line of Pope's; while, in the case of the Duke of Ormonde's remark on his son, "The sublimity of the sentiment consists in its being the secret possession of the Father" (Knight, ii.181). Gray's epitaph on his mother, *"the careful and tender Mother of many Children, one of whom alone had the misfortune to survive her," is more severely criticized. The thought is admitted to be "searching" (Knight, ii.180); but the occasions to which it would have been appropriate are few, and remote from general experience: it is "too peculiar." It is, "if searched to the bottom," a case of "lurking and sickly selfishness." It is unnatural, a disturbance and inversion of "the order of things." It commemorates the mourner rather than the deceased, and is therefore incongruous with its own purpose (Knight, ii.180–81).

Even the admired Chiabrera has occasionally failed for the reasons suggested in this section. Wordsworth does not specify the faults, but they are clear enough: the fictions involved in the personifications of Savona and *Sebeto, and the untempered expression of grief.

*"Chiabrera has here neglected to ascertain whether the passions expressed were in kind and degree a dispensation of reason or at least commodities issued under her licence and authority" (Knight, ii.183–84). For "the excellence of writing, whether in prose or verse, consists in a conjunction of Reason and Passion, a conjunction which must be of necessity benign" (126.5–7): a Coleridgean dictum which, as we shall see, in a broader form dominates most of Wordsworth's Essays.

vi General Truth

Wordsworth's conception of general truth broadens between 1800 and 1802. In the Preface of 1800, it is confined, on the whole, to "the great and simple affections of our nature," such as "the maternal passion," reactions to death, "fraternal ... attachment," "characters of which the elements are simple, ... such as exist now and will probably always exist," "the great and universal passions of men, the most general and interesting of their occupations, and the entire world of nature" (20.2–21; 25.18–20). And in the Preface of 1802 these ideas reappear, as "the general passions and thoughts and feelings of men," connected with "our moral sentiments and animal sensations, and ... with the operations of the elements and the appearances of the visible universe; with storm and sun-shine, with the revolutions of the seasons, with cold and heat, with loss of friends and kindred, with injuries and resentments, gratitude and hope, with fear and sorrow" (54.8–15). But also in 1802 there appears, in Wordsworth's letter to John Wilson, a much broader conception of general truth, which imposes upon the poet the task not merely of reminding men of these great commonplaces which tend to slip out of sight, but also of expanding their mental and spiritual horizons beyond the commonplace: "to rectify men's feelings, to give them new compositions of feeling, to render their feelings more sane, pure, and permanent. ... [The poet] ought to travel before men occasionally as well as at their sides" (72.17–21). In *The Idiot Boy*, "the feelings ... delineated are such as men *may* sympathise with. ... It is not enough for me as a Poet, to delineate merely such feelings as all men *do* sympathise with; but it is also highly desirable to add to these others, such as all men *may* sympathise with." (74.32–75.2) And in 1815, he wrote of genius, which he was not averse to attributing to himself, that its "only infallible sign is the widening the sphere of human sensibility ... the introduction of a new element into the intellectual universe" (184.20–23).

Such later utterances, which suggest, in their stress on novelty, the observations of eighteenth-century theorists such as William Duff and Alexander Gerard on the scientific rather than the artistic genius, are in a measure matched in Wordsworth's poetry by a search for the matter of fact, even for the obscure matter of fact, from which to illustrate the general principle; and in his prose, even in the Preface of 1800, by such a quasi-scientific explanation of a poem as the account of the psycho-physical event with which *Goody Blake* deals (28.26–30).[8]

In spite of the tendency which we may thus trace beginning in 1802, or earlier, and persisting up to 1815, the *Essays upon Epitaphs* revert to the simpler and more traditional view of the subject which is, on the whole, that of the Preface of 1800; and they offer a fuller and more satisfying account of that view. In the broadest terms: "a sepulchral Monument is a tribute to a Man as a human Being; and ... an Epitaph ... includes this general feeling and something more" (96.11–14). Because the dead are usually buried in churchyards, "with us the composition of an Epitaph naturally turns still more than among the Nations of Antiquity, upon the most serious and solemn affections of the human mind; upon departed Worth – upon personal or social Sorrow and Admiration – upon Religion individual and social – upon Time, and upon Eternity" (99.7–12). It may well deal in commonplaces of affection or grief (99.17 ff.). Indeed, *"it is not only no fault but a primary requisite in an Epitaph that it shall

8/See p. 92.

contain thoughts and feelings which are in their substance common-place, and even trite. It is grounded upon the universal intellectual property of man; – sensations which all men have felt and feel in some degree daily and hourly; – truths whose very interest and importance have caused them to be unattended to, as things which could take care of themselves" (117.31–118.1). Upon this proposition Wordsworth erects two corollaries: the undesirability of excessive detail, especially when conveyed in antithetical form; and the need for freshness in the presentation.

The first of these is introduced early and is almost all-pervasive. The pious commonplace "is the language of a thousand Church yards; and it does not often happen that any thing, in a greater degree discriminate or appropriate to the Dead or to the Living, is to be found in them" (99.27–29). It is unnatural that it should:

"to analyse the Characters of others, especially of those whom we love, is not a common or natural employment of Men, at any time. ... The affections are their own justification. ... We shrink from the thought of placing [the] merits and defects [of friends and kindred] to be weighed against each other in the nice balance of pure intellect; nor do we find much temptation to detect the shades by which a good quality or virtue is discriminated in them from an excellence known by the same general name as it exists in the mind of another; and least of all do we incline to these refinements when under the pressure of Sorrow, Admiration, or Regret, or when actuated by any of those feelings which incite men to prolong the memory of their Friends and Kindred, by records placed in the bosom of the all-uniting and equalizing Receptacle of the Dead." (100.7–25)

Therefore the epitaph "should speak, in a tone which shall sink into the heart, the general language of humanity as connected with the subject of Death ... and of life. To be born and to die are the two points in which all men feel themselves to be in absolute coincidence" (100.26–101.1).

Yet some detail is necessary: the perfection of the epitaph lies "in a due proportion of the common or universal feeling of humanity to sensations excited by a distinct and clear conception, conveyed to the Reader's mind, of the Individual ... at least of his character as, after death, it appeared to those who loved him and lament his loss" (101.6–11). The two aspects, generality and particularity, are to be interwoven: they should "temper, restrain, and exalt each other" (101.17–18). Yet it remains necessary that "what was peculiar to the individual shall still be subordinate to a sense of what he had in common with the species" (Knight, ii.182), and therefore the individualization should be made "implicitly where it can, rather than explicitly" (101.20–21).

An excess of detail, on the other hand, is a defect: "It suffices ... that the Trunk and the main Branches of the Worth of the Deceased be boldly and unaffectedly represented. Any further detail, minutely and scrupulously pursued, especially if this be done with laborious and antithetic discriminations, must inevitably frustrate it's own purpose" (102.24–28). It is a mark of insincerity: "the Understanding having been so busy in it's petty occupation, how could the heart of the Mourner be other than cold?" (102.34–35). It is indecorous with the mode and with the traits of universality which characterize the occasion: "For in no place are we so much disposed to dwell upon those points, of nature and condition, wherein all Men resemble each other, as in the Temple where the universal Father is worshipped, or by the side of the Grave which gathers all Human Beings to itself, and 'equalizes the lofty and the low'" (103.2–7). It is indecorous with the mood in which we approach the occasion: "We suffer and we weep with the same heart; we love and are anxious for one another in one spirit; our hopes look to the same quarter; and the virtues by which we are all to be furthered and supported ... are in an equal degree the concern of us all" (103.7–11).

With these "acknowledgments to our common nature," "a balance of opposite qualities or minute distinctions in individual character" is incongruous. Even when "true and just," such distinctions are, in the last resort, unsuited to the audience which the writer of epitaphs postulates: for "an Epitaph is not a proud Writing shut up for the studious: it is exposed to all, to the wise and the most ignorant"; to the thoughtless, the busy, the ignorant, the old, the young, and the stranger: "it is concerning all, and for all: – in the Church-yard it is open to the day; the sun looks down upon the stone, and the rains of Heaven beat against it" (103.12–29).

Excessive detail of itself is thus contrary to the purpose of the epitaph; when handled in the antithetical manner of Pope, it is deplorable. We saw earlier that Pope's metrical form encourages the use of a particular rhetoric: a rhetoric of antithesis, which balances and contrasts detail against detail; which therefore encourages the search for detail. In certain literary genres, in particular in the characteristic satirical genre of English neo-classicism, the mode is appropriate to the genre: *"Pope's mind had been employed chiefly in observation upon the vices and follies of men. Now, vice and folly are in contradiction with the moral principle which can never be extinguished in the mind; and therefore, wanting this controul, are irregular, capricious, and inconsistent with themselves" (120.10–15).

A man who, for his own profit, adopts consciously a course of vice rather than of virtue is, inevitably, at odds with himself; for no man can submit utterly to the diabolic canon, "Evil, be thou my good!" Hence *"It is reasonable ... that ... Dryden and Pope [in their satirical portraits] should represent qualities and actions at war with each other and with themselves: and that the page should be suitably crowded with antithetical expressions" (120.26–121.5). In short, as we saw earlier (p. 107–9), the moral stance of the satirist, concerned to expose deviations from an implicit norm, is opposed to that of Wordsworth, who is concerned, in *Lyrical Ballads*, to show that superficial deviations by no means indicate an absence of a moral or social norm, and, in the epitaph, to deal with "truths whose very interest and importance have caused them to be unattended to, as things which could take care of themselves" (117.35–118.1).

The Augustan manner is therefore unsuited to the epitaph. At the simplest level, its striving after balance leads to the empty line:

> *"'Here rests a Woman good without pretence
> Blest with plain reason'—

from which, *sober sense* is not sufficiently distinguishable." (116.22–24)

Here is a case in which *"one half of the process is mechanical, words doing their own work, and one half of the line manufacturing the rest" (118.21–22); in which "a balance of opposite qualities or minute distinctions in individual character ... when examined, resolve[s itself] into a trick of words" (103.14–16).

The manner has its jargon: in "No conquest she but o'er herself desir'd," for example, *"the word, *conquest*, is applied in a manner that would have been displeasing even from its triteness in a copy of complimentary Verses to a fashionable Beauty; but to talk of making conquests in an Epitaph is not to be endured" (116.36–117.3). A milder example is found in Mason's line: "And if so fair, from vanity so free": *"the word *fair* is improper; for unquestionably it was not intended that their title to receive this assurance [of heaven] should depend at all upon their personal beauty" (124.4–6).

The empty line is a negative fault, and jargon, as Wordsworth demonstrates in other cases, may merely conceal an "under current ... natural and pure" (113.6–7). The admired double antithesis of Denham's famous lines[9] is achieved in Pope's epitaph on Mrs. Corbett: "So firm yet soft, so strong yet so refined." Wordsworth does not go into detail; he probably considers the first half of the line as bordering on nonsense, the second as an antithesis in form which has no backing in sense: refinement is not necessarily opposed to strength (118.19–25). So, at any rate, he attacks Lord Lyttleton's epitaph on his wife. The result of the contrived antithesis is here false; for since the purpose of the epitaph is to praise the deceased, and since, therefore, the qualities ascribed to the deceased must be

9/*Cooper's Hill*, 191–92. Cf. Johnson, *Lives*, i.78–79.

favourable and congruous one with another, to place them in contrast is pointless, if not nonsensical: *"In the mind of the truly great and good every thing that is of importance is at peace with itself. ... A lovely quality, if its loveliness be clearly perceived, fastens the mind with absolute sovereignty upon itself; permitting or inciting it to pass, by smooth gradation or gentle transition, to some other kindred quality" (121.8–14).

Meekness is not antithetical to magnanimity; but Lyttleton, following the pernicious model of Pope, has forced these virtues into antithesis (121.14–29). Without the model of Pope's characteristic form, there is no reason to suppose that he would have done so. Thus *"the thoughts have their nature changed and moulded by the vicious expression in which they are entangled, to an excess rendering them wholly unfit for the place which they occupy" (116.18–21). In so far as Pope's manner is dictated or fostered by his metrical form, it is clear that Wordsworth will regard the form with suspicion: any form which demands, or encourages, the "changing and moulding" of the thought away from the shape which sincerity imposes upon it is antagonistic to the very purpose which the writer of epitaphs has, or should have, in mind.

This account is far removed from the narrower thesis of the Preface to *Lyrical Ballads*, whereby Wordsworth sought to impose upon all poetry a single, clumsily defined "language," and offered vague accusations at "poetic diction" which were unsupported by any argument save that a conventional diction is – vaguest of terms – "unnatural." In the Essays he does not commit himself to a definition of a "language" which aspires to permanence or to any other particular virtue. He is even willing to admit that the Augustan manner is congruous with a particular poetic genre. And he justifies his attack on it as unsuitable for the epitaph, as he rightly claims, with "reasons not lightly given" (120.2). His implications are, of course, wider. He had a low opinion of satire as a genre, as he makes clear in the Preface of 1815: "personal and occasional Satire rarely comprehending sufficient of the general in the individual to be dignified with the name of Poetry" (142.30–32); and by subtle hints that the epitaph is an epitome of most kinds of poetry which it is worth the poet's while to write, he makes it clear that much of the Essays' doctrine is of wider application.

The second corollary which Wordsworth establishes upon the basis of his notion of general truth is the concept of freshness. Of this there is an obscure foreshadowing in the Preface to *Lyrical Ballads*: Wordsworth there proposed "to make the incidents of common life interesting," or, in the more detailed phrasing of texts later than 1800, "to choose incidents and situations from common life" (the best available representatives, as the Preface proceeds to claim, of general truth), and "to throw over them a certain colouring of imagination, whereby ordinary things should be presented to the mind in an unusual way" (18.2; 40.29–34).

In the Essays this notion receives fuller statement. The epitaph is based on commonplaces, on "truths whose very interest and importance have caused them to be unattended to, as things which could take care of themselves." But its presentation of such commonplaces must rise above the commonplace: *"it is required that these truths should be instinctively ejaculated or should rise irresistibly from circumstances; in a word that they should be uttered in such connection as shall make it felt that they are not adopted – not spoken by rote, but perceived in their whole compass with the freshness and clearness of an original intuition" (117.35–118.6).

This passage recalls, first, the phrase in the Preface of 1802 concerning general truth "carried alive into the heart by passion," and, secondly, the obscure but suggestive account of "emotion recollected in tranquillity" and of the subsequent poetic process which Wordsworth casts out as an *obiter dictum* in his discussion in the Preface of the pleasurable effects of metrical form (50.21–22; 57.37). From this account we gather that the poetic process reveals, not only the original emotion, but also the poet's perception of its significance, of its relation to general truth (see Chapter III, sec. ii). The poet writes either having acquired, or acquiring as he writes, knowledge of the meaning of his emotional experience. He at once feels his emotion and, as it were, stands outside it, in the attitude of a sympathetic but calm observer, who, like the scientist concerned with particular obscure problems, or like any man concerned with the "passions and thoughts and feelings of men" (54.9), takes pleasure in his final mastery of the subject: a mastery given him by time, by his habits of meditation, and by the processes of the imagination.

So, in the Essays, the poet's masterly knowledge of the significance of his subject is eloquently stressed: *"The Writer must introduce the truth with such accompaniment as shall imply that he has mounted to the sources of things – penetrated the dark cavern from which the river that murmurs in every one's ear has flowed from generation to generation" (118.6–10). Such an account is, again, removed from the stress on novelty, on "widening the sphere of human sensibility ... the introduction of a new element into the intellectual universe," which Wordsworth imposed in his letter to John Wilson and in the *Essay, Supplementary to the Preface*. There is to be novelty, indeed, but it is a novelty of emphasis, a sharpening of man's focus on ideas which are in fact within the scope of his ordinary observation. A contemporary philosopher, Dugald Stewart, distinguished between Invention and Discovery: "The object of the former ... is to produce something which had no existence before; that of the latter, to bring to light something which did exist, but which was concealed from common observation."[10] Oddly enough, he claims that Invention belongs to the arts and Discovery to science. Wordsworth, in the mood of the Essays, would have disagreed: the poet here described is a discoverer. For it is not to "new elements of the intellectual universe," but to "universally received truths," that the poet must give "a pathos and spirit which shall re-admit them into the soul like revelations of the moment" (124.11–12).

10/*Elements of the Philosophy of the Human Mind* (London, 1792), p. 310. Cf. C.N.B., i.387, n.

vii *The Epitaph as Poetic Epitome*

It was hinted earlier that to Wordsworth the epitaph is a kind of essence or epitome of all poetry; that it stands in relation to all poetry as, in the Preface of 1800, the rustic stood in relation to all men (p. 104). In so far as the themes of the Preface are generally applicable to all poetry, and in so far as these themes are resumed in the Essays (documents nominally dealing with a single poetic genre), this view is, in a sense, obvious. And we have seen in the preceding section that, where a rhetoric of which Wordsworth on the whole disapproves can be justified as decorous in another genre, then that genre is one of which Wordsworth has no very elevated opinion.

There are, however, certain passages in the second and third Essays which urge this view more positively. The general form of such passages is a statement that what is a virtue or a defect in all or most genres is especially so in the epitaph. Thus Wordsworth claims "to place in a clear view the power and majesty of impassioned faith, *whatever be its object*: to shew how it subjugates the lighter motions of the mind, and sweeps away superficial difference in things": *"And this I have done ... with a wish to bring the ingenuous into still closer communion with those primary sensations of the human heart, which are the vital springs of sublime and pathetic composition, *in this and in every other kind*" (107.1–9; my italics). Insincerity "is worse in a sepulchral inscription, precisely in the same degree as that mode of composition calls for sincerity more urgently than any other" (107.20–22); and again, "the occasion of writing an epitaph ... forbids more authoritatively than any other species of composition all modes of fiction, except those which the very strength of passion has created" (115.11–15). The Augustan mode is represented by examples *"where the thoughts and feelings had no vital union; but were artificially connected, or formally accumulated, in a manner that would imply discontinuity and feebleness of mind *upon any occasion*; but still more reprehensible here!" (122.26–29).

The epitaph is an index of the impermanence imposed on art by changes of taste: this impermanence "is in nothing more evinced than in the changeful character and complexion of that species of composition which we have been reviewing" (124.20–22); *"the Reader need only look into any collection of Epitaphs to be convinced, that the faults predominant in the literature of every age will be as strongly reflected in the sepulchral inscriptions as any where; nay perhaps more so, from the anxiety of the Author to do justice to the occasion: and especially if the composition be in verse; for then it comes more avowedly in the shape of a work of art; and, of course, is more likely to be coloured by the works of art holden in most esteem at the time" (124.26–33). In the collection of epitaphs given in Vicesimus Knox's *Elegant Extracts*, "there is scarcely one which is not thoroughly tainted by the artifices which have over-run our writings in metre since the days of Dryden and Pope" (125.4–6). If upon such an occasion sincerity cannot thrust aside the canons of bad taste, it speaks poorly for the *"taste, intellectual Power, and morals of a Country" in the age which produced such epitaphs: *"how could the tyranny of bad taste be brought home to the mind more aptly than by shewing in what degree the feelings of nature yield to it when we are rendering to our friends this solemn testimony of our love? more forcibly than by giving proof that thoughts cannot, even upon this impulse, assume an outward life without a transmutation and a fall?" (126.8–16).

By such means Wordsworth succeeds in widening implicitly the scope of the Essays from a discussion of what is, superficially, a minor genre to a general statement of Wordsworthian poetics.[11]

VIII *Reconciliation of Opposites*

It is at first glance curious that a work which devotes so much space to an attack on the Augustan rhetoric of balance and antithesis

11/On the relation of many of Wordsworth's poems, and of "Romantic lyricism" generally, to the epitaph, see Geoffrey H. Hartman, *Wordsworth's Poetry 1787–1814* (New Haven and London, 1964), pp. 12–13.

should be dominated in its major arguments by the Coleridgean concept of "the *antithetical* balance-loving nature of man" (*S.C.*, ii.5); but the paradox is not real. The *Essays upon Epitaphs* are concerned (to use Coleridge's words again) with the "effort of the mind ... to reconcile opposites and qualify contradictions, leaving a middle state of mind more strictly appropriate to the imagination than any other, when it is, as it were, hovering between images" (*S.C.*, ii.103). The Augustan manner is concerned, not to reconcile and to unify, but to put asunder what nature has joined together; to disjoin, to the point of falseness, qualities which, unless in the perverted, cannot be separated either logically or emotionally. The process of the Wordsworthian and Coleridgean imagination is the reverse of this.

The concept is a broad one: it includes, and perhaps develops from, the eighteenth-century notion of the perception of similitude in dissimilitude and the reverse, the distinction between copy and imitation which Coleridge drew from Adam Smith and perhaps other sources, the reconciliation of judgment and genius, of reason and passion, and the like (*S.C.*, i.177–78 and Raysor's n.).

Wordsworth was aware of the principle in 1800; for the Preface to *Lyrical Ballads* mentions the principle of similitude in dissimilitude (27.13 ff.), and the theory of metre there expounded relies heavily on it, in its view of metrical form as an artificial, non-realistic element in poetry which tempers and is reconciled with the realistic, "natural" language of passion which Wordsworth proposed to use in *Lyrical Ballads* (Chapter II above). In the Preface he is probably handling, with a considerable degree of originality, an eighteenth-century commonplace; in the Essays, the much wider use of the notion suggests either continued meditation or the influence of Coleridge (we remember that the Essays were written for *The Friend*); or, indeed, both, for the notion is too firmly embedded in the Essays to be due to mere verbal reminiscence of Coleridge's talk.[12]

In a sense, the idea is in evidence in Wordsworth's first argument,

12/Further from the eighteenth-century terminology of the Preface to *Lyrical Ballads* and nearer to Coleridge is the opening paragraph of *Prel.*, XII, which links "Genius" with "interchange Of peace and excitation" and with "emotion" opposed to "calmness," "energy" opposed to "stillness."

which traces the origin of memorial structures and epitaphs to the sense of immortality; for at first sight it appears paradoxical that a memorial should be required for one who is yet living, and Wordsworth does not even draw on the resolved paradox of the Christianized pastoral elegy to emphasize his point. Rather, he assumes that the sense of immortality will become self-evident after due reflection on natural ways of thinking, and therefore he does not need to draw upon the doctrinal support, implicit or explicit, on which an elegy such as *Lycidas* relies. What he has in mind emerges more clearly in the possible attitudes to death revealed in the contrasting anecdotes of Simonides and "another ancient Philosopher" (95.1 ff.). On examination, it emerges that the opposed attitudes of respect and contempt for the dead body which the anecdotes describe are not, as might be thought, irreconcilable. It is a matter of emphasis: on the mortal or on the immortal part of man, either of which is, from an appropriate viewpoint, worthy of respect. Indeed, the very action of Simonides reveals that his respect for the corpse involved also a respect for the immortal soul: "we may be assured that, if he had been destitute of the capability of communing with the more exalted thoughts that appertain to human Nature, he would have cared no more for the Corse of the Stranger than for the dead body of a Seal or Porpoise which might have been cast up by the Waves. We respect the corporeal frame of Man, not merely because it is the habitation of a rational, but of an immortal Soul" (95.15–21). The attitudes, superficially contrasted, are capable of unity: "Each of these Sages was in sympathy with the best feelings of our Nature; feelings which, though they seem opposite to each other, have another and a finer connection than that of contrast. – It is a connection formed through the subtle progress by which, both in the natural and the moral world, qualities pass insensibly into their contraries, and things revolve upon each other" (95.21–27). Consideration of death leads to thoughts of immortality; thoughts of immortality, to consideration of "transitory things – of sorrow and of tears" (96.3).

Therefore, "On a midway point ... which commands the thoughts and feelings of the two Sages ... does the Author of [epitaphs] take his stand" (96.4–7). He reconciles the opposed attitudes, assuming the "middle state of mind" connected by Coleridge with the imagination.

In another sense also, closer to Coleridge's, the poet's state of mind may be seen as a reconciliation of opposites: the reconciliation of reason and passion. We have already glanced at the relevant ideas in connection with the concept of reticence (sec. v above); we can now see that reticence is to be achieved by the process just indicated: "though the Writer who would excite sympathy is bound in this case more than in any other, to give proof that he himself has been moved, it is to be remembered, that to raise a Monument is a sober and a reflective act ... the thoughts and feelings expressed should be permanent ... liberated from that weakness and anguish of sorrow which is in nature transitory. ... The passions should be subdued, the emotions controlled; strong indeed, but nothing ungovernable or wholly involuntary" (103.30–104.4). And, as we saw earlier, the fiction whereby the deceased is represented "as speaking from his own Tomb-stone" is a means whereby "the Survivors bind themselves to a sedater sorrow, and employ the intervention of the imagination in order that the reason may speak her own language earlier than she would otherwise have been enabled to do" (104.18–30). And Wordsworth justifies his long discussion of bad taste as certain epitaphs reveal it "From a deep conviction ... that the excellence of writing, whether in prose or verse, consists in a conjunction of Reason and Passion, a conjunction which must be of necessity benign" (126.5–7). In an only partially successful epitaph, Chiabrera *"neglected to ascertain whether the passions expressed were in kind and degree a dispensation of reason or at least commodities issued under her licence and authority" (Knight, ii.184).

Thus much of the poet's state of mind. The principle under discussion reappears in Wordsworth's views on the manner in which the deceased is to be presented to the world in his epitaph: as a blending and reconciliation of the general and the particular in humanity. The excellence of the form "will be found to lie in a due proportion of the common or universal feeling of humanity to sensations excited by a distinct and clear conception ... of the Individual. ... The general sympathy ought to be quickened, provoked, and diversified, by particular thoughts, actions, images ... and these ought to be bound together and solemnized into one harmony by the general sympathy. The two powers should temper, restrain, and exalt each other" (101.6–18). Again, the basic contrast between death and immortality may be resolved, as it was in the anecdotes of the two philosophers, in the selective presentation of the character of the deceased: "The composition and quality of the mind of a virtuous man, contemplated by the side of the Grave where his body is mouldering, ought to appear and be felt as something midway between what he was on Earth walking about with his living frailties, and what he may be presumed to be as a Spirit in Heaven" (102.18–23). In a more general way, the serene spectacle of the uniformly favourable records of the dead which may be found in a country churchyard may well be tempered, but not destroyed, by *"a consciousness ... of the anxieties, the perturbations, and, in many instances, the vices and rancorous dispositions, by which the hearts of those who lie under so smooth a surface and so fair an outside have been agitated" (Knight, ii.146).

Finally, the concept appears in incidental details of the Essays. The Greek and Roman practice of burying by the wayside had the advantage that the art of the epitaph could blend with the "surrounding images of Nature" (96.27–28) to yield a heightened composite impression of the meaning of life and death which neither aspect of the combination could provide of itself: the natural analogies suggested "must have given, formerly, to the language of the senseless stone a voice enforced and endeared by the benignity of that Nature with which it was in unison" (97.10–12). In modern times, burial in a village churchyard "combines many of the best tendencies which belong to the mode practised by the Ancients, with others peculiar to itself"; and the churchyard becomes "a visible centre of a community of the living and the dead" (98.33–99.4), a tangible symbol of the reconciliation of opposites.

ix *Imagination and Fancy*

The reconciliation of opposites is, in Wordsworthian and Coleridgean terms, the task of the Imagination; if, therefore, the view
expressed in the preceding section, that this concept pervades the
Essays upon Epitaphs, is correct, we shall expect to find in the work
at least hints of Wordsworth's later view of the Imagination and the
Fancy. This is the case; though in fact neither word occurs with any
frequency in the Essays.

We have, however, already found one use of *imagination* in its
anticipated context. The fiction of the deceased speaking from his
tombstone is a means of reconciling passion and reason, of disarming
death of the sting without which it is no longer death. This fiction is
achieved by "the intervention of the imagination in order that the
reason may speak her own language earlier than she would otherwise
have been enabled to do. This shadowy interposition also harmo-
niously unites the two worlds of the Living and the Dead by their
appropriate affections" (104.28–32). This is, I believe, the only such
occurrence in the Essays; but the concept appears in more general
terms in several other contexts.

The "lively and affecting analogies" which Nature supplies to the
traveller who rests by a wayside burial-ground are essentially imaginative: they are "like a refreshing Breeze that comes without warn-
ing, or the taste of the waters of an unexpected Fountain" (96.37–
97.9), a figure which recalls the "mild creative breeze, A vital breeze
which travell'd gently on O'er things which it had made," of the
opening lines of *The Prelude*. Indeed, the whole drift of the Essays,
that the epitaph should dwell, not upon the petty distinctions of the
Understanding (102.24 ff.), but upon commonplaces stated "with the
freshness and clearness of an original intuition" (118.6), is a claim
that the Imagination is the master-faculty at work in the form.

More often, however, the Essays present hints of the later discrimination between Imagination and Fancy. The author of Sir
George Vane's epitaph calls forth Wordsworth's doubts whether he
might not have *"prided himself upon what he might call a clever

hit: I mean that his better affections were less occupied with the several associations belonging to the ... ideas [of 'Sir George' and 'St. George'] than his vanity delighted with that act of ingenuity by which they had been combined" (Knight, ii.153). Wordsworth is suspicious lest the writer should have thought the pun its own justification; if he did, he was using his Fancy, and the connection is "unstable [and] transitory" (153.21), unlike that other punster cited earlier in the Essays (Knight, ii.151), who punned on the name *Palmer* to some slight imaginative effect because the connection between the two senses of the word went deeper than mere identity of verbal form. But Wordsworth is willing to give his author the benefit of the doubt, supposing that *"the sense of worldly dignity associated with the title ... which at this time we can but feebly sympathize with, and the imaginative feeling involved, viz. the saintly and chivalrous Name of the Champion of England, were unaffectedly linked together" (Knight, ii.153); "and," he adds, significantly for the present discussion, *"that both were *united and consolidated* in the Author's mind."

Of the quality of Montrose's epitaph on Charles I Wordsworth has no doubts. Here is a case in which the fictions are justified by the "very strength of passion" (115.14): *"His soul labours; – the most tremendous event in the history of the Planet, namely, the Deluge, is brought before his imagination by the physical image of tears, – a connection awful from its very remoteness and from the slender band that unites the ideas: – it passes to the region of Fable likewise; for all modes of existence that forward his purpose are to be pressed into the service" (108.15–20). In a sense, the concept of reconciliation of opposites is still present: the conjunction of great and small, of deluge with tears, of the fabulous with the merely human. But rather we catch in this passage the first glimpse of the concept on which Wordsworth dwells at some length in the Preface of 1815: the modification of one image by another. *Deluge* raises the power of *weep* so that the enormousness of the event lamented is made clear; *weep* yet maintains the event at the level of human understanding.

The fabulous references, similarly, tend to elevate the event beyond human experience; *trumpets*, *blood*, and *wounds* ensure that it remains at an intelligible level. Thus, finally, as the poem hovers between the human and the superhuman levels, we are led back to the reconciliation of opposites: *"Hyperbole in the language of Montrose is a mean instrument made mighty because wielded by an afflicted Soul, and *strangeness is here the order of Nature*" (110.13–15).

From this account there emerges a concept which is not, perhaps, repeated by Wordsworth and is only implicitly touched on by Coleridge: that sincerity acts as a stimulus to the Imagination.[13] It is because the author of Vane's epitaph felt sincerely the connection between Sir George and St. George that the linkage may, perhaps, be regarded as imaginative; it is because Montrose's soul is "afflicted" that his hyperboles are permissible and indeed valuable. On the other hand, the "wit" who adapted du Bellay's lines to serve as an epitaph for Philip Sidney, though he had an inkling that the occasion must be important, did not sincerely feel its impact: *"Accordingly, an Epitaph is adopted in which the Writer has turned from the genuine affections and their self-forgetting inspirations, to the end that his understanding, or the faculty designated by the word *head* as opposed to *heart*, might curiously construct a fabric to be wondered at" (110.8–13).

Where the feelings are not sincerely involved, the Imagination fails, and the Understanding and Fancy work in its place; as in this instance, and in Lord Lyttleton's epitaph on his wife: *"there is no under current, no skeleton or stamina, of thought and feeling. The Reader will perceive at once that nothing in the heart of the Writer had determined either the choice, the order, or the expression, of the ideas – that there is no interchange of action from within and from without" (112.19–24). Where the Fancy works, it works languidly:

13/Emotions felt in "real life," notably fear, are, of course, stimulants to the Imagination, but do not necessarily stimulate towards poetry. See Havens, Chapter III, especially p. 49.

*"the connections are mechanical and arbitrary, and the lowest kind of these – Heart and Eyes – petty alliterations, as meek and magnanimous, witty and wise" (112.24–26), and the Understanding throws in "oppositions in thoughts where there is no necessary or natural opposition" (112.26–27). In Mason's epitaph, the sentence "She bow'd to taste the wave – And died" combines jargon with a fanciful attempt at a pathetic (or sublime?) compression which does not succeed: "bow'd" and "wave" are merely factually false; "and died" "would have been a just expression if the water had killed her." In sum, *"the expression involves a multitude of petty occupations for the fancy ... a shock of surprize is given [by the compression of statement involved in 'and died'], entertaining perhaps to a light fancy but to a steady mind unsatisfactory – because false" (123.13–23).

Indeed, "truth is the soul of passion" (Knight, ii.183), as Mason in this instance, and Chiabrera in another, forgot. But Chiabrera's epitaph on *Baldi is "a perfect whole"; "there is nothing arbitrary or mechanical" (that is, there is no intrusion of Understanding or Fancy), "but it is an organized body of which the members are bound together by a common life and are all justly proportioned" (it is a production of the Imagination) (Knight, ii.183).

With this concept we have completed the full circle of the argument, which began with the view that the epitaph is peculiarly adapted to serve as the epitomizing form of Wordsworthian poetics, because it demands the emotional involvement of the poet as the *sine qua non* of its accomplishment. Without emotional involvement, the epitaph cannot succeed, because in its absence Imagination fails, the Fancy is languid, and the disintegrating Understanding is the master-faculty of composition.

Seven ✳ The Preface of 1815

1 *The Background*

The nominal purpose of the Preface is to justify the curious classification of Wordsworth's poems which first appeared in the edition of
1815.[1] Wordsworth had begun to consider such a grouping six years
before, when, having more or less completed the troublesome task of
putting into print his pamphlet on *The Convention of Cintra*, he had
"been much employed lately in the arrangement of his published
poems, as he intends to blend the 4 volumes together whenever they
are reprinted."[2] In a letter of May 1809 we find him drafting for
Coleridge's inspection a scheme of which elements remain in the
edition of 1815 and later editions. It comprises the following divi-
sions: (1) "Poems relating to childhood"; (2) "all those emotions,
which follow after childhood, in youth and early manhood"; (3)
"natural objects and their influence on the mind either as growing or
in an advanced state"; (4) "Naming of Places, as a Transition to"
(5) "the Poems relating to human life"; (6) "those relating to the
social and civic duties"; (7) "those relating to Maternal feeling, connubial or parental";[3] (8) poems on "old age" (M.Y., i.334–6). In

---

1/This is clearer in the original second paragraph of the text (140.7–13),
removed after 1836, than in the standard text.
2/M.Y., i.326 (1 May 1809); "the 4 volumes" are *Lyrical Ballads* and the
Poems of 1807.
3/It is not clear whether Wordsworth means "maternal or connubial or parental feeling" or "the feeling of a mother directed either towards her husband or

each group, it is usually stated or in any case implied, the poems are to "ascend in a gradual scale of imagination"; or, as Wordsworth says at the end of the letter, "The principle of the arrangement is that there should be a scale in each class and in the whole, and that each poem should be so placed as to direct the Reader's attention by its position to its *primary* interest."

The scheme outlined here is considerably simpler and more logical than that actually adopted in 1815 and in later editions. The classification is based entirely on the subject-matter of the poems, and it is given recognizable shape by running more or less parallel to the course of human life from childhood to old age. The shape is not rigorously maintained: thus group 3, "natural objects," bears no necessary chronological relation to 2 and 4–5, which deal with adolescence and "Naming of Places, as a Transition to those relating to human life" respectively; and 6 and 7, "social and civic duties" and "Maternal feeling," though no doubt seen by Wordsworth as both connected with maturity, again bear no particular time-relation to each other or to what precedes. Nevertheless a rough shape can be seen, and the proposed arrangement approximates to a chronological "history or science of feelings" (13.27) covering man's mortal span.

The next information we have on Wordsworth's plans appears three years later, when Crabb Robinson reports that "Wordsworth purposes as soon as the two last volumes are out of print to reprint the four volumes, arranging the poems with some reference either to the fancy, imagination, reflection, or mere feeling contained in them" (*H.C.R.*, p. 89 [31 May 1812]). If this report represents Wordsworth's intentions completely, the scheme differs widely from that of 1809. With the possible exception of the grouping according to "mere feeling" contained in the poems, which may be analogous to "Maternal feeling" of the earlier scheme, subject-matter is now ignored as a

---

her child." Conceivably, "parental," though perfectly clear in the manuscript of this letter (now in the Wordsworth Library, Grasmere), was miswritten for "paternal": *The Childless Father*, though not named in the letter, is eventually grouped with the poems concerned.

criterion of classification;[4] and attention is now directed to "the powers of mind *predominant* in the production of" the poems (143.2). This is in accord with the marked interest in the psychology of literary creation which Robinson reports of Wordsworth about this time.[5]

The scheme eventually adopted in 1815 is a conflation of the two just described, with excisions, interpolations, and additions. The headings "Childhood," "Naming of Places," and "Old Age" survive from the scheme of 1809; "Fancy," "Imagination," and "[Sentiment and] Reflection,"[6] from the scheme of 1812. Obviously interpolated are: "Juvenile Pieces," "Miscellaneous Sonnets," "Sonnets Dedicated to Liberty," and "Inscriptions"; added are "Epitaphs," and the *Immortality Ode* as a section by itself.[7] "Poems founded on the Affections" is mainly a conflation of groups 2 and 7 of the scheme of 1809.

The resulting scheme has neither the shape which was provided by the rough parallel to human life in the scheme of 1809, nor the purely psychological interest of the scheme of 1812. To be sure, Wordsworth cites authority for classifying poems "either with reference to the powers of mind *predominant* in the production of them; or to the mould in which they are cast; or ... to the subjects to which they relate" (143.1–3); but classification in terms of all these three diverse notions is not likely to be very significant. Wordsworth, ignoring this obvious difficulty, proceeds to insist that a chronological scheme like that implicit in 1809 is, "as far as it was

4/The "mere feeling" may be that of the poet, or of his characters; the phrase itself might correspond to the class "Affections" or to the class "Sentiment [and Reflection]" in the scheme of 1815. Examples are given of poems of fancy, imagination, and reflection, but not of "mere feeling," so that we cannot be sure of Wordsworth's intention.

5/See *H.C.R.*, pp. 89, 90, 93. It is tempting to conjecture that this interest arose from renewed contact with Coleridge, after the reconciliation engineered by Robinson in early May 1812; but I know of no direct evidence.

6/In a draft list of the poems under appropriate headings in a copy of *Poems* (1807) now in Yale University Library (Tinker 2335, i.103), the words "Sentiment &" are interpolated into the heading "Poems of Reflection."

7/In 1809 the *Ode* was to conclude the section on childhood (*M.Y.*, i.334).

possible," maintained: "the following Poems ... , that the work may more obviously correspond with the course of human life, for the sake of exhibiting in it the three requisites of a legitimate whole, a beginning, a middle, and an end, have been ... arranged ... according to an order of time, commencing with Childhood, and terminating with Old Age, Death, and Immortality" (143.4–10).

This apology is relevant to, perhaps, the first three and the last three classes (out of thirteen) of 1815. By moving in the direction of "Death, and Immortality,"[8] Wordsworth is enabled to include in the scheme, in particular, his epitaphs, and to keep the *Ode* as a climax of the collection, while he maintains a superficial resemblance to "the course of human life." The interpolation of the "Juvenile Pieces" he justifies on the ground that "they were the productions of youth, and represent implicitly some of the features of a youthful mind" (144.5–7); that is, they cast some light on the adolescent mind though they are not explicitly "about" that subject as the first class is "about" children and the child's mind. The third class of 1815, "Affections," is, as we have seen, mainly made up from the second group of 1809 (which is appropriate to the pattern of human life) and the seventh (which is sometimes appropriate, sometimes not),[9] and in three editions (1820, 1827, 1832) it concludes with *Michael* (which is wholly inappropriate).[10]

But what bearing Wordsworth's apology has on the "middle" classes, "Fancy," "Imagination," "Sentiment and Reflection," "Miscellaneous Sonnets," "Sonnets Dedicated to Liberty," "Poems on the Naming of Places,"[11] and "Inscriptions," is far from clear. To

8/If any reason for this addition is necessary, it can perhaps be found in Wordsworth's meditations on the essential continuity with life of death and immortality, in the first *Essay upon Epitaphs.*

9/Some of Wordsworth's mothers are clearly young women, others as clearly are not.

10/*Michael* was to conclude the group on old age in the scheme of 1809 (M.Y., i.336). In the edition of 1815 it was followed by *Laodamia*, which in later editions was moved to an earlier position.

11/In 1809 this comes between "natural objects" and "human life," "as a Transition" (M.Y., i.335); that is, it shows (at least one aspect of) man's response to the influence of natural objects.

some extent the order of the poems concerned in 1815 resembles that of 1809: most of those in group 3 of 1809 can be found under either "Fancy" or "Imagination" in 1815, and thus follow those of group 2 which appear under "Affections"; all the named poems in group 6 of 1809 appear in 1815 under "Sentiment and Reflection," and are thus located near the "Sonnets Dedicated to Liberty" which contain the "political Sonnets" of group 6. But we have already seen that group 3 of 1809 bears no necessary chronological relation to group 2, and that a similar lack of connection applies to group 6. Moreover, most of the named poems of group 5 are placed under "Imagination," and all those in group 7 under "Affections"; in both cases, whatever chronological significance the ordering of 1809 had is lost in 1815. The function (logical if not chronological) of "Naming of Places," "as a Transition [from 'natural objects and their influence on the mind'] to those [poems] relating to human life," is lost also, since in 1815 the poems appear between "Sonnets Dedicated to Liberty" and "Inscriptions."

It is clear, therefore, that the scheme of 1815, seen as a parallel to "the course of human life," lacks, to a much greater degree than the scheme of 1809, a convincing "middle"; and this defect arises from Wordsworth's partial rejection of subject-matter as the basis of classification and from his introduction of literary form and of the psychology of literary creation as alternative bases. Confusion is evident in the admission that the classes "Fancy" and "Imagination" "might without impropriety have been enlarged from that consisting of 'Poems founded on the Affections'; as might this latter from those" (143.30–32); the reader who asks the obvious question, "Then on what basis has your classification actually been decided?" receives only an unsatisfactory answer in terms of "The most striking characteristics of each piece, mutual illustration, variety, and proportion" (143.33–34). No single basis, therefore, underlies the classification, and no meaningful interpretation can be given it as a whole.

The second feature claimed for the scheme of 1809, that "there should be a scale [of imagination] in each class and in the whole," seems of uncertain application in the classification of 1815; and indeed Wordsworth does not insist on it in the Preface. Some traces, however, can be found. The poems of group 1, "relating to childhood," appear to be arranged in the letter to Coleridge "in a gradual scale of imagination,"[12] and those that reappear in 1815 under the corresponding heading are in almost identical order.[13] Wordsworth thought that "An address to an Infant," "which the Reader will find under the Class of Fancy ... , exhibits something of this communion and interchange of instruments and functions between the two powers; and is, accordingly, placed last in the class, as a preparation for that of Imagination which follows" (154.23–27). Here, certainly, is an attempt to preserve "a scale ... in the whole"; but elsewhere the principle seems elusive. For instance, "Poems founded on the Affections" begins with *The Brothers*, though the corresponding group 2 of 1809 was to "conclude with Ruth or The Brothers" (*M.Y.*, i.335). More important than this,[14] the latter part of the poems on "Affections" in 1815 is, as we have seen, composed almost entirely of the poems on "Maternal feelings" of group 7. The suspicion arises, therefore, that the collocation of such poems springs from the accident of the bodily transfer of the group from a different place in the scheme of 1809 (in which the collocation was justified by unity of subject-matter), rather than that, by accident or by some quality inherent in "Maternal feeling," this subject called forth the imagination of the

12/M.Y., i.334. Wordsworth says that "The class ... would ascend ... to Hartley, 'there was a Boy,' and it would conclude with the grand ode, 'There was a time.' " The list next given ends: "To H.C. Six Years Old, There was a Boy, Ode," which suggests that the list is arranged in a "scale of imagination." The two poems at the end of this list, of course, do not appear in this class in 1815.

13/The only marked shift is that of *The Pet Lamb*, third in twelve poems in 1809 and specifically placed early in the group, as illustrating "the simplest dawn of the affections or faculties"; but placed twelfth in sixteen poems in 1815. In the Yale draft (see n.6 above), it is eighth in fourteen poems.

14/Wordsworth had doubts about *The Brothers* in 1809 ("this last might be placed elsewhere"), and *Ruth* does in fact appear near the end of those poems of group 2 which were classified under "Affections" in 1815. In the edition of 1827, *Laodamia, Ruth*, "& one or two more, from the close of Affections," were moved to "Imagination" to replace "the Scotch Poems," which became a separate class (*C.R.*, pp. 160–61). The other poem moved was "Her eyes are wild," which in 1820 was fairly near "the close of Affections," though *Ruth* and *Laodamia* were not, except in the sense just indicated.

poet more imperiously than some others, and therefore justified the placing of the poems towards the end of the section. Lastly, we observe that in 1809 the third group is to "conclude with the highly imaginative as the Tintern Abbey," that in 1815 *Tintern Abbey* is, in fact, the last of the "Poems of the Imagination," but that in 1826 Wordsworth thought that it should occupy that place, not as being the most imaginative, but "as being more admired than any other," and that the *Ode to Enterprise* ought not to precede it immediately, not because it showed markedly less imagination than *Tintern Abbey*, but because the poems were recognizably written at markedly different periods.[15] From considerations such as these, it is reasonable to suppose that, probably by 1815 and certainly by 1826, Wordsworth had abandoned this feature also of the scheme of 1809.

II *The Imagination*

After a curious paragraph pleading for "an animated or impassioned recitation" of his poems (144.21 ff.), the Preface now hastens to what is obviously Wordsworth's main concern, the distinction between Imagination and Fancy, which occupies the rest of the operative text. It is difficult to estimate Wordsworth's motive in devoting most of a preface to expounding this distinction which applies to only two of the several classes in the edition of 1815, but some can be suggested.

A partial motive is perhaps to be found in the supplementary Essay and one paragraph of the Preface (151.13–24) echoing the indignant assertion of Wordsworth's merits as a poet which is the basic theme of the Essay.[16] The preceding account of the Imagination not only

15/M.Y., i.335; C.R., p. 165. In the edition of 1827, the arrangement of which is under discussion with Robinson, the *Ode to Enterprise* appears in "Memorials of a Tour on the Continent"; it is transferred to "Imagination" in 1845.

16/See *Essay, Supplementary to the Preface, passim;* Chapter VIII, below; W. J. B. Owen, "Wordsworth and Jeffrey in Collaboration," *R.E.S.,* N.S., xv (1964), 161–67.

expounds but also glorifies: some of the operations of the faculty proceed "from, and [are] governed by, a sublime consciousness of the soul in her own mighty and almost divine powers" (149.22–23); they produce "splendour" (150.7); the faculty may be found in a "grand store-house" (150.19). Later, we hear that "the Imagination is conscious of an indestructible dominion; – the Soul may ... not [be] able to sustain its grandeur ... Imagination [is given] to incite and to support the eternal [part of our nature]" (153.23–29). Great names are associated with it: "this mighty Poet ... our great epic Poet," Milton, in whom "all things tended ... towards the sublime" (150.2, 28; 151.2); Spenser, associated with "universality and permanence ... the highest moral truths and the purest sensations" (151.5–8); and Shakespeare. With these attributes and these great names Wordsworth associates himself in the paragraph concerned. As in the Essay Wordsworth consoles himself against failure and the attacks of Jeffrey with the thought that he shares the neglect and misunderstanding which all great poets since Spenser have suffered, so here he links himself with the greatest of these on the ground that "I have given, in these unfavourable times,[17] evidence of exertions of [the Imagination] upon its worthiest objects ... which have the same ennobling tendency as the productions of men, in this kind, worthy to be holden in undying remembrance" (151.19–24). It is improbable that Wordsworth wrote a whole preface merely to have the opportunity of an incidental fling at "the Ignorant, the Incapable, and the Presumptuous," to wit Francis Jeffrey (151.15–16); but he took the opportunity when it presented itself.[18]

17/Neither the Preface nor the Essay (which argues that in all ages genius is neglected) makes it clear why Wordsworth's age should be especially "unfavourable" to the appreciation of poetry, though there is more on this in the Preface to *Lyrical Ballads* (43.37–44.24). Possibly Wordsworth recalls Milton's "fall'n on evil dayes, On evil dayes though fall'n and evil tongues" (*Paradise Lost*, VII.25–26).

18/The postulate implicit in the two documents, that Genius and Imagination (both of which Wordsworth attributes to himself) are interrelated, indeed that Imagination is the mark of Genius, is made explicit in some eighteenth-century psychologists whose ideas resemble Wordsworth's in other ways, e.g., Duff, p. 6: "Imagination is the quality of all others most essentially requisite to the

A more convincing motive, or set of motives, may be found in Wordsworth's renewed interest in the psychology of literary creation which we have noticed before as emerging about 1812. Of the Imagination Wordsworth had written at length, and in terms not very different from those of the Preface, in *The Prelude*, ten years and more earlier; but *The Prelude* says little of the distinction which now concerns us: it is more concerned to balance the creative Imagination against the disintegrating Understanding, and in any case the poem was unpublished. The distinction is explicit in the note to *The Thorn* of 1800, but is there confined to a sentence; it is implicit in the *Essays upon Epitaphs*, but two of these were, like *The Prelude*, unpublished in 1815.[19] It may well be that Wordsworth, with the confidence which is given by the discovery, or the new and full understanding, of an idea, thought the time ripe to announce it in print. Two accessory motives may have urged him in the same direction. He was well aware, as his quotation from Taylor's *British Synonyms* (145.13–27), at the beginning of his discussion, shows, that his usage of the terms Fancy and Imagination was new, or at least unfamiliar. It is true that the usage of Wordsworth and Coleridge had occasionally been anticipated by eighteenth-century psychologists and aestheticians; but when a handbook of usage published as recently as 1813 could repeat a conventional eighteenth-century view of the terms concerned, Wordsworth must have realized that his classification of his poems under "Fancy" and "Imagination" risked profound misunderstanding if he left the terms unexplained. The distinction was no doubt Coleridge's; but all that Coleridge had published on the subject to date was an *obiter dictum* in a book of

existence of Genius"; p. 89: "ORIGINAL GENIUS is distinguished from every other degree of this quality, by a more vivid and a more comprehensive Imagination"; Gerard, *Genius*, p. 36: "genius of every kind derives its immediate origin from the imagination"; Dugald Stewart, *Elements of the Philosophy of the Human Mind* (London, 1792), p. 479: "An uncommon degree of Imagination constitutes *poetical genius*."

19/*Prel.*, VIII.511 ff., seems to be the only extended discussion of Fancy in the poem. In *Prel.*, XIII.279 ff., Wordsworth apologizes for omitting a full account of Fancy. See also Zall, 12.18–22; Chapter VI, secs. viii and ix above.

quaint knowledge.[20] And the possibility of an extended exposition by Coleridge, Wordsworth must have realized also, was remote; how right he was is clear from the unsatisfactory account of the distinction which appeared in *Biographia Literaria*, two years after his own.

Whatever his prime motive, it is from dissatisfaction with the conventional distinction represented by Taylor's account that Wordsworth moves to his own exposition. Brushing aside the notion of "images that are merely a faithful copy, existing in the mind, of absent external objects" (146.13–14), he proceeds to define "Imagination, in the sense of the word as giving title to a Class of the following Poems" (146.11–12), by a series of illustrations which are arranged more or less in order of increasing power and complexity. Within this order they are arranged according to (1) the independence (146.16–148.21), or (2) the interaction (148.22–149.17), of the images; or (3) the creative power of the Imagination (149.18–150.8).

In the case of category 1 (subdivided into images of sight and images of sound), the most striking feature is that all Wordsworth's illustrations involve figurative language. Vergil's "pendere" and Shakespeare's "Hangs" (as Wordsworth interprets the passage)[21] involve mild metaphor which is justified, in the first instance, because the objects concerned present "to the senses something of such an appearance" and because in such cases the metaphorical usage gives "gratification" to the mind.[22] The difference between these cases and that of Milton's image which follows (147.1–16) and which, Wordsworth says, shows "the full strength of the imagination involved in the word, *hangs*," is hardly clear. The discrepancy between reality and appearance, between what "we know and feel" and the fleet's "appearance to the senses," is again emphasized, as is the "gratification of the mind"; these are the same justifications as were advanced previously. Other aspects of Milton's simile which are later discussed in detail (149.23 ff.) are here hinted at: "the Fleet, an aggre-

20/*Omniana* (London, 1812), ii.12–14; the account cited by Wordsworth later in the Preface (152.14).

21/It is quite possible to read the passage (*King Lear*, IV.vi. 15–16) without drawing on the metaphorical sense of "Hangs" which Wordsworth postulates.

22/How the "gratification" arises is not explained.

gate of many Ships, is represented as one mighty Person ... the motion and appearance of the sublime object to which it is compared," and these are relevant to "the full strength of the imagination ... exerted upon the whole image"; but it is hard to see how this affects the metaphorical use of *hangs*.[23]

The "images of ... sound" which are next discussed are more convincing, because Wordsworth's discussion now launches forth into the connotations of individual words used metaphorically, as it does not in the case of the "images of sight." The stock-dove *broods* rather than *coos*: *broods* retains most of the onomatopoeic effect of *coos*, but has overtones which *coos* lacks. The primary meaning intended is that the bird appears to meditate upon the sound of its voice, repeating its call so that it may be the more accurately studied; the secondary, that it appears to cherish its voice as if it were its offspring or its potential offspring still in the egg.[24] The metaphor operates, according to Wordsworth, because "the affections are called in by the imagination" (147.25–26); he appears to mean that the observer (or reader) empathically shares the bird's delight in the sound and the quasi-maternal feelings of its incubation. The metaphor in *buried* in the next example, as Wordsworth tells us, connotes: (1) the bird's "love of *seclusion*"; (2) the muffled quality of

23/In particular, the use of *hang* would be valid whether or not the fleet were seen as "one mighty person" or as individual vessels. The optical illusion involved is common in certain weather conditions on the North Wales coast, and Wordsworth reports it from the same general region in 1811: "It was about the hour of sunset, and the sea was perfectly calm, and in a quarter where its surface was indistinguishable from the western sky, hazy, and luminous with the setting Sun, appeared a tall sloop-rigged vessel, magnified by the atmosphere through which it was viewed, and seeming rather to hang in the air than float upon the waters"; he refers to Milton's image, and proceeds: "the visionary grandeur and beautiful form of this *single* vessel, could words have conveyed to the mind the picture which Nature presented to the eye, would have suited his purpose as well as the largest company of Vessels that ever associated together with the help of a trade wind, in the wide Ocean. Yet ... his image is a permanent one, not dependent upon accident" (*M.Y.*, i.508). I find the following in a family magazine: in Cyprus "there is no horizon, for the hazy blue of the flat calm sea merges into the blue of the sky, and steel-grey warships, shimmering in the heat, seem to be suspended in air" (*Ideal Home*, July 1958, p. 15).

24/Wordsworth refers to the bird in the poem (*Resolution and Independence*, 5) as masculine, in the Preface as feminine. Either is appropriate, since the male stock-dove assists in incubation.

the bird's song; (3) the inaccessibility of the song (as well as of the bird), such that only the breeze can "convey it to the ear of the listener" (148.5). The synecdoche of the final example is adequately expounded in the text; it is similar to the examples from Vergil and Shakespeare, in that it relies on sense-data for its effect, but upon sense-data accumulated and pondered on ("the memory that the Cuckoo is almost perpetually heard throughout the season of Spring, but seldom becomes an object of sight," 148.11–13), rather than upon sense-data immediately available. The processes so far discussed are summed up in the paragraph beginning "Thus far of images" (149.14–21); it is essentially a résumé of the processes of metaphor.

The next part of the Preface (148.22–149.17) broadens the discussion to "a consideration of [Imagination] employed upon images in a conjunction by which they modify each other." In Wordsworth's examples, figure is again wholly or partially involved. In the passage from Vergil, the effect of the metaphor in "pendere" is enhanced by the contrast with the situation "of the Shepherd, contemplating [the goat] from the seclusion of the Cavern in which he lies stretched at ease and in security." Wordsworth means that the situation of the goat appears the more perilous from the contrast with the security of the shepherd; he may also mean that the shepherd appears the safer from the contrast with the danger of the goat's situation, but it seems doubtful whether modification in this sense actually occurs, since degrees of safety are hardly a concept relevant to the shepherd's situation. Rather, the security of the shepherd provides, what is lacking in the image of the goat "taken separately," a datum-line, an absolute point of reference by which we estimate the degree of the goat's danger.[25]

The double simile of the stone and the sea-beast (from *Resolution and Independence*) which is next analysed operates differently, and

25/A similar contrast probably operates in the passage from *King Lear*: Wordsworth may have thought so when he misquoted the first half-line as "half way up" in the text of 1815 (it was corrected to "half way down" in 1820).

provides a striking instance of a Coleridgean reconciliation of opposites. The animate and the inanimate merge (as the shepherd and the goat do not) into an "intermediate image" which defines Wordsworth's perception of the leech-gatherer with a precision not otherwise to be achieved (149.11). The whole complex image defines a complex perception with the same precision as Vergil's "pendere" and Shakespeare's "Hangs" define a simple "appearance to the senses" (147.13). Less complexly, in the image of the cloud which Wordsworth does not discuss, the cloud, by a kind of personification achieved in "heareth," acquires a personality and a will,[26] and the old man, as in the preceding image, acquires the inanimateness of a natural object.[27]

Wordsworth's main example of the Imagination's power to create (149.23–35) is less impressive. It is true that in the passage from *Paradise Lost* the attention is directed to the fleet now as "one body," now as a "Multitude of Ships," but what creative purpose is thus served is not made clear. A lawn is a green plane but also a mass of individual blades of grass; a woollen garment is a solid body when we wear it, a texture of interwoven threads when we darn a hole in it; the audience of a lecture is a pattern of flesh and garment, or a

26/That is, a seeming determination not to obey "the loud winds when they call." The phenomenon involved may be that of a high cloud which either remains motionless or moves as a whole (without changing shape or tending to disintegrate) while winds at ground level blow with such force that the observer is surprised to see no effect on the cloud. Mr. Malcolm Chisholm suggests to me, alternatively, a phenomenon seen in the Lake District and in North Wales, when a cloud is built up on the windward side and disintegrates on the leeward side, maintaining a more or less constant volume and not moving bodily. Cf. also *Prel.*, p. 53, textual n.: "see with the lofty winds These [clouds] hurrying out of sight in troops, while that, A lonely One upon the mountain top, Resteth in sedentary quietness." In the poem, the image carries the not quite fortunate connotation that the poet expected the old man to be disturbed by his approach as the observer expects the cloud to be disturbed by the "loud winds."

27/The functions so far analysed (and, by implication, the creative function about to be discussed) are recorded by Wordsworth as early as 1804 in MS. W of *The Prelude*, which lists the quasi-imaginative workings of Nature: she "moulds, exalts, indues, combines, Impregnates, separates, adds, takes away And makes one object sway another ... By unhabitual influence or abrupt" (*Prel.*, p. 483, textual n.).

medley of attentive, puzzled, or bored faces: these shifts of attention or point of view, from unity to multeity or the reverse, are determined by practical considerations, and no particular effort is involved in making them. It is an advantage to Milton that the fleet can be seen as "compact," otherwise the comparison would be pointless; but this instance of "consolidating numbers into unity" would not seem to have cost Milton a supreme creative effort, for the effort, if any is involved, has already been made (as the existence of the collective noun indicates) by all users of the language, and the word *fleet* has no more striking effect than has a dead metaphor. Nor do the "dissolving and separating" of this "unity into number" appear to have any marked value in enforcing the point of the simile.[28] Wordsworth, to the contrary, seems to consider that the mere act of shifting the attention in such cases from unity to number, and vice versa, is a notable achievement of the individual's imagination.

The next Miltonic example is markedly different in effect. The "indefinite abstraction 'His coming!'" (150.7–8) operates "like a new existence" (148.21) because the mind does not usually unite such individuals into such a collective; whereas we habitually unite a multitude of ships into the collective *fleet*. This is not merely a case of the original *versus* the commonplace, nor of what T. S. Eliot called "the element of *surprise* so essential to poetry"[29] as opposed to the conventional. The commonplace and the conventional are here *inevitable*, rather than usual: *whenever* practical considerations

---

28/Unless it is to impress the size of the fleet upon the reader: largeness of number is more easily perceived than largeness of dimension. Wordsworth's phrases "Multitude of Ships" and "many Ships" (149.26–27, 147.11) suggest that he reads this into the passage; but it is not in Milton's words except in so far as connotations of a large number of individuals are present in *fleet* (cf. the colloquial "a whole fleet of ..."); nor is the multeity which Wordsworth stresses relevant to our conception of Milton's Satan. Milton's image operates, first, by the fleet's "appearance to the senses" (147.13), and, secondly, by the associations of a lengthy voyage; but to neither of these impressions is the sense of number particularly relevant.

29/*Selected Essays* (London, 1934), p. 308. When Nature works as if with imaginative power, she exerts an *"abrupt and unhabitual* influence" (*Prel.*, XIII.80).

require that several ships be regarded as a unit, we[30] call them a fleet. No such inevitability drives us to unify a number of persons advancing upon us into a "coming": the poet chooses such a collective as will suit his purpose, and this may well be, as it is here, a word which is not felt as a collective at all, except in the unique context in which the poet places it. It is for this reason that such an image operates "like a new existence," is "creative," or provides the "element of *surprise.*" In Coleridgean terms, unification of *ships* into *fleet* is the work of the primary imagination; of the Messiah and the saints into "his coming," of the secondary imagination (*Biog. Lit.*, i.202). Of this distinction, which marks the difference between the ordinary man and the poet, between language and poetry, Wordsworth is here evidently unaware.

With the exception of the double simile from *Resolution and Independence* (148.32 ff.), the examples of the workings of Imagination so far discussed are essentially verbal: they deal usually with single words used in metaphorical or other figurative senses.[31] Such a mode of operation is, curiously enough, not very typical of the Wordsworthian Imagination; and, curiously again, the very mode which is typical, that described in the quotation from Lamb (150.15–18), Wordsworth decides not to discuss. A poem such as *Nutting*, with its descriptions of natural things superficially in the manner of Thomson's *Seasons*; the similar descriptions of the ruined cottage and garden in the first book of *The Excursion*; the impression of continuity in nature and in the human experience of nature which is the underlying theme of *Tintern Abbey*; the eternal and inexhaustible

---

30/"We" means "all users of the same language," here the English of Milton, which does not differ essentially from nineteenth- or twentieth-century English in this instance. Some other languages might not possess such a facility of unification, and some varieties of English (e.g., that of very young children) might also lack it.

31/In terms of the valuable distinction of R. A. Foakes, *The Romantic Assertion* (London, 1958), pp. 32 ff., most of the images analysed are examples of the "image of thought, which is seen in its greatest refinement in the swift realization of relationships by means of an active verb"; the example from *Resolution and Independence*, as Professor Foakes notes, is an "image of impression" (p. 34).

discharge of energy which is the theme of the description of the Simplon Pass in *The Prelude*, VI.556–72: these are far more typically Wordsworthian, and also far more impressive, examples of the operation of the Imagination than most of the examples which the Preface discusses. In such passages, figure is often not in question, and, if it is involved at all, it is involved only incidentally, as a means of presenting the thing perceived with more precision than is otherwise possible. The main effort of the Imagination in such poems is, in Lamb's phrase, to "draw all *things* to one." Thus in *Nutting* the images of the "violets of five seasons ... unseen by any human eye" and of the "green stones ... fleeced with moss" converge upon the one concept of a piece of nature utterly inviolate, upon which even the sky is an intruder (l.53); in *The Excursion*, the encroachment of weeds and sheep and the decline of garden and cottage symbolize the decay of a human spirit, until, paradoxically, the decay ends in a peace which is symbolized by the final victory of nature over its humanly imposed bounds. Such passages gain in power, moreover, because the natural objects are at once literal signs and poetic symbols of what is signified. The presence of the moss on the stones directly implies the absence of the disturbing foot; the decay of the cottage is caused by the "sleepy hand of negligence" of its owner; but the effect is larger than these individual implications, because by them and others the mind is induced to see a unity, a meaning towards which all details point. The process involves the coadunation of which Wordsworth and Coleridge speak, and may, as in the passage from the sixth book of *The Prelude*, involve selection of details available to the poet.[32] The distinctively Wordsworthian quality of such passages can perhaps be seen best by comparison with the "fanciful" manner of Thomson in a passage such as *Summer*, 458 ff., where the man who prudently shelters from the noonday summer sun is seen as an

32/Intermediate manuscripts show that Wordsworth's memory retained other details of the scene which he attempted to work in but eventually rejected. See above, pp. 49–50.

"Emblem instructive of the virtuous man,
Who keeps his tempered mind serene and pure,
And every passion aptly harmonized
Amid a jarring world by vice inflamed";

or with the manner of Bowles or such early poems of Coleridge as *Lines to a Beautiful Spring* and *On Bala Hill*. Thomson's emblem depends for its effect upon nothing more substantial than a kind of punning identification of the notions of *heat* used literally and metaphorically; in Wordsworth, the identification of object and symbol is real.[33]

III *The Fancy*

The characteristics of Fancy are described in Wordsworth's account of the distinction between the Fancy and the Imagination, and we must obviously inquire whether Wordsworth is successful in establishing the distinction which it is the main object of the Preface to assert. His account will best be seen against the background of the sharp distinction between the faculties made by Coleridge and others.[34]

Some critics of Coleridge urge that his discrimination, clear enough in his own examples, fails when the borderline case is in question. Some images or passages, it is urged, are clearly fanciful, some are clearly imaginative; but how shall we discriminate between cases of Fancy working strongly and Imagination working feebly? Between

33/". . . a symbol [as distinct from an allegory] always partakes of the reality which it renders intelligible; and while it enunciates the whole, abides itself as a living part in that unity of which it is the representative. The others are but empty echoes which the fancy arbitrarily associates with apparitions of matter" (Coleridge, *Statesman's Manual* [London 1839], pp. 230–31). For a more profuse discussion, see James A. W. Heffernan, "Wordsworth on Imagination: The Emblemizing Power," *PMLA*, lxxxi (1966), 389–99.

34/I rely on Coleridge's major statement in *Biog. Lit.*, i.202. Some other remarks by Coleridge, such as that on Spenser's "imaginative fancy," seem to blur the distinction (*Miscellaneous Criticism*, ed. Raysor [London, 1936], p. 38).

fanciful success and imaginative failure? The intensity of working is judged by observable effects, and at some intermediate point between clearly definable extremes, it is argued, there must be an observable effect which is not clearly definable as that of Fancy or Imagination, and which is therefore better defined as the effect of a single operator working at a particular intensity. So, we might say, a substance at a particular temperature may be solid, at another, liquid; intermediately, it is, as we say, "soft" or "plastic." Since varying intensities of the same operator, heat, produce these effects, it is pointless to give names to the extremes, or at any rate names which suggest that one operator produces solidity and another liquidity.[35]

On such an argument two major observations can be made. The first is that, even if the argument were valid, the naming of extremes might be useful; we mean something, and know what we mean, when we say *hot* or *cold* or *warm*. Secondly: the argument depends upon the borderline case, and the assumption that any particular case is borderline is itself based on the assumption of a single operator, which is what the argument sets out to prove. Only when it is assumed that Fancy and Imagination are faculties of the same kind, that a maximal intensity of Fancy is in some way equivalent to a minimal intensity of Imagination (if only the point and nature of the equivalence could be defined), and that the creative process may be measured on a scale which is essentially continuous even though its lower reaches are marked in degrees of Fancy and its higher in degrees of Imagination – only on these assumptions is it possible to assert that a particular case is borderline between Fancy and Imagination.

35/For a representative account of this viewpoint, see Barbara Hardy, "Distinction without Difference: Coleridge's Fancy and Imagination," *E. in C.*, i (1951), 336–44. Mrs. Hardy's version of the scale-of-temperature analogy involves hot water and steam (p. 339); I prefer that given above, since the softening solid provides an analogue, missing from her account, for the borderline image on which she bases her criticism of Coleridge. The influential discussion of I. A. Richards in *Coleridge on Imagination* (London, 1934), Chapter IV, is essentially of the same kind. Such an account is encouraged, it must be admitted, by such comments of Coleridge as: "*How many* images and feelings are here brought together ..." in a passage from *Venus and Adonis* (*S.C.*, i.189; my italics).

Coleridge would have denied these assumptions, and certainly, if pressed, ought to have denied that the borderline case exists. Since Fancy and Imagination are, to Coleridge, "two distinct and widely different faculties" (*Biog. Lit.*, i.60), their respective effects ought to be discernible in any particular case. The case postulated, which is defined by the critics as produced *either* by strong Fancy *or* by feeble Imagination (or by Imagination failing in its task),[36] will no doubt be observably different from clearly definable extreme cases. But in Coleridgean terms such a case ought to be defined, not as it has just been defined, but as one in which Fancy is strong (or present) *and* Imagination weak (or absent). Since "imagination must have fancy" in order to work at all,[37] there will be Fancy wherever there is Imagination, though Fancy can operate without Imagination.[38] Therefore, whether there is Fancy only, or Imagination of whatever intensity working upon the basis of Fancy, the operation of each faculty should, in Coleridgean theory, be observable and distinguishable; and in this sense the borderline image or passage or poem is not like the fanciful solid on the point of turning into the imaginative liquid – it does not, indeed, exist in such a sense.[39]

36/Cf. Hardy, p. 340: "once we recognize the similarity or the identity of the successes of Fancy and the failures of Imagination, we begin to wonder whether the door between [the two faculties] *can* be slammed." The notion of a (complete) failure of Imagination introduced here has no relevance to Coleridge's theory of Imagination, though Mrs. Hardy's phraseology seems to give it some. The student who (it is reputed) describes himself as "B.A. (failed)" is still an undergraduate in the eyes of all universities; and the result of adding zero Imagination (which is what Mrs. Hardy's "failure of Imagination" means) to Fancy must always be Fancy and Fancy only.

37/Coleridge, *Table Talk*, 20 August 1833.

38/Mrs. Hardy recognizes this in the first two paragraphs on p. 340, yet proceeds: "If Imagination and Fancy are always and essentially different in kind, what happens when Imagination fails? If it fails to unify, may the result not bear a strong resemblance to the casual connections of Fancy?" The answer to the second question is "Yes, of course"; except that "a strong resemblance" is not the phrase required. The result in such a case not only resembles, but *is*, an example of the "casual connections of Fancy"; for if Imagination fails, or fails to unify, it is simply absent, and whatever connection exists must be the work of Fancy.

39/I am not concerned here to discuss whether this position is defensible in practice (that is, whether convincing examples can be found); but it appears to follow necessarily from Coleridge's definitions.

In the Preface and elsewhere, some of Wordsworth's statements appear to be based implicitly on one side of this argument, some on the other. Two early statements, in the note to *The Thorn* and in the final book of *The Prelude*, distinguish the faculties fairly sharply:

"imagination ... the faculty which produces impressive effects out of simple elements ... fancy, the power by which pleasure and surprize are excited by sudden varieties of situation and by accumulated imagery." (12.18–22)

> "having track'd the main essential Power,
> Imagination, up her way sublime,
> In turn might Fancy also be pursued
> Through all her transmigrations, till she too
> Was purified, had learn'd to ply her craft
> By judgment steadied." (*Prel.*, XIII.289–94)[40]

In the classification of 1809, however, the poems were "to ascend in a scale of imagination ... in each class and in the whole"; whence it appears that at that date Wordsworth considered that all his poems, including those subsequently classified as fanciful, could in some sense be classified according to "degrees" of imagination.[41] This seems to imply the postulate of the single operator, unless we take seriously Wordsworth's remark of 1812, that the sonnet "How sweet it is" was at that date "almost the only [poem] of pure fancy," and

40/The definition of Imagination in the note is clearly parallel to the account of "higher minds" which "build up greatest things From least suggestions" (*Prel.*, XIII.90–99). *Prel.*, XIII.289–94 virtually disappears from the text of 1850.
41/*M.Y.*, i.335–6. There is no mention of Fancy in this scheme. Most of f the "Poems of the Fancy" appear in group 3, "Poems relating to natural objects and their influence on the mind." This group is to "begin with the simply human and conclude with the highly imaginative"; the progress is obscurely described as "from objects as they affect the mere human being from properties with which they are endowed, and as they affect the mind by properties conferred; by the life found in them, or their life given." With the phrases "properties conferred" and "life given" we should perhaps understand: "by the imaginative mind which observes them." The poems concerned, except the "highly imaginative," are unfortunately listed in the letter "at Random."

conclude that all other poems have at least a tinge of Imagination.[42]
A statement early in the Preface, on the other hand, appears to be
congruous with Coleridge's theory of distinct faculties: the poems
"are placed according to the powers of mind, in the Author's conception, predominant in the production of them; *predominant*, which
implies the exertion of other faculties in less degree. Where there is
more imagination than fancy in a poem it is placed under the head
of imagination, and vice versa." (143.25–29) Here is implied the
position stated above, that the effects of Fancy and Imagination in
any poem can always be discriminated. Wordsworth is in error,
according to Coleridge, when he claims that "To aggregate and to
associate, to evoke and to combine, belong as well to the Imagination
as to the Fancy" (152.15–17); he has "mistaken the co-presence of
fancy with imagination for the operation of the latter singly" (*Biog.
Lit.*, i.194); that is, in images where both Fancy and Imagination are
present – where, in fact, Imagination has worked upon the aggrega-
tions and associations of Fancy – Wordsworth has attributed the
whole creative effort to Imagination, instead of recognizing that the
labour is actually divided between the faculties. It would be true, in
Coleridge's view, that the faculties work upon different materials,
and Wordsworth's "materials [not] susceptible of change in their
constitution" (152.19–21) correspond clearly enough to Coleridge's
"fixities and definites" (*Biog. Lit.*, i.202); but Wordsworth's implication in this passage, that the faculties work similarly upon dissimilar
materials – an implication which opens the way for the theory of the
single operator, whose observably different effects can be attributed
to difference in materials – was obviously unacceptable to Coleridge.
It is extremely doubtful whether Coleridge regarded the Fancy as a
"creative faculty" (153.31) in any sense. It is clear that in Coleridgean theory "Imagination stoops to work with the materials of
Fancy" (153.32–33), but that this happens, as Wordsworth's implication is, in borderline and unusual cases, is to Coleridge not true: it

---

42/H.C.R., p. 94. Coleridge thought that Wordsworth's "fancy seldom dis-
plays itself, as mere and unmodified fancy" (*Biog. Lit.*, ii.124).

happens invariably, and Imagination cannot otherwise operate at all. The view that "Fancy ambitiously aims at a rivalship with Imagination" (153.31–32), on the other hand, is untenable; it again hints at the possibility of a single operator, or at any rate at the possibility that Fancy's mode of operation is in some way similar to Imagination's. Yet Wordsworth's examples of these postulated processes are in fact capable of analysis in Coleridgean terms: in the lines from Chesterfield and Milton the connection of dew or rain with tears is the associative work of the Fancy; the remaining effects of the two passages are attributable to the presence or (complete or partial) absence of Imagination. In the *Address to my Infant Daughter* (154. 21–27), the basic association of the age of the child with the period of the moon is accidental and fanciful; but upon this basic association the Imagination works.[43]

Whatever the agreements and disagreements of Wordsworth's theory with Coleridge's, and whatever lack of self-consistency in Wordsworth's a comparison of it with Coleridge's reveals, there can be no doubt that the poems actually classified in the edition of 1815 as fanciful have a distinctive tone which is markedly different from that of the "Poems of the Imagination." There are twenty such poems, all but two of which remained under the heading "Fancy" in later editions; they should therefore provide a firm basis for discussion.[44]

43/The attempt to generalize the significance of the notion of "one month" (*Address*, 6–8), and the general identification of growing child and moon (46–50), might be called imaginative. The alternative images contrasting human life and the moon's period (52–65) are perhaps imaginative in themselves, but in that they are alternative, neither being inevitable to the poet in the mood of writing, they are fanciful. The image in "both are free from stain" (51) is fanciful: it depends (apart, perhaps, from unexpressed connections with the myth of Diana) entirely on the identification of two senses, one literal, the other metaphorical, of the word *stain* (cf. the passage from Thomson cited above, p. 167).

44/The poems will be referred to in what follows by the roman numerals prefixed to them in the edition of 1849–50 and standard editions. They are, as arranged in the edition of 1815: *To the Daisy* ("Fancy," vii); *"A whirl-blast"* (iii); *"With how sad steps"* (*Misc. Son.*, ii.xxiii); *The Green Linnet* ("Fancy," ix); *To the Small Celandine* (xi, xii); *The Waterfall and the Eglantine* (iv); *The Oak and the Broom* (v); *The Redbreast Chasing the Butterfly* (xv); *To the Daisy*

Many of these poems ("Fancy," vII, vIII, IX, XI, XII, XIV, XV, XXXI, and "Sentiment and Reflection," IX) represent a kind of exaggeration or inflation of the mode of *Lyrical Ballads*. Whereas the characteristic *Ballads* sought general truth in the simple and the commonplace in humanity, these poems seek it, or at least seek significance, not only in the commonplace but also in the positively trivial. Whereas in *Lyrical Ballads* Wordsworth pleaded, explicitly or (more usually) implicitly, for recognition of the dignity and importance of the commonplace, he now wittingly inflates the importance of the trivial, well aware of the inflation which his treatment gives the subject, and usually offering the reader ample notice of his intention.[45] This mode is seen in: personifications of, and apostrophes to, not indeed "abstract ideas" (44.29–30), but the most trifling of natural things – the commonest of wild flowers (Poems vII, vIII, XI, XII), small birds (IX, X, XV, XXXI, 63 ff.), or a kitten (XXXI); in ingenuous "lessons from Nature" (IV, V, X, XXXI);[46] in fable (IV, V) and fairy tale (XIII); in mythological convention used at its face value ("With how sad steps"). Above all, the mode is seen in short, exaggerated, ingenious comparisons (especially noticeable in vIII), and in the poet's stated or implied sense of the exaggeration, triviality, or ingenuity of these,[47] or of the arbitrary, non-inevitable, or tentative use of them.[48]

(vIII); *To the Daisy* ("Sentiment and Reflection," IX); *To a Sky-Lark* ("Fancy," x); *To a Sexton* (vI); "Who fancied" (xIV); *Song for the Wandering Jew* (xxIII); *The Seven Sisters* (xIII); *Stray Pleasures* (xxIV); *The Kitten and Falling Leaves* (xxxI); *The Danish Boy* (xxII); *Address to my Infant Daughter* (xxxII).

45/xI.13–16: "I'm as great as they, I trow, Since the day I found thee out, Little Flower – I'll make a stir, Like a sage astronomer." It is difficult to see here, or in the lines cited just below from Poem vIII, a "tone of defiant apology" which "can be said to conceal an uncertainty ... of moral response" (Scoggins, p. 81); or if such a tone is there, it is one of mock-heroic defiance. The final stanza of Poem xI, especially in the latest text which removes the common-sense word "lanes," shows in its unqualified exaggeration the risks to which this mode exposes the poet.

46/Cf. *Prel.* (1850), xIV.315–20: "Nature's secondary grace ... The charm more superficial that attends Her works, as they present to Fancy's choice Apt illustrations of the moral world, Caught at a glance, or traced with curious pains."

47/See the discussion of Poem vIII below.

48/xxxII, 42: "parallels have risen"; 71–72: "or shall those smiles be called Feelers of love ...?"

The most characteristic form of such poems is seen best developed in Poem VIII; it consists of a simple "subject" which the poet states simply and then proceeds to adorn (rather than develop) with a series of images of the kind just indicated. The poem has no noticeable argument; the images are all of equal value and each is alternative to another, whence it follows that none impresses as being peculiarly appropriate or inevitable. The poet is well aware of his own ingenious triviality: he "plays with similes, Loose types of things" (10–11); he gives the daisy "many a fond and idle name ... As is the humour of the game" (13–15). One image replaces another: "That thought comes next – and instantly The freak is over, The shape will vanish" (27–29). The poem reaches a kind of climax or conclusion in the last stanza, but it is, not the high point of Fancy, but a return to reality and common sense: "Bright *Flower!* for by that name at last, When all my reveries are past, I call thee, and to that cleave fast" (41–43); a *piano* ending to the somewhat strained and disjointed *scherzo*, as it were, which is the body of the poem.

Several other poems of the group tend towards or achieve this shape. The series of alternative questions in XIV and XV are similar to the series of alternative images in VIII; and similar again is the series of images of similitude and difference which begins at XXXII, 46. The closest parallel in the group, in layout though not in tone, is XXIII, in which six images of action followed by repose, each a stanza long, contrast with the final image of the Wandering Jew.[49]

We may return to our text by observing that Wordsworth's most extensive example of Fancy, Cotton's *Winter*, conforms to the shape of the poems described above. In the passage summarized by Wordsworth (155.4–15), a single simple subject, as in Wordsworth's "With little here," is taken and embellished with a series of brief and ingenious comparisons. The poet "evokes" all the physical manifesta-

49/The convergence of the images towards a single idea in this poem suggests the coadunating faculty of the Imagination; yet any one of them could be omitted without much damage to the poem.

tions of winter he can think of, and "combines" (152.16) them with more or less appropriate aspects of an invading army:

> "The squadron nearest to your eye,
> Is his forlorn of infantry,
> Bow-men of unrelenting minds,
> Whose shafts are feathered with the winds.
>
> *
>
> Bold horse on bleakest mountains bred,
> With hail instead of provend fed.
>   Their lances are the pointed locks,
> Torn from the brows of frozen rocks,
> Their shields are crystals and their swords,
> The steel the crusted rock affords.
>
> *
>
>   Their caps are fur'd with hoary frosts,
> The bravery their cold kingdom boasts;
> Their spungy plaids are milk white frieze,
> Spun from the snowy mountains' fleece.
>   Their partizans are fine carved glass,
> Fringed with the morning's spangled grass;
> And pendent by their brawny thighs,
> Hang scimitars of burnished ice."[50]

The stanzas which Wordsworth quotes (155.20 ff.) proceed in the same manner to embellish the notions of wine and drinking. In each passage the images are brief, and, in some of the earlier stanzas which deal with "forms" (155.19), not particularly accurate: it is difficult to visualize "shafts ... feathered with the winds"; hail is not a particularly convincing food even for such horses;[51] and, though snow on mountains is aptly imaged as fleece, it is hard to imagine

---

50/*Poems of Charles Cotton*, ed. Beresford (London, 1923), pp. 64–65.

51/Unless we regard it, with the Old English poet, as "corna caldast" (*The Seafarer*, 33); but Cotton's image is too brief to sustain this identification.

"milk white frieze, Spun" from it: the poet is thinking of a sheep's fleece only, rather than of an "intermediate image" (149.11) of snowfleece. The passage is effective because it relies on the rapid succession of brief images: the reader is given no time to consider the accuracy and power of any particular identification; or, as Wordsworth puts it, "Fancy depends upon the rapidity and profusion with which she scatters her thoughts and images, trusting that their number, and the felicity with which they are linked together, will make amends for the want of individual value" (153.14–18).

Other characteristics of Fancy as the Preface describes it should now emerge more clearly. Two seem especially noteworthy: (1) there is little or no modification of the "materials" of Fancy (152.19–22). So, for instance, the daisy is not elevated by being called a queen, nor debased by being called a starveling, in adjacent lines in Poem VIII; snow, in Cotton's poem, is soft and white, like a fleece, but the notions of snow and fleece do not interact sufficiently to support the notion of frieze woven from snow. (2) The resemblance of Fancy depends "upon outline of form and feature" and upon "casual and outstanding ... properties" (153.8–10). So in Poem VIII, the images of queen,[52] Cyclops, shield, and star, and in Cotton's stanzas the images of weapons, depend upon mere geometrical similarity, or similarity of texture, in the objects compared. Poem XIII depends upon "casual" numerical coincidence of sisters and islands; Poem XXXII, similarly, upon the accidental coincidence of the child's present age and the period of the moon.

The most marked characteristic which emerges from these poems and theoretical considerations is that the image of Fancy is not inevitable, and that the poet is aware that it is not inevitable: alternative views of the subject, alternative attitudes of the poet towards his subject, are possible. Consideration of a fanciful image will not produce a growing "sense of the truth of the likeness" (153.5–6); it will, rather, suggest another image. The poet's mind works to the pattern: "It's like this – or like this – or like that," and the expected

52/The "rubies" are evidently the red tips on the petals of a young flower.

response of the reader is perhaps only "Oh, yes?". Imagination, on the contrary, works to the pattern: "It's like this – because of that, and that, and that"; the reader's response on such an occasion is "Ah, yes!" The coadunation of object and symbol, of tenor and vehicle, is real and complete.

Whatever we think, therefore, or whatever Coleridge may have thought, of the logic of Wordsworth's psychology in the Preface, the distinction at which Wordsworth aims is valid. At least we can say that the poems in each class do in fact hang together, that they are in fact distinct in tone, and in the approach of poet to subject, from the poems in the other class. Eventually, Wordsworth himself seems to have been satisfied with such a modest view of his classification and its usefulness: "Miscellaneous poems ought not to be jumbled together at *random* ... one poem should shade off happily into another ... as to the classification of Imagination &c – it is of slight importance as matter of Reflection, but of great as matter of *feeling* for the Reader by making one Poem smooth the way for another."[53] This genial good sense, though by no means an adequate apology for the whole complex scheme, is a better justification of some such classification than the insistent theoretical distinctions of 1812 and 1815.

iv *Faculty and Subject*

A more fundamental criticism of Wordsworth's logic, which is possibly more revealing of the workings of his mind than Coleridge's doubts on the accuracy of his psychology, is concerned, not with the distinction between Fancy and Imagination, but with the question whether certain of Wordsworth's poems are accurately classified

53/*C.R.*, p. 161 (6 April 1826); the distinction had been criticized as pointless by Lamb and Robinson (*C.R.*, p. 152). There is no suggestion in this letter that "Probably Wordsworth himself came to think of the terms *fancy* and *imagination* as mere labels denoting degrees of merit" (Scoggins, p. 214); though it is easy to agree with Mr. Scoggins that some later "Poems of the Imagination" tend to share the characteristics of earlier "Poems of the Fancy."

"according to the powers of mind ... predominant in the production of them" (143.25–27). We need to inquire, that is, whether some poems are in fact "produced" by the Fancy or the Imagination, or whether they are classified under these headings because of some other connection with the faculty concerned.

Elsewhere in these pages it is observed that Wordsworth is sometimes concerned with the presentation of an event for its own sake, or for the sake of the *power* which resides in it; and that such a presentation may be achieved with or without the intervention of what may be called, according to the point of view, literary art or the Imagination – with or without additions to, or transformations of, the factual basis of the event (Chapter VIII, sec. v). Among the poems of Fancy and Imagination, it is possible to find what appear to be merely factual records of events which, in some sense, share the qualities of Fancy and Imagination but which in their presentation are not modified by either of these faculties.

Such a poem is "A whirl-blast from behind the hill." It is a poem about what might be called a fanciful natural phenomenon, rather than a poem produced by the poet's Fancy. Except for the last four lines of the standard text which introduce a somewhat unnecessary simile, nothing here is significantly "aggregated and associated" by the mind of the poet: the odd behaviour of the holly-leaves, as it were a fanciful freak of Nature akin to the fanciful freaks of the poet's mind seen in the poems of the Fancy discussed earlier, is the major point of the poem; and this the poet faithfully records without significant modification or addition. The poem says little more, in effect, than the laconic entry in Dorothy Wordsworth's *Journal*: "sheltered under the hollies, during a hail-shower. The withered leaves danced with the hailstones" (i.12–13); and the concluding lines of the manuscript version, which lacks both the simile just mentioned and the moralizing comment which appeared in the text of *Lyrical Ballads*, indicate clearly enough that Wordsworth originally considered such a record as sufficient material for a poem: "This long description why indite? Because it was a pleasant sight"

(*P.W.*, ii.128). What is fanciful in the poem is, indeed, a datum which the poet reproduces, rather than a product of his own Fancy.[54]

If we were to substitute for the phrase "pleasant sight" something like "moving experience," the lines just quoted would serve as a corresponding apology for certain poems of the Imagination. For instance, in his general account of the poems of the Imagination of 1815 (151.25 ff.), Wordsworth, in describing "There was a Boy," is describing a poem about the Imagination, rather than a poem produced by the Imagination; that is, he gives the impression that the poem describes (whether "imaginatively" or merely factually does not appear, and is not relevant to Wordsworth's account) an event in which the Imagination of the protagonist, but not necessarily that of the poet composing the poem, is emphatically active. The remainder of this paragraph lists the "objects" upon which the Imagination "exerts itself" in the other poems of the group; and, again, it is not always clear whether the exertion is the poet's during composition or the protagonist's (usually also the poet's) during the events described. *A Night-Piece*, for instance, like "There was a Boy," seems to be primarily a factual account of certain natural phenomena and their effect upon the poet's mind (perhaps upon his Imagination), rather than an imaginative poem.[55] *St. Paul's*, a poem never published by Wordsworth, similarly describes an external scene which reacted strongly upon the Imagination of the poet; but the poem itself does not differ significantly from Wordsworth's prose

54/The poet's mind here is indeed in that state which Scoggins attributes to the Fancy in his discussion of this poem: "fancy is dependent upon 'the accidents of things'; it must, therefore, assume an essentially passive state towards Nature, waiting, so to speak, for the fortuitous circumstance" (pp. 68–69). That the typical Wordsworthian poem of the Fancy is marked by such a passive state of mind is, I hope, disproved by the preceding section of this chapter.

55/Wordsworth himself thought this "among the best for the imaginative power displayed in [it]" (*H.C.R.*, p. 166). It is hard to see why, and Robinson, in spite of his efforts to understand Wordsworth's notion of the Imagination, confessed that "I believe I do not understand in what [its] excellence consists." The Fenwick note shows clearly that the poem is a memorial, not an imaginative, reconstruction: "I distinctly recollect the very moment when I was struck, as described 'He looks up at the clouds, etc.'" (*P.W.*, ii.503).

account of the scene in a letter to Sir George Beaumont,[56] and is clearly a product of the memory rather than of the Imagination. Most readers, whatever their general view of the poem, would agree that some parts at least of *The Thorn* are the product of Wordsworth's Imagination; but it is not wholly clear whether this is the reason for its inclusion in this class, or whether the main reason is, rather, that Wordsworth considered the poem to be about a superstitious man with "a reasonable share of imagination ... the faculty which produces impressive effects out of simple elements" (12.18–20).[57] Two similar poems placed under "Imagination" in 1815, *The Horn of Egremont Castle* and *Goody Blake and Harry Gill* – which, according to the Preface of 1800, shows that "the power of the human imagination is sufficient to produce such changes even in our physical nature as might almost appear miraculous" (28.27–29) – are so described in a note of 1815 as to reveal the ambiguity of the classification: "This poem [*Egremont Castle*] and [*Goody Blake*], as they rather refer to the imagination than are produced by it, would not have been placed here but to avoid a needless multiplication of the Classes" (*P.W.*, iv.439). The poems remained under the heading "Imagination" until 1845, when they were degraded to the new and unmeaningful category of "Miscellaneous Poems," and when the account of *Goody Blake* just quoted disappeared from the Preface to *Lyrical Ballads*. But the other poems mentioned remained under "Imagination," with no such explanation as the note of 1815 provided for *Egremont Castle* and *Goody Blake*. We shall compare

56/*P.W.*, iv.374–75; *M.Y.*, i.209. The differences in the poem are mainly Miltonic mannerisms, e.g., the repetition of "gift" (8–9), and especially Miltonic series of adjectives in 17, 22, 25.

57/This case differs from the others in that the material is fictitious and Wordsworth is not recording his own experience, as he is in the others. To make a fictitious character speak imaginatively (if we grant that the protagonist of *The Thorn* does so), the poet must evidently exert his own imagination as he composes. Or we may say that Wordsworth is recording his own experience in the sense that he found the thorn impressive (see the Fenwick note, *P.W.*, ii.511), like the sea-captain, and that the poem is his imaginative response to this impressiveness. Whichever of these accounts may be acceptable, this motive for classifying the poem as imaginative is not necessarily the major one.

"There was a Boy" and *A Night-Piece* with two sorts of poem described earlier, in an attempt to see their significance and their connection with the Imagination which evidently led Wordsworth to place them in the class concerned.

In the most successful exposition which the Preface offers of the Imagination, the description of the double simile of *Resolution and Independence* (149.6–15), Wordsworth is describing the workings of the mind of the poet upon the data of memory. In "There was a Boy," on the other hand, he is describing the workings of the mind of the boy upon sense-data actually present; and in the account of this poem in the Preface (151.25–152.6), he is not describing how the poem came to be written, or how his mind worked upon the incident as it lay ten years deep in his memory, but glossing the poem, translating the event which the poem describes into psychological terms in an effort to ensure that the reader understands the event. The Preface, that is to say, illuminates the event with which "There was a Boy" deals; but in the discussion of *Resolution and Independence* it illuminates, not the analogous event, Wordsworth's meeting with the leech-gatherer, but a quite different event – the poet's transformation of this encounter into an imaginative poem. It is, of course, perfectly possible, but far from inevitable, that a poem such as "There was a Boy" might be an imaginative poem, the subject-matter of which was an event involving the imaginative activity of the protagonist; what is significant here is that the account of "There was a Boy" in the Preface is evidently intended as a justification for the appearance of the poem among "Poems of the Imagination" (that is, among poems "produced by" the Imagination), as the account of *Resolution and Independence* justifies the inclusion of that poem in this class. In brief, the description of "There was a Boy" leads us to believe that, in some important instances, there was for Wordsworth no adequate distinction between a poem produced by the Imagination and verse describing, without the exertion of the poet's Imagination during composition, an imaginative act.

A Night-Piece and *St. Paul's* are similar poems. In each of the events described, the Imagination of Wordsworth as protagonist was evidently active in some sense; in each poem the description is what is commonly called vivid. But in each case no creative effort by the poet appears to be involved; as in "A whirl-blast," what is presented is a seeming effort on the part of Nature, which the poet merely reports.[58] We are faced, as a critic of "There was a Boy" puts it, with an "attempt to reenact the processes of private experience";[59] with an exercise, we might say, of the power "to observe with accuracy things as they are in themselves, and with fidelity to describe them, unmodified by any passion or feeling existing in the mind of the Describer: whether the things depicted be actually present to the sense, or have a place only in the memory" (140.15–19); with an attempt at "Copying the impression of the memory";[60] or with an attempt to produce a verbal *copy* (in Coleridge's vocabulary) of private experience, as far as words can be used for such a purpose. But poetry draws on the power of accurate observation and reporting "only in submission to necessity," Wordsworth adds immediately, "and never for a continuance of time, as its exercise supposes all the higher qualities of the mind to be passive, and in a state of subjection

58/The mind's "delight" mentioned at the end of *A Night-Piece* is analogous to the "pleasure" which the poet took in observing the dancing holly-leaves. The Imagination is not mentioned in *A Night-Piece*, though it is in *St. Paul's*. The general point made here is made by Scoggins (p. 115), but without indication of its significance in the interpretation of the Preface. Indeed, on p. 120 Mr. Scoggins describes such poems as dealing "with the earliest impressions and influences on that faculty [the Imagination] of 'various objects of the external universe' "; this is a possible characterization of the poems, but a misrepresentation of Wordsworth's statement, which says that "The Poems ... exhibit the faculty exerting itself upon various objects of the external universe" (152.6–8).

59/Herbert Lindenberger, *On Wordsworth's Prelude* (Princeton, 1963), p. 43.

60/*Prel.*, VII.146. The "things depicted" are, or are presented as being, "actually present to the sense" in *A Night-Piece* and "A whirl-blast"; they are presented as "only in the memory" in "There was a Boy," *St. Paul's*, and the description of London in *Prel.*, VII. Because of the nature of the material and of its handling, the difference does not usually amount to more than a difference between present and past tense. *Prel.* VII is by no means wholly a copy of "the impression of the memory," as is clear from (for instance) such brief but vivid similes as "Escaped as from an enemy," "Still as a shelter'd place when winds blow loud" (*Prel.*, VII. 185, 187; cf. 354 ff., 374 ff., 387 ff., 394 ff.).

to external objects" (140.21–23); the poetry of the Imagination does not copy, it does not attempt (as the Preface makes abundantly clear) to preserve the "private experience" unchanged; on the contrary, it works by enabling the object or experience "to react upon the mind which hath performed the [imaginative] process, like a new existence" (148.20–21).

A further contrast is clear between poems like "There was a Boy," on the one hand, and, on the other, the superficially similar poems described earlier such as *Nutting, Tintern Abbey, The Prelude*, VI.556–72 (which eventually appeared in "Poems of the Imagination" as *The Simplon Pass*), and parts of the first book of *The Excursion*.[61] Such poems also describe natural phenomena, with the same precision and vividness as "There was a Boy" and the like, but the final effect is different. It is different because the poems of the second group show a purposeful selection of scenic details which, in Lamb's phrase, "draws all things to one; which makes things ... take one colour and serve to one effect" (150.16–18); in short, these poems show, what the other group lacks, the coadunating power of the Imagination applied by the poet in the act of composition. Whether the unity towards which the details point is stated, as it is in *The Prelude*, or whether it remains implicit, as in *Nutting, Tintern Abbey*, and the story of Margaret, these poems mean more than the first group because they rise above particularities of scene towards "general truth," or an idea; because, in Robinson's words, they demonstrate "the capacity of the *sensible* produced to represent and stand in the place of the abstract intellectual conception," and that "imagination is the faculty by which the poet conceives and produces – that

---

61/See above, pp. 165–67. The events described in these poems also differ, usually, from the occasions of "power" described in *The Prelude* and elsewhere: see below, Chapter VIII, sec. iii. Such occasions usually depend on "An ordinary sight" (*Prel.*, XI.309) which is transmuted by the Imagination of the observer; whereas the poems now under consideration deal with natural phenomena already so transmuted by the quasi-imaginative workings of Nature, with "abrupt and unhabitual influence" (*Prel.*, XIII.80), that they are extraordinary. Of the occasions of power cited in Chapter VIII, below, only the sunset of *Exc.*, II.829 ff. resembles such unusual phenomena.

is, images – individual forms in which are *embodied universal ideas or abstractions*" (*H.C.R.*, pp. 93, 191). No such embodiment is achieved by "There was a Boy," *A Night-Piece,* and *St. Paul's.*

In what sense, then, are such poems to be connected with the Wordsworthian Imagination? Imaginative minds, says Wordsworth in *The Prelude,* "build up greatest things From least suggestions";[62] in these poems, on the contrary, the suggestion in the poet's mind is powerful and the building insignificant. But in the same context, Wordsworth describes, in terms which suggest that he does not fully appreciate the difference, what is in a sense the opposite case. In certain natural phenomena such as the scene upon Snowdon (and, we may add, the scenes of *A Night-Piece*[63] and *St. Paul's*), Nature works as if with imaginative power, coadunating scenic details, which may be otherwise commonplace and unremarkable, into a whole. Imaginative minds

> "for themselves create
> A like existence, and, *whene'er it is*
> *Created for them, catch it by an instinct* ...
> Willing to work and *to be wrought upon* ...
> By sensible impressions ...
> ... quicken'd, rouz'd, and made thereby more fit
> To hold communion with the invisible world."
>
> (*Prel.,* XIII.94–105)

Poems like "There was a Boy" describe such an "existence ... Created for" the perceiving mind, which "catches" it and is "wrought upon" by it, but does not, or does not necessarily, "work" upon it. The Imagination of the observer in such contexts of events is active, but it is active in receiving, not in transforming or creating; and the observer need not be a poet as such. Indeed, when the manifestations of Nature's quasi-imaginative works are especially powerful, "even

---

62/*Prel.,* XIII.98–99. Cf. the sentence quoted above from the note to *The Thorn.*
63/Which closely resembles the scene upon Snowdon; see pp. 50–51 above.

the grossest minds must see and hear And cannot chuse but feel."[64]
It is evidently this activity (if activity is the right word) of the Imagination which is involved in the events reported in these poems; and this activity is to Wordsworth the justification for the inclusion of the poems among "Poems of the Imagination." It is hardly a valid justification: the imaginative act concerned is part of Wordsworth's biography, not of his poetry. It is, perhaps, analogous to the reading, hearing, or performing of a musical score, each of which may be an imaginative act but none of which closely resembles the composition of music: the creative act resides in the mind of the composer, and its issue is a datum which the performer reports.

It may be significant that the three poems discussed describe events of a particular kind in the Wordsworthian experience. They deal with events which were felt the more strongly when, and because, the mind had been occupied previously with something else.[65] The characteristic of these events is the sudden power with which the scene is perceived.[66] It seems possible that this sudden power resembles that access of power which accompanies, for most writers, the achievement of the right word, or of the figure which seems peculiarly illuminating or appropriate: in short, the achievement of

64/*Prel.*, XIII.83–84; "men, least sensitive, see, hear, perceive" etc., in the text of 1850. Cf. the discussion of the inevitable effect of the "simple and direct" pathetic in the *Essay, Supplementary* (185.1 ff.); also the ending to "A whirl-blast" in *Lyrical Ballads*: "Oh! grant me Heaven a heart at ease, That I may never cease to find, Even in appearances like these, Enough to nourish and to stir my mind!" Here again the mind receives but does not necessarily transform.

65/"The Boy, there introduced, is listening, with something of a feverish and restless anxiety, for the recurrence of the riotous sounds which he had previously excited; and, at the moment when the intenseness of his mind is beginning to remit, he is surprised into a perception of the solemn and tranquillizing images which the Poem describes" (152.1–6).

66/"... a gentle shock of mild surprise Has carried far into his heart the voice Of mountain-torrents" ("There was a Boy," 19–21); "a Light upon the turf Fell like a flash; a startling gleam, yet mild The shock and gentle" (*Prel.*, XIII.39–40, reading A²); "any impressive visual object ... is carried to the heart with a power not known under other circumstances" (De Quincey, *Reminiscences of the English Lake Poets*, ed. Jordan [London, 1961], p. 122, fn.; describing a similar incident).

the "incarnation of the thought" (125.27)[67] by an act of Imagination, such as makes significant the leech-gatherer or the hazel-grove of *Nutting* or the Simplon Pass – things not seen, as far as we know, in the peculiarly Wordsworthian context of events which contains the others. Or we may say that the creative power of Wordsworth's poetic Imagination enabled him to see a figure like the leech-gatherer, or a scene like the Simplon Pass, with the same vividness as he saw the moon "on the road between Nether Stowey and Alfoxden" (*P.W.*, ii.503) or the snow-scene in London. We may say that it was indifferent to him whether the imaginative power which worked on the elements of such scenes was his own or that which seems to reside in Nature; that in either case the effect upon some recipient faculty – call it the Imagination as receiver, or the "feelings,"[68] the "heart,"[69] the "soul,"[70] or even the "capacity of apprehension"[71] – was the same or similar.[72] Exactly what effect the scenes created by Nature had for Wordsworth can hardly be precisely known,[73] except to those who recognize, or think they recognize, similar effects in their own

67/See above, pp. 44–47.
68/Called "recipient ... powers," 114.9–10.
69/"There was a Boy," 20; De Quincey's report.
70/*St. Paul's*, 10 (*P.W.*, iv.374).
71/De Quincey's report.
72/After the Imagination has "conferred" or "abstracted," the object on which it has operated is enabled "to react upon the mind which hath performed the process, like a new existence" (148.17–21). Here the mind as receiver of the completed product of the Imagination is clearly envisaged, and for this act of reception it might seem indifferent whether the conferring or abstracting has been performed by the mind which eventually receives or by some other agency. Again, in the Fenwick note to the *Immortality Ode* (*P.W.*, iv.463), Wordsworth says of his childhood that "I was often unable to think of external things as having external existence, and I communed with all that I saw as something not apart from, but inherent in, my own immaterial nature"; cf. *Prel.*, II.368–71. The confusion of the objective and the subjective discussed above seems similar.
73/Effects are described, but the descriptions are imprecise: "a gentle shock of mild surprise" ("There was a Boy," 19; cf. *Prel.*, XIII.40, reading A²); "delight" or "deep joy" (*A Night-Piece*, 24 and textual n. in *P.W.*, ii.209); "My Soul in her uneasiness received An anchor of stability" (*St. Paul's*, 10–11; cf. *Airey-Force Valley*, 16: "soothe his thoughts").

experience; but the very fact that Wordsworth recognizes in such scenes analogues of the products of the poetic Imagination indicates that they acted upon him in the manner of an imaginative poem. In this virtual identification (some would say confusion) of causes from the identity or close similarity of their effects upon him, we may see a reason why Wordsworth wrote such poems, and why he felt justified in calling them "Poems of the Imagination."

Eight ✳ Essay,
Supplementary to
the Preface

1 *The Argument*

The major argument of the Essay, extending from the beginning to
a point a few paragraphs from the end (159.15–182.14), is a defence,
on which Wordsworth had been brooding for several years, against
previous and anticipated criticism. There are, he says, four classes
among readers of poetry: the young, the middle-aged, the middle-
aged religious, and habitual readers (159.15–28). Only the fourth
class produces good critics; each of the other classes is prone to peculiar errors of judgment (159.29–164.4). Not only the best, however,
but also the worst critics are found in the fourth class (164.5–165.5).
In this situation, we should expect that poetry of permanent merit
would be neglected by the audience contemporary with the poet
(165.6–28). The Essay continues with an account of English poetry
of the preceding two centuries designed to prove this thesis (165.29–
181.21), from which it follows that the unfavourable reception of
Wordsworth's poems indicates that they are likely to survive
(181.22–182.14).

The argument is in particular a defence against the criticism of
Jeffrey,[1] who is clearly aimed at in the opening paragraph of the text
of 1815 (158.1–159.14) and also in the account of the bad critics of
the fourth class of readers described in 164.5–165.5. As a defence of

1/See W. J. B. Owen, "Wordsworth and Jeffrey in Collaboration," *R.E.S.*,
N.S., xv (1964), 161–67.

Wordsworth's poetry, the argument is passable rhetoric but poor logic; for it is, in its simplest terms, an attempt to prove the following proposition:

All poetry of permanent value is neglected by the contemporary audience.
My poetry is neglected by the contemporary audience.
Therefore, my poetry has permanent value.

Here the fallacy of the undistributed middle appears immediately.

Even if we take a kindlier view and urge that Wordsworth is arguing by analogy rather than by invalid syllogism, it is clear that the argument is conclusive neither as a whole nor in details. The account of Shakespeare hovers between two concepts of his "mighty genius" (166.13) which are mutually inconsistent.[2] The discussion of Thomson, whose "case appears to bear strongly against" Wordsworth, is marked by hair-splitting "between wonder and legitimate admiration" and by unsupported implication such as that Thomson's descriptions of "the most obvious and important phenomena ... the visible universe" filled a pressing need in the mind of the contemporary audience (173.5–174.14), whereupon Wordsworth proceeds to denigrate, as far as he dares, other qualities of Thomson's poetry, lest his general proposition that bad poetry is admired by its contemporaries should appear to be weakened. The burlesque tone of Shenstone's *Schoolmistress* is attributed to "timidity" in the face of possible public reactions, and "the People" are right to "read in seriousness, doing for the Author what he had not courage openly to venture upon for himself" (Knight, ii.243, fn.; first printed 1827). Shenstone, we are asked to believe, deliberately trivialized a poem which, in terms of his basic purpose, was seriously intended. The attack on Macpherson's Ossian (178.2–180.26) is aimed at the forgery as much as at the bad literature.

2/The Coleridgean view of "Shakespeare's judgement equal to his genius" (*Biog. Lit.*, i.22) and the notion of genius prostituted to popularity.

Contrarily, it would be easy to interpolate into Wordsworth's survey examples of poets popular in their time who seem to have acquired a fame more permanent than Wordsworth's argument would suggest. The clearest example is that of Donne and others "of that class of curious thinkers whom Dr. Johnson has strangely styled Metaphysical Poets" (169.18–19). The immense gain in the prestige of these poets in the first half of this century; the corresponding decline in reputation of Spenser, Milton, and the Romantics and Victorians; and signs within the last few years of a reversal of these processes: all suggest, if any conclusions are possible, not the steady rise or decline of reputations decided by the ultimate judgment of "the People" (186.32), but a kind of cyclic development in the reactions of the audience of poetry. Indeed, with the decline in the audience of poetry and the elevation of the art to a subject of academic study, it becomes increasingly difficult to assign a meaning to Wordsworth's faith in the judgment of the People; and increasingly easy to see the reputation of particular poets undergoing in the mind of a minority such a cyclic development, of which the utterances of influential critics may be either symptoms or directors.

Thus the major argument of the Essay fails in logic if not in persuasion: some "good" poets take time to establish a reputation, some establish one immediately (and both sorts may lose it temporarily); some "bad" poets establish a transient reputation; of those "bad" poets who fail to establish any reputation at all we must assume the existence, but we are not likely to find a record of them unless, like Blackmore and his kind, they happen to have attracted the immortality of a *Dunciad* or a Johnsonian Life.

The conclusion which Wordsworth really wishes to establish, we have seen, is that which has "particular relation ... to these Volumes" of 1815: "the products of my industry will endure" (181.29–182.14). From this point he proceeds to discuss another "conclusion," which is not necessarily proved by the preceding discussion nor necessarily connected with the particular case of Wordsworth, but which demands much more consideration: the difficulties in which an original poet is involved in his attempt to secure the approval of an intelligent audience; or, in the Coleridgean phrase which Wordsworth borrows, "every Author, as far as he is great and at the same time *original*, has had the task of *creating* the taste by which he is to be enjoyed" (182.17–19).[3] This proposition is not necessarily proved by what precedes since Wordsworth is earlier concerned, because of his own situation in 1815, to demonstrate an inevitable time-lag between publication and appreciation of a good poet. In fact, such a time-lag is not inevitable, as (for instance) the profusion of manuscripts of Donne's poems during his lifetime and of printed editions after his death indicates.

II *Power and Knowledge*

Stated as baldly as Wordsworth states it, Coleridge's proposition is almost a truism: it would be hard to conceive, without rendering the adjective almost meaningless, an "original" author who found "the taste by which he is to be enjoyed" already existing in the contemporary audience.[4] But the subsequent discussion on "the real difficulty of creating that taste by which a truly original Poet is to be relished" (182.28–29) is, if we concede that the difficulty is real but that it does not necessarily require an appreciable time for its solution, a passage of considerable importance and interest.

The discussion opens with a list of certain effects upon his audience at which the serious poet will aim and which might be considered as difficulties standing in the way of the creation of a new taste (182.28–183.5). They are not, in fact, difficulties, Wordsworth concludes, if they "are to be attained by the mere communication of *knowledge*" (183.6–7). There follows a digression upon the inappropriateness of the word *Taste* as commonly used, and of the metaphor involved in its use, on the ground that "the pathetic and the sublime

3/It is attributed to Coleridge by Wordsworth in a letter of 21 May 1807 (83.19–22). Coleridge is, of course, the "philosophical Friend" of 182.20; cf. 156.29 ff.

4/Wordsworth approaches this position in the discussion of Thomson (174.15 ff.).

... are neither of them ... objects of a faculty which could ever without a sinking in the spirit of Nations have been designated by the metaphor – *Taste*. ... Because without the exertion of a co-operating *power* in the mind of the Reader, there can be no adequate sympathy with either of these emotions" (183.30–36). The real difficulty involved, Wordsworth concludes, is that the original poet has "to call forth and bestow power, of which knowledge is the effect" (184.32–33).

Apart from an *obiter dictum* admitting the competence of taste to deal with such aesthetic elements as "proportion and congruity" (183.25–26), it is clear that we have to do here with a Wordsworthian discrimination which was never fully expounded by its author in print and for which we have to rely on late and probably much amplified accounts by De Quincey: the distinction between the Literature of Knowledge and the Literature of Power.

De Quincey's account of the distinction, which he owed "to many years' conversation with Mr. Wordsworth," appears in his third *Letter to a Young Man whose Education has been Neglected* (1823) and his article on Pope (1848).[5] The distinction may be outlined as follows:

The word *literature* is ambiguous, for it is used in a wide sense to mean "the total books of a language." More accurately, literature is opposed to "Books of Knowledge," which include "all books in which the matter to be communicated is paramount to the manner or form of its communication." Hence (i) the defining characteristic of literature thus conceived is that it communicates (not *pleasure*, as the conventional Horatian antithesis has it, but) *power*: "All that is literature seeks to communicate power; all that is not literature, to communicate knowledge" (Masson, x.46–48). (ii) Its function is to *move* rather than to *teach* (xi.54). Yet (iii) though it "speaks ... *through* affections of pleasure and sympathy," though "it does and must operate ... on and through that *humid* light which clothes itself

5/*Collected Writings of Thomas De Quincey*, ed. Masson (Edinburgh, 1889–90), x.46 ff. and xi.54 ff.

in the mists and glittering iris of human passions, desires, and genial emotions," nevertheless it may secondarily speak "to the higher understanding or reason ... it may travel towards an object seated in what Lord Bacon calls *dry* light" (xi.54–55). (iv) The Literature of Power makes us aware of "emotions which ordinary life rarely or never supplies occasions for exciting, and which had previously lain unawakened, and hardly within the dawn of consciousness";[6] or it *"informs"* otherwise lifeless abstractions such as space;[7] or it provides *"power*, that is, exercise and expansion of your own latent capacity of sympathy with the infinite."[8] Finally, (v) individual examples of the Literature of Power are not superseded, but survive as individuals, inimitable and unmodifiable; whereas individual examples of the Literature of Knowledge can always be modified, improved upon, and eventually superseded (Masson, xi.57–59).

It is obvious that much of this account can be paralleled in Wordsworth's Essay and other critical writings. The basis of it may be found as early as 1800, in the Preface to *Lyrical Ballads*: "the ... philosophical [contradistinction] of Poetry and Science" (24.fn.15), a distinction echoed early in the Essay (160.2–7). As De Quincey rejects the Horatian antithesis *prodesse aut delectare*, so in the Essay we hear nothing significant about the pleasures of poetry, a constant theme in the Preface to *Lyrical Ballads*;[9] we hear, rather, as far as the audience is concerned, of poetry *"as a study"* (159.28); of "admiration," of reason, understanding, and judgment.[10] None of these characteristics, to be sure, is incompatible with the reader's pleasure in poetry; but the emphasis has been altered, in that the reader's response is now conceived as more laboured and more intellectual, and the figure of the poet, once "a man speaking to men," now

---

6/Masson, x.48 (*King Lear* cited in illustration, x.49).
7/Masson, x.49 (*Paradise Lost* cited).
8/Masson, xi.56 (*Paradise Lost* cited).
9/See Chapter IV, sec. iv, n.28. The Essay tends to associate this theme with pleasure in *bad* poetry (159.32–161.23, 174.5–8).
10/See 165.17, 166.21, 169.20, 170.25, 171.3, 172.20, 173.6, 174.5, 181.20, 182.4, 186.21; 160.10, 161.4, 161.26, 164.15.

becomes more portentous and oracular, more remote, more like Blake's Bard "Who Present, Past, and Future, sees."

The major antithesis between knowledge and power lies behind Wordsworth's whole discussion of the difficulty of creating a new taste. To proceed, if one could proceed, to alter taste by the "mere communication of *knowledge*" (183.6–7) would be easy; but this is not the poet's function. The poet's function is to stir the reader's mind to action; to stimulate "the exertion of a co-operating *power* in the mind of the Reader" (183.34–35); to achieve "an advance, or a conquest" (184.26); to ensure that the reader "is invigorated and inspirited by his Leader, in order that he may exert himself" (184.29–31).

As De Quincey concedes that power may secondarily lead to knowledge, so Wordsworth asserts that "knowledge is the effect" of power called forth and bestowed (184.33). With De Quincey's fourth point, that the Literature of Power makes us aware of "emotions which ordinary life rarely or never supplies occasions for exciting, and which had previously lain unawakened, and barely within the dawn of consciousness," we may compare, as well as some notable passages in the *Essays upon Epitaphs* (especially 107.1–12, 117.33–118.10), Wordsworth's discussion, developed largely from John Dennis, of the "simple" and the "complex" emotions with which poetry may deal (185.1–26).[11] In making his reader aware of "simple"[12] emotions the poet faces no particular difficulty; it is in the case of emotions which are "complex and revolutionary ... against which [the heart] struggles with pride" (185.8–9); of "meditative ... pathos ... enthusiastic ... sorrow; a sadness that has its seat in the depths of reason, to which the mind cannot sink gently of itself – but to which it must descend by treading the steps of thought" (185.17–20) – it is here, and in the case of the sublime, that the poet must exert himself "to call forth and bestow power" (184.32–33).

11/See sec. v below.

12/The adjectives *direct, human,* and *ordinary* are used as more or less synonymous with *simple* (185.7, 17, 18).

Lastly, we match De Quincey's claim that individual examples of the Literature of Power survive with Wordsworth's that "this advantage attends [good poetry], that the *individual*, as well as the species, survives from age to age" (186.22–24). The contrasting members of the antithesis differ: for De Quincey, it is the Literature of Knowledge; for Wordsworth, it is "vicious poetry" (186.20). But their claims are essentially similar; and Wordsworth's harks back to the much earlier arguments of the Preface to *Lyrical Ballads* and the *Essays upon Epitaphs*, where he tried to define, by contrast to the transience of poetic dictions or bad epitaphs, the qualities which make for permanence of poetic appeal, in poetry in general and in the epitaph in particular (see Chapters I; VI, sec.ii).

De Quincey's discussion, though it elucidates the nature of the distinction in terms of which Wordsworth is thinking in the passage under consideration, does not wholly clarify the metaphorical texture of Wordsworth's language. We shall therefore consider Wordsworth's concept of power at greater length.[13]

III *The Concept of Power*

In ordinary usage the word *power* demands, or at least implies, a context: we expect it to be followed by an infinitive, or by such a group as *of* plus verbal noun, or to be qualified by an adjective or its equivalent; or, if such a context is not present, we expect it to be easily inferred. Among the 600-odd occasions on which Wordsworth uses the word or its plural in his verse, all the expected contexts can no doubt be found.[14] But there is also to be found a usage

13/For some instances of De Quincey's experiences of power which seem comparable to Wordsworth's described in the next section, see John W. Bilsland, "On De Quincey's Theory of Literary Power," *U.T.Q.*, xxvi (1957), 469–80.

14/In *The Prelude* and *The Excursion* I find the following usages or senses: (1) *power* + infinitive (often equivalent to the verb *to be able*), e.g., *Prel.*, VIII.3; X.577; XII.282; XIII.387, a usage notably commoner in the text of 1850, e.g., V.107; VII.548; X.139, 254; and in *Exc.*, e.g., I.145, 660, 683, 919, and many others; (2) *power* defined by adjective (often less idiomatic than the preceding or other idioms), e.g., *Prel.*, I.407: *voluntary power* = "power of will," cf. *C.L.*, ii.953:

196 Wordsworth as Critic

which is seemingly peculiar to Wordsworth, the use of the word
without such a context stated or easily inferred – a case which pro-
vokes in the reader the questions, "Power for what?" "Power to do
what?" and the like. This usage appears in our text in the passage
under consideration, and adds to the difficulty of interpretation.

The passages concerned are two (184.16, 33); a probable third
occurs slightly earlier (183.34). In the two certain cases, *power* is a
quality which the great poet "calls forth" from the reader, and which
he also "communicates" to, or "bestows" on, the reader. In the third
case (183.34), *power* is a faculty of the reader's mind which he
"exerts."[15] Thus *power* in these passages is an attribute of the mind
– the poet's mind, perhaps, and certainly the reader's, and it is also,
as we shall see, an attribute of other things; but it is not an attribute
of the artefact, which is rather the means by which power is communicated. By the process which Wordsworth calls elsewhere "action
from within and from without,"[16] the reader, it would appear,
achieves the quality of power and, perhaps, the same state of power
as that which obtains in the mind of the poet. Power is thus, it seems,
at once objective and subjective: the power of the poet is perceived
by the reader, but in the act of perception the power of the reader is
also felt by himself.

There are analogues to this process in various incidents narrated
in *The Prelude*. When Wordsworth first entered London, he experi-

Coleridge is "diseased in voluntary power"; II.330 and v.619: *visionary power*
= ?"power to see visions"; II.381: *plastic power* = "power to mould"; III.370:
winning power = "power to win me"; *Exc.*, I.167, 265, 480; (3) *power* = "faculty,
aspect of the mind," e.g., *Prel.*, II.221 (= "reason"), 310; III.164; text of 1850,
I.77 (= "Imagination"), 166; *Exc.*, I.157; II.614; (4) *power* = "physical, political,
military, divine or quasi-divine power," e.g., *Prel.*, I.198; IV.156; v.166; *Exc.*, I.16,
217; (5) *power* = "powerful being, divine or quasi-divine nature" (very similar
to the preceding), e.g., *Prel.*, VIII.393; IX.48 (?); x (1850).420; *Exc.*, I.217; III.353;
cf. 166.9: Spenser "was a great power"; (6) *power* = "artistic power," e.g., *Prel.*,
VII.259; text of 1850, VII.406, 625; *Exc.*, I.615; IX.138 (text of 1814–20).

15/This is ambiguous since it may be an instance of the usage noted under
2 in the preceding note: "co-operating *power*" may mean simply "power (ability,
capacity) to co-operate"; but the italicization militates against this sense.

16/See 112.23–24; *Prel.*, XII.377. In the second passage, "power" is a mark
"Both of the object seen, and eye that sees" (XII.379).

enced "weight and power, Power growing with the weight," at the moment when he "seem'd to know The threshold now is overpass'd." He was moved to this experience by the realization that he was now within a great city:

> "that vast Metropolis,
> The Fountain of my Country's destiny
> And of the destiny of Earth itself,
> That great Emporium, Chronicle at once
> And Burial-place of passions and their home
> Imperial and chief living residence."
>
> (*Prel.*, VIII. 697–706, 746–51)

That is to say, London appeared to him a place of power, and its effect upon his mind was to "call forth" power. And, aptly to the view expressed above, that power is in some sense, perhaps primarily, an attribute of the mind, Wordsworth thinks it remarkable that "aught *external* to the living mind Should have such mighty sway." Power was "left behind" in Wordsworth's mind by his boyhood experience on the Penrith Beacon, and contributed "radiance more divine" to his later visit; what appears to be the same power, associated with "a strong Confusion," led him to connect Coleridge with this scene, though the association was not warranted by historical fact (*Prel.*, XI.279–326; VI.239–48). In this case a strong emotion, fear, appears to have been the prime source of power.[17]

Such episodes do not define the Wordsworthian concept of power; they define rather the context of events in which he was likely to feel power exerted upon himself. And, in general, it is difficult to extract a simple definition of the concept from his autobiographical verse: the most we can usually do is to define the associations of power or the mode by which it operates.

It is associated, commonly, as we might expect, with notions of greatness, including, apparently, mere physical size. The Wanderer of

17/The episode of the horses which follows (*Prel.*, XI.345 ff.) left, according to MS. V, "a kindred power Implanted in my mind."

The Excursion, in a passage which obviously records Wordsworth's
own experience, "saw the hills Grow larger in the darkness," and

> "In such communion, not from terror free, ...
> Had he perceived the presence and the power
> Of greatness; and deep feelings had impressed
> So vividly great objects that they lay
> Upon his mind like substances."   (*Exc.*, 1.127 ff.)

In a vivid Lakeland sunset, the Solitary saw

> "fixed resemblances ...
> To implements of ordinary use,
> But vast in size, in substance glorified
> ... forms uncouth of mightiest power
> For admiration and mysterious awe";
>   (*Exc.*, II.864–69)

and in America he thought that nothing in Europe compared

> "for power
> And majesty with this gigantic stream,
> Sprung from the desert."   (*Exc.*, III.881–84)

The physical size of London contributed to the effect it had on
Wordsworth as he describes it in the passage discussed above: it was
the "great City," "that vast Metropolis ... That great Emporium."[18]
Physical size in natural objects, coupled with what Wordsworth calls
"simplicity," which seems to mean simplicity in visual outline – these
are associated with power in a passage which claims that the influence of such objects strengthens the ability of the mind to impose
unity upon multeity; examples are the desert, the sea, and the
mountain.[19]

18/*Prel.*, VIII.693 ("thy vast dominion," text of 1850), 746, 749; cf. 825, 837–38.
19/*Prel.* (1850), VII.740 ff. The text of 1805 mentions only mountains, and
Wordsworth's fragmentary essay on the Sublime and Beautiful, discussed in the

The operation of power is associated in the first place with strong emotion: in the case of London, "a swell of feeling" (*Prel.*, VIII.743); in the cases of the Beacon and of the Wanderer's observation of nature, with fear; and in the case of the sunset, with "admiration and ... awe." It is subsequently associated with a strong impression on the memory: Wordsworth will "Never ... forget the hour The moment rather say" when he entered London, and though on this occasion there was "no thought embodied, no Distinct remembrances," yet he remembered "that it was a thing divine."[20] Clearly, the two "spots of time" recorded in Book XI of *The Prelude*, as well as many others not specifically linked with these two, made a powerful impression on his memory.[21]

In some instances, as in our text, power is distinguished, but not necessarily dissociated, from knowledge. Of schoolboys behaving "naturally" Wordsworth writes:

next section of this chapter, deals mainly with the mountainous scenery of the Lake District. In terms of the Preface of 1815, the faculty involved would be the Imagination. As early as 1800, Wordsworth had "a deep impression of certain inherent and indestructible qualities in the human mind, and likewise of certain powers in the great and permanent objects that act upon it, which are equally inherent and indestructible" (21.28–22.1). Cf. Gerard, *Taste*, p. 15: in the appreciation of the sublime, "Large objects can scarce indeed produce their full effect, unless they are also *simple*. ... Objects cannot possess that largeness, which is necessary for inspiring a sensation of the sublime, without simplicity. Where this is wanting, the mind contemplates, not one large, but many small objects." Wordsworth's fragment on the Sublime and Beautiful calls for "a feeling or image of intense unity without a conscious contemplation of parts" in the perception of the sublime.

20/*Prel.*, VIII.689–710. Cf. II.334–37: "the soul, Remembering how she felt, but what she felt, Remembering not, retains an obscure sense Of possible sublimity."

21/His inability "To paint the visionary dreariness" of the later part of the episode of the Beacon (XI.309–16) may be analogous to the failure to embody thoughts and remember distinctly the experience of entering London. On the importance to Wordsworth of the memorable, see Christopher Salvesen, *The Landscape of Memory* (London, 1965). Mr. Salvesen's pithy summary (p. 169), "To remember was, for Wordsworth, to be a poet," may represent accurately Wordsworth's own view; for reasons suggested in Chapter VII, sec. iv, above, it is not the view of this book that the mere presentation of the event of power necessarily results in poetry. The importance of the memorable event, scene, image, or phrase is stressed in the theorizings of T. S. Eliot; see especially *The Use of Poetry and the Use of Criticism* (London, 1933), pp. 147–48.

> "May books and nature be their early joy!
> And knowledge, rightly honor'd with that name,
> Knowledge not purchas'd with the loss of power!"
>
> *(Prel.*, v.447–49)

Power, according to a late text of *The Prelude* (which seems to reverse the claim of the Essay [184.33] that knowledge "is the effect" of power), "waits On knowledge";[22] and, according to the same text, Wordsworth in London was

> "seeking knowledge at that time
> Far less than craving power; yet knowledge came,
> Sought or unsought, and influxes of power
> Came, of themselves, or at her call derived
> ... when whate'er was in itself
> Capacious found, or seemed to find, in me
> A correspondent amplitude of mind."[23]

Some of the points discussed above which concern the operation of power may be seen summarized in the description of the Pastor's narratives at the beginning of Book vii of *The Excursion*:

> "Strains of power
> Were they, to seize and occupy the sense ...
> And, when the stream
> Which overflowed the soul was passed away,
> A consciousness remained that it had left,
> Deposited upon the silent shore
> Of memory, images and precious thoughts,
> That shall not die, and cannot be destroyed."[24]

22/Text of 1850, iii.391–92. The text of 1805 speaks of "a sense ... of what holy joy there is In knowledge."

23/Text of 1850, viii.599–606. The text of 1805 mentions only the acquisition of power, not of knowledge.

24/*Exc.*, vii.22–30. The use of *power* here approaches, but does not, I think, coincide with, two usages defined in n.14 above, 1 and 6.

Here we have the effect of power defined, as in the passages cited above, as, at first, strongly emotional, and, latterly, strongly memorable; whether "images and precious thoughts" may be considered "knowledge" is debatable.

A more exact definition of the concept of power is promised by two passages in *The Prelude* which have already been cited, verbally or by implication: viii.752 ff., and xi.258 ff. They are imprecise enough, but at least they refer specifically to the mind where power resides. The earlier describes the effect of London:

> "all objects, being
> Themselves capacious, also found in me
> Capaciousness and amplitude of mind";

or, in the version of 1850:

> "whate'er was in itself
> Capacious found, or seemed to find, in me
> A correspondent amplitude of mind."

"Capaciousness and amplitude" is, in a way, merely a metaphor substituting itself for the metaphor involved in "power." Yet the passage is valuable in that it throws light on the process by which power is communicated. It is here, rather than a merely passive absorption by the receiving mind, a process both active and passive, "action from within and from without," a notion which we have already seen implied in the relevant passage of the Essay, and which occurs in other passages (p. 196 above). It is a process of adaptation, an active sympathetic identification of the perceiving mind with the object perceived, by which the mind, far from merely passively receiving, is changed (and, in Wordsworth's view, permanently changed) by every access of power.[25] By taking thought on such an occasion, a man adds a cubit to his intellectual stature.

25/A similar notion, of Longinian origin, is put forward by eighteenth-century writers on the Sublime: the mind is sympathetically "expanded" by the contemplation of vast objects. See the following section of this chapter, and Samuel H. Monk, *The Sublime: A Study of Critical Theories in XVIII-Century*

The second passage is that which introduces the two notable "spots of time" in Book XI:

> "There are in our existence spots of time,
> Which with distinct pre-eminence retain
> A vivifying Virtue, whence ...
>
> our minds
> Are nourished and invisibly repair'd ...
> This efficacious spirit chiefly lurks
> Among those passages of life in which
> We have had deepest feeling that the mind
> Is lord and master, and that outward sense
> Is but the obedient servant of her will."[26]

England (New York, 1935), pp. 73 ff. Cf. Dennis, i.360: the sublime "has this peculiar to it, that it exalts the Soul, and makes it conceive a greater Idea of it self, filling it with Joy, and with a certain noble Pride, as if it self had produced what it but barely reads. ... The more the Soul is moved by the greatest Ideas, the more it conceives them; the more it conceives of the greatest Ideas, the greater Opinion it must have of its own Capacity." And cf. Gerard, *Taste*, p. 14: "We always contemplate objects and ideas with a disposition similar to their nature. When a large object is presented, the mind expands itself to the extent of that object, and is filled with one grand sensation, which totally possessing it, composes it into a solemn sedateness, and strikes it with deep silent wonder and admiration: it finds such a difficulty in spreading itself to the dimensions of its object, as enlivens and invigorates its frame: and having overcome the opposition which this occasions, it sometimes imagines itself present in every part of the scene, which it contemplates; and, from the sense of this immensity, feels a noble pride, and entertains a lofty conception of its own capacity." Wordsworth's imagination was made "restless" by "images of danger and distress, And suffering among awful Powers, and Forms" (*Prel.*, VIII.211–13), i.e., amid "sublime" scenery; and the "rocks and precipices ... snows and streams Ungovernable ... terrifying winds" of the Lake District "seize the heart with firmer grasp" (*Prel.*, VIII.353–55) than does a milder pastoral plain in Germany.

26/*Prel.*, XI.258–73. MS. V has, after "our minds," the line "Especially the imaginative power." At the crucial point 270–72, the text of 1850 reads: " ... life that give Profoundest knowledge to what point, and how, the mind is lord and master." The contrast between "the mind" and "outward sense" appears since Wordsworth was previously discussing that period when

> "the eye was master of the heart,
> When that which is in every stage of life
> The most despotic of our senses gain'd
> Such strength in me as often held my mind
> In absolute dominion" (XI.172–76),

that is, when he sought mere sensual pleasure from the natural scene.

In the episode of the Beacon which follows, "the mind Is lord and master" since a powerful emotional tone is imposed upon a natural scene which in itself (that is, as perceived by "outward sense") has nothing remarkable about it. The place of the gibbet was indeed recognized from the letters in the turf, but the gibbet and its appurtenances had gone, and the terror which drove the boy away sprang from his prior knowledge and this recognition: that is, from the mind, and in particular from the imagination, not from the visible scene as "outward sense" recorded it. Similarly, the pool, the beacon, and the girl with the pitcher constituted, as Wordsworth says, "An ordinary sight"; but were invested, by (we must suppose) imaginative effort persisting from the immediately preceding experience, with a "visionary dreariness" which Wordsworth now finds it impossible to "paint."[27] Again, the mind is active as well as recipient; in this case, to a greater degree than in that previously discussed, more active than recipient, in that the external scene is adapted to the mind rather than that the mind is adapted to the outward scene of London.

IV *The Power of the Sublime*

The concepts which we have thus extracted with some labour from Wordsworth's verse are illuminated by references to *power* in an unpublished essay on the Sublime and Beautiful which the poet designed at one stage as an introduction to his *Guide to the Lakes* and

27/Presumably a case of "commutation and transfer of internal feelings, co-operating with external accidents, to plant, for immortality, images of ... sight, in the celestial soil of the Imagination" (151.29–152.1). Cf. Gerard, *Taste*, pp. 169–70: "Ideas, which are thus compounded [by the imagination], or which are even, without composition, only associated, communicate, by the closeness of their relation, their qualities to one another. The disposition with which the mind contemplated the first, by its own firmness, which makes force requisite to destroy or change it, and by the strength of the union, which keeps this force from being applied, continues while we view the others. And we imagine, by a kind of illusion, that they produced the disposition, which in reality was brought to the perception of them; and we ascribe to them the qualities which are necessary for its production. A perception, by being connected with another, that is strong, pleasant, or painful, becomes itself vigorous, agreeable or disagreeable."

which is based mainly on the mind's reaction to the mountainous scenery of the Lake District.[28] The essay confirms the connections in Wordsworth's mind between power and eighteenth-century notions of the sublime which have been hinted at in the preceding discussion. The explicit connection suggests that he may have derived the concept of power from such discussions.[29]

Wordsworth proposes as a typical natural object which may give rise to feelings of the sublime "the Pikes of Langdale & the black precipice contiguous to them." These objects must be seen on a particular scale: not "so distant that ... they are only thought of as the crown of a comprehensive Landscape," but so that "the mountain is almost the sole object before our eyes, yet not so near but that the whole of it is visible" (MS., pp. 4–5). The "sensation of sublimity" which results from such a spectacle consists of three components: "a sense of individual form or forms; a sense of duration; and a sense of power" (MS., pp. 5–6). Sublimity may, "in the works of Man," be conveyed by the first two of these: "But in works of Nature it is not so: with these must be combined impressions of power, to a sympathy with & participation of which the mind must be elevated – or to a dread and awe of which, as existing out of itself, it must be subdued" (MS., pp. 6–7). We are not here concerned with the concept of duration,[30] nor, immediately, with that of "individual form"; but

28/Dove Cottage MS., Prose 28. The text cited here has been edited.
29/See, for instance, Burke, *On the Sublime and Beautiful,* in *Works* (London, 1886), i.94: "I know of nothing sublime, which is not some modification of power"; Richard Payne Knight, *An Analytical Inquiry into the Principles of Taste* (2nd edition, London, 1805), pp. 55–56, on "the grandeur or sublimity of sound; which can no otherwise arise from its loudness, than as that loudness excites an idea of power in the sonorous object, [for instance,] artillery and lightning are *powerful* engines of destruction; and with their *power* we sympathize, whenever the sound of them excites any sentiments of sublimity; which is only when we apprehend no danger from them; or at least no degree of danger sufficient to impress fear: for so far is terror from being a source of the sublime, that the smallest degree of fear instantly annihilates it, as far as relates to the person frightened." Wordsworth and Coleridge knew this book: see Edna Aston Shearer, "Wordsworth and Coleridge Marginalia in a Copy of Richard Payne Knight's *Analytical Inquiry into the Principles of Taste,*" H.L.Q., i (1937), 63–94.
30/Duration as a mark of sublimity "in the works of Man" is best seen in

rather with the source of power and with the reaction, or possible reactions, of the observing mind to power. The mind perceives power in such a scene, according to Wordsworth, by "the sense of motion which in the mind accompanies the lines by which the Mountain itself is shaped out. These lines may either be abrupt and precipitous, by which danger & sudden change is expressed; or they may flow into each other like the waves of the sea, and, by involving in such image a feeling of self-propagation infinitely continuous and without cognizable beginning, these lines may thus convey to the Mind sensations not less sublime than those which were excited by their opposites, the abrupt and the precipitous" (MS., p. 7). Associated details of such scenes are torrents, clouds, height, storms, and "the triumphant ostentation with which [the mountain's] snows defy the sun." In a passage largely deleted from the fragment, Wordsworth claims that "these outlines also affect us not merely by sensations referable to motion, but by dim analogies which they bear to such parts of organized bodies, as height of stature, head, neck, shoulder, back, breast, &c., which are dignified in our estimation as being the seats & instruments of active force" (MS., pp. 7–8).

The sources of power are thus perceived as: potential danger to the observer ("the abrupt and the precipitous"); a type of infinity ("self-propagation infinitely continuous and without cognizable beginning"); great physical size and energy (torrents, clouds, height); and "dim analogies" with a gigantic human or, at any rate, animal body.

Wordsworth's reaction to London, which included "a sense Of what had been here done, and suffer'd here Through ages, and was doing, suffering, still," which was "like the enduring majesty and power Of independent nature"; further, "out of what had been, what was, the place Was thronged with impregnations, like those wilds In which my early feelings had been nurs'd" (*Prel.*, VIII.780–91). The text of 1850 includes the reading: "There I conversed with majesty and power Like independent natures," where "natures" apparently means "existences," unless "natures" is a mistake for "nature's" (the reading of MS. D of the poem) – as the general drift of the following lines (1850, ll.632–38 = 1805, ll.785–95) suggests. London, as these and other passages indicate, in fact has the quality of power even though it is among "the works of Man."

Two possible reactions of the observing mind to such manifestations of power have already been indicated: "impressions of power, to a sympathy with & participation of which the mind must be elevated — or to a dread and awe of which, as existing out of itself, it must be subdued" (MS., p. 7). Here we have the sympathetic adaptation of the mind to the power of the natural scene, such as we recognized in various episodes from Wordsworth's biography outlined in the preceding section; and an attitude of mind characterized by "dread and awe" and recognizable as akin to various emotional reactions to the natural scene indicated in *The Prelude* and *The Excursion* which are marked by a component of fear or something resembling it.

From these two reactions to power Wordsworth proceeds to derive a feature which he claims as common not only to these two but also to two further reactions described a little later in the fragment. The common feature Wordsworth calls "unity":

"Power awakens the sublime either when it rouses us to a sympathetic energy & calls upon the mind to grasp at something towards which it can make approaches but which it is incapable of attaining — yet so that it participates force which is acting upon it; or, 2dly, by producing a humiliation or prostration of the mind before some external agency which it presumes not to make an effort to participate, but is absorbed in the contemplation of the might in the external power, &, as far as it has any consciousness of itself, its grandeur subsists in the naked fact of being conscious of external Power at once awful & immeasurable; so that, in both cases, the head & the front of the sensation is intense unity." (MS., pp. 10–11)

The answer to the obvious question, "Unity of what with what?" is clear in the first situation envisaged: it is a unity, or an approximate unity, of the observing mind with the power of the sublime object. In the second situation, where the sympathetic identification of the mind with the power is specifically denied by Wordsworth, the nature of the unity he postulates is less clear at first sight: for here the subject and object appear to be separated to such a degree as to make any concept of unity irrelevant. And indeed Wordsworth concedes that in certain circumstances this is so:

"For whatever suspends the comparing power of the mind & possesses it with a feeling or image of intense unity without a conscious contemplation of parts, has produced that state of the mind which is the consummation of the sublime; but if personal fear be strained beyond a certain point, this sensation is destroyed, for there are two ideas that divide & distract the attention of the Spectator with an accompanying repulsion or a wish in the soul [that] they should be divided: the object exciting the fear & the subject in which it is excited." (MS., p. 10)

The second part of this sentence states, what is commonplace in eighteenth-century theories on this subject, that "personal fear" destroys the sense of the sublime.[31] The first part implies the conditions under which the "unity" essential to the perception of the sublime exists: the "comparing power" of the mind is "suspended," that is, the whole attention of the mind is given to the object, and the mind in its contemplation of the object is thus unified, homogeneous in its attention; and, secondly, the object is perceived as a "unity without a conscious contemplation of parts," that is, as a whole and unified thing, an "individual form" (as Wordsworth's earlier discussion puts it), which, though it may have parts, is perceived not as a conglomerate of parts but as the unified sum of them.[32] In this situation, unity is both of the mind and of the object; it is a uniform attention of the mind given wholly to the object which it perceives as a unity.

31/See, for instance, Burke (n. 29 above), i.149: "if the pain and terror are so modified as not to be actually noxious; if the pain is not carried to violence, and the terror is not conversant about the present destruction of the person ... they are capable of producing delight; not pleasure, but a sort of delightful horror, a sort of tranquillity tinged with terror ... its object is the sublime"; and the passage from Payne Knight cited above, n. 29.

32/See the passage from Gerard cited above, sec. iii, n. 19; and cf. *Prel.*, VII.707–12, on the imaginative mind which "sees the parts As parts, but with a feeling of the whole."

Two further reactions of the mind to power are sketched by Wordsworth in this fragment, and both are reconciled to the overriding concept of unity. The third reaction seems to be connected closely in Wordsworth's mind with the second, just discussed; at any rate, it is insinuated, with negligible preliminary discussion, into the argument as follows: "power produces the sublime either as it is thought of as a thing to be dreaded, to be resisted, or that can be participated" (MS., p. 14). Here "dreaded" and "participated" correspond to the two reactions first described by the fragment; "resisted" introduces a new concept into the list. Wordsworth proceeds:

"as power, contemplated as something to be opposed or resisted, implies a twofold agency of which the mind is conscious, this state seems to be irreconcilable to what has been said concerning the consummation of sublimity, which ... exists in the extinction of the comparing power of the mind, & in intense unity. But the fact is, there is no sublimity excited by the contemplation of power thought of as a thing to be resisted & which the moral law enjoins us to resist, saving only as far as the mind, either by glances or continuously, conceives that that power may be overcome or rendered evanescent, and as far as it feels itself tending toward the unity that exists in security or absolute triumph (when power is thought of under a mode which we can & do participate, the sublime sensation consists in a manifest approximation towards absolute unity.)" (MS., p. 14)

In this reaction, the "unity" or "individual form" of the object is still implicit, and the unity of the mind's effort of attention is stated; but, further, this unity is here specifically defined by the mind's relation to the object: it is a relation of *superiority* which, for as long as it exists, permits the object to be perceived as sublime.[33]

The fourth reaction of the mind to power again involves the concept of resistance, but not the resistance of the mind to power:

33/Cf. the passages from Dennis and Gerard cited above, sec. iii, n. 25, on the soul's great "Opinion ... of its own capacity ... a lofty conception of its own capacity."

"If the resistance contemplated be of a passive nature (such for example, as the Rock in the middle of the fall of the Rhine at Chaf-hausen, as opposed for countless ages to that mighty mass of Waters), there are undoubtedly here before us two distinct images & thoughts ... these objects will be found to-have exalted the mind to the highest state of sublimity when they are thought of in that state of opposition & yet reconcilement, analogous to parallel lines in mathematics, which, being infinitely prolonged, can never come nearer to each other; & hence ... the absolute crown of the impression is infinity, which is a modification of unity." (MS., pp. 14–15)

In this reaction, the resistance of the mind to power is replaced by its observation of the resistance of one natural object to the power of another. The curious terms in which Wordsworth here defines the unity of impression ("infinity, which is a modification of unity") suggest the possibility of varying the definition of this and other reactions of the mind to power. For what the mind observes here is an instance of an eternal (or seemingly eternal) *stability*, the rock eternally resisting the eternal assault of the Rhine waters. This sta-bility or equilibrium is the product of a balance of forces which the observing mind perceives as an eternal balance.[34] Similarly, in those reactions described earlier where the mind stands in awe of the power, or resists the power, of the sublime object, we have instances of relations which are stable as long as the sensation of the sublime lasts. These relations are of the inferiority ("humiliation or prostra-tion of the mind," or, in another passage, "humiliation & submis-sion") or the superiority ("security or absolute triumph") of the mind to the exciting object. And in these instances also, the stability is achieved in a kind of balance between the mind and the object; by

34/So, in the passage on the Simplon Pass discussed earlier (*Prel.*, vi.556–72; see Chapters iii, sec. ii; vii, sec. ii), the scene is perceived as an eternal balance between the forces of decay and the forces of renewal. The connection between this concept and that discussed in Chapter vi, sec. viii, will be obvious. "Dura-tion" as a quality of the sublime (see n. 30 above) may likewise be considered as a state of stability, the result of the balance between the forces of decay and the inherent strength of the object, natural or artificial.

virtue of "action from within and from without" (112.23–24; *Prel.*, XII.377), the mind grasps the object, by imposing on it a unity, and the object grasps the mind, by claiming its total attention. Lastly, in the reaction which the fragment first describes, in which the mind strives to identify itself with power or with the source of power, the interaction of mind and object is such that a stable unity coextensive with both mind and object, which Wordsworth calls "a manifest approximation to absolute unity," is achieved.

Whatever terms we prefer for the definition of these various reactions to the power of the sublime, for our present purpose the most important common feature is the active participation of the observing mind.

v *The Nature of Power and the Difficulty of Communication*

We have examined power as an experience of the poet, recorded in his autobiographical poems; and as a quality of things, of the natural scene or of some man-made things like a great city. This, clearly, may be what the poet "communicates" to the reader, in so far as some Wordsworthian poems try to communicate the poet's experience of power, or the power of this or that natural scene, or of London. But it is not all that Wordsworth communicates, and certainly it is not what he "calls forth" from the reader. Our view of power is, at the moment, too limited.

For the poet, as for the observer of the Lake District, power may reside in natural objects, and the poet may communicate the power of such objects, as Wordsworth does, say, in the scene of the Simplon Pass in Book VI of *The Prelude*. Or power may reside in what may be called events or experiences, as in the boy Wordsworth's experience on the Penrith Beacon (*Prel.*, XI.279 ff.); and the poet may attempt to communicate the power of this experience. The experience took place against, and was enhanced by, a natural scene; but the scene itself was not especially impressive. Power may reside also, we must suppose, in a different type of event, the human situation where the natural background, though it may be present, sinks in importance before the human situation itself, as in the poet's encounter with the leech-gatherer in *Resolution and Independence,* or in the conduct of Michael under spiritual stress. We may draw analogies between all these situations and subjects which Wordsworth actually used for poems, and the characteristics of power as seen in the natural objects of the Lake District and elsewhere. The parallel between the Simplon Pass and these natural objects needs no elaboration. In the episode of the Beacon, the scene did not supply the characteristics of power: they were added to it, in the form of "danger" or "dread and awe," by the boy's imagination. In the human situations of the leech-gatherer and Michael, the power resides in the more or less indomitable spiritual energy of the protagonists, or in their dogged resistance to the assaults of circumstance, analogous to the resistance of the observer to the natural scene, or of the rock at Schaffhausen to the Rhine waters; or, as in the climax of *Michael,* power resides in the overcoming of this spiritual energy or power of resistance by some great and conflicting feeling.

If we ask how the poet communicates the power of all these scenes and situations, we shall ask, in particular, this question: does the power of the poet lie in the events which he communicates, or in his communication of them? In (as we say) his subject-matter, or in his presentation of that subject-matter? Is the poet a mere colourless medium for the communication of the power which resides in "real" objects or events of which he gives as literal a transcript as possible, or is his verbal art a means of communicating power to, or of enhancing the power of, the matter with which he deals?

The contrast between these seeming alternatives is not real. Wordsworth's meeting with the leech-gatherer was to him evidently an event of power; but the poem which resulted was not a literal transcript of that event. Wordsworth alters the facts, in particular by omitting the presence of his sister at the meeting; the force of the meeting is thereby enhanced.[35] Not only does he thus tamper with matter of fact, but he enhances the event, in at least one passage (as he is at pains to point out in the Preface of 1815, 148.32–149.15), by what he calls the Imagination and by what others might call literary art – the use of elaborate simile. Yet the art is exerted, not as "the adversary of Nature" (124.17), but so that "nature," the event itself as the poet experienced it,[36] may exert its power the more effectively. The imagery of the description of the Simplon Pass is obviously the result of careful selection towards a foreseen end, and some of the figures used are highly complex. Yet the final effect is the presentation of the object itself, with its power implicit; just as a "faithful image ... truth ... of the highest order" in the presentation of the deceased, for a particular purpose and from a particular viewpoint, is achieved in the epitaph which says less than the whole truth (101.28–102.23).[37] On the other hand, the literary effectiveness of the line from *Michael*, "And never lifted up a single stone," lies in its literal presentation of action, or rather inaction, which in its factual context has power; and the literary art, here and also in the presentation of the episode of the Penrith Beacon, lies, paradoxically, in Wordsworth's recognition that in these cases, though not necessarily in others, no "literary" art is required to enhance the power of the event.

35/See *Journals*, i.63, for a literal version of the encounter.
36/Sara Hutchinson in 1802 is rebuked for her failure to appreciate the poem always in terms of the event: Wordsworth, assuming that the event will be factually clear whatever his artistic success or failure, finds it incredible that she should not respond to the power of the event: "the figure presented in the most naked simplicity possible. ... I then describe him, whether ill or well is not for me to judge ... but ... I cannot conceive a figure more impressive than that of an old Man like this. ... Such a figure, in such a place ... telling such a tale! ... it is of the utmost importance that you should have had pleasure from contemplating the fortitude, independence, persevering spirit, and the general moral dignity of this old man's character" (*E.Y.*, pp. 366–67).
37/See *Prel.*, vi.556–72; pp. 49–50 above; and Chapter vi, sec. iv. Here too belongs the reticence of the best of *Lyrical Ballads* (see p. 22), and of the epitaph which makes its points "implicitly ... rather than explicitly" (101.20–21).

The reader's reaction to such poems is therefore as to the event with which the poem deals. He is meant to react as the poet himself reacted, with or without the obvious assistance of the poet's art; and it is necessary that he should exert "a co-operating *power*," that power should be both called forth and communicated, because he is faced with a situation in which "the mind is lord and master." It is necessary that the reader's mind should be active; that, like the poet's, it should (for instance) impose upon the scenery of the Alps such a meaning as will make it seem the type and symbol of Eternity; that, like the poet's, it should see the significance of Michael's inaction.

To suggest a general definition of power is still difficult. In the natural scene, it is, first, the analogue in the scene of various elements of our experience connected with *power* in the physicist's sense: "any form of energy or force available for application to work" is a definition from the *Oxford English Dictionary* (sense 13), where *work* means the overcoming of resistance. This is something like the sense in which Shelley uses the word in his *Mont Blanc*. From a nearby point of view, which might also be Shelley's, power is that which can act outside of itself; which can affect things beyond its own limits.[38] And this point of view is useful in the aesthetic sense; for in that sense the power of the natural scene is the power to grasp and dominate the mind, to seize the mind's attention, so that, in Wordsworth's phrase, the "comparing power of the mind" is "suspended." The natural scene itself is such that it, and it alone, grasps the attention and retains it for as long as the power is felt. In other experiences, not necessarily involving the natural scene, the same is true: the young Wordsworth entering London was gripped by the power of the place: the place itself, its long history (the concept of *duration* is

38/Cf. *O.E.D.*, sense 1: "Ability to do or effect something or anything, or to act upon a person or thing"; sense 2: "Ability to act or affect something strongly. ..." Shelley's Power which "dwells apart in its tranquillity" acts beyond its own limits while yet seeming "Remote, serene, and inaccessible" (*Mont Blanc*, 96–97).

relevant); its size, its political power, its moral power (for good or evil), its cultural power – these all gripped his mind and acted upon it, contributing what Wordsworth calls, in the subjective sense, power to the mind, as well as knowledge. In human incidents, those which Wordsworth himself experienced, or those which happen to characters in his poems, the experience holds the mind, by some emotion which dominates the mind – fear, delight, joy, in some instances; awe, rather than fear, in some other passages, especially those which describe the mind faced by the natural scene, and more especially the sublime natural scene which the eighteenth-century mind had sought, and sought to define and understand. The boy awe-struck by the recognition that here a man had died, ignominiously, by the vengeance of society, on a gibbet; the knowledge that the leech-gatherer had a quality in him which could act beyond himself – the incident of the gibbet and the encounter with the leech-gatherer were like that in Wordsworth's experience, having the power to drive him from the place or draw him from his despondency. The inaction of Michael is significant, powerful, resembling, in a way, an "individual form" of nature, seizing the reader's mind and making it homogeneous in its attention to this crucial fact of a man's betrayal and the breaking of his courage by this betrayal.

From the reader's point of view, the power which, Wordsworth says of the episode of the Penrith Beacon, is "left behind," is perhaps akin to knowledge, with which Wordsworth connects it, or to wisdom: the event and its taking-in, the natural scene and its taking-in, the personal experience of the poet or the vicarious experience of dramatic or narrative character and its taking-in – these make the mind which takes them in larger. The mind, says the eighth book of *The Prelude*, needs to be capacious, to have amplitude, when faced with those things which themselves have capaciousness and amplitude; the mind grows by being stretched, as it were, to the measure of those things which have capaciousness, amplitude, power. De Quincey, in one of the more useful sentences of his report of Wordsworth's distinction between the literature of power and the literature of knowledge, says that literature provides *"power,* that is, exercise and expansion of your own latent capacity of sympathy with the infinite."[39] We cannot always press the phrase "with the infinite," though Wordsworth, in some moods, would have accepted it; but at least we can accept "exercise and expansion of your own latent capacity of sympathy" with something larger than ourselves. The mind's own power is enhanced because it has, somehow, acquired the power which resides in the powerful thing which it has received into its own capaciousness. The mind is changed with each access of power: it grows, by accepting the power of nature, or the power of art, or the power of another man's mind. To assist the reader so to add to himself, to add to his own store of power – this, according to Wordsworth, is the purpose of poetry and the task of the poet.

Why are the communication and evocation of power more difficult for "an original Writer, at his first appearance in the world" (184.17–18), than for a classic? The answer can hardly lie, as Wordsworth just before seems to imply, in the mere familiarity of the classic; the individual reader may be no more familiar with the classic than with the contemporary poet. The answer lies elsewhere, and in particular in Wordsworth's immediate concession that the degree of difficulty involved varies according to the nature of the occasion of power which the poet handles. Drawing largely upon the ideas of John Dennis,[40] he proceeds (185.1–26) to distinguish three kinds of occasion: the "simple and direct" pathetic, the "complex and revolutionary" pathetic, and the sublime. The first of these is distinguished from the others since by it "all men, possessed of competent knowledge of the facts and circumstances,[41] [are] instantaneously affected"

39/*Collected Writings,* ed. Masson (Edinburgh, 1889–90), xi.56.

40/For a fuller exposition of Wordsworth's indebtedness, see W. J. B. Owen, "Wordsworth, the Problem of Communication, and John Dennis," in *Wordsworth's Mind and Art,* ed. A. W. Thomson (Edinburgh, 1969), pp. 140–56.

41/That is, the facts and circumstances of the event of power with which the poet deals; the "subject-matter" of the artefact, not the artefact itself, is still in question.

(185.2–4). The sublime, we assume, presents a difficulty even greater than the "complex and revolutionary" pathetic. We shall need to understand the distinction between the "simple" and the "complex" pathetic if we are to grasp Wordsworth's meaning fully.

In a letter of late 1814 or early 1815[42] which shows specifically his debt to Dennis, Wordsworth claims that in at least three passages in *The Excursion* can be found "emotions of the pathetic" which are "simple and direct ... human ... ordinary":

"One word upon ordinary or popular passion. Could your correspondent read the description of Robert, and the fluctuations of hope and fear in Margaret's mind, and the gradual decay of herself and her dwelling without a bedimmed eye, then I pity her. Could she read the distress of the Solitary after the loss of his Family and the picture of his quarrel with his own conscience (though this tends more to meditative passion) without some agitation then I envy not her tranquillity. Could the anger of Ellen when she sate down to weep over her Babe, though she were but a poor serving-maid, be found in a book, and that book be said to be without passion, then [Wordsworth is glad not to be connected with the person who says so]." (136.5–17)

The "description of Robert" probably means *The Excursion*, 1.566–91; the "fluctuations" and "decay" begin at 1.646.[43] The other passages concerned are III.680–705; III.778–991, especially 842–69; and VI.973–82.[44]

The characteristic which most of these passages share is that in each the main figure of the episode is faced with a current situation, a combination of "real" circumstances, which stimulates in him an

42/On the date, see my paper cited in n. 40.

43/The Wanderer calls the story of Margaret "a common tale, An ordinary sorrow of man's life" (1.636–37). In MS. E (1801–2), however, he added that it was "to the grosser sense But ill adapted, scarcely palpable To him who does not think" (*P.W.*, v.29).

44/Zall (136.fn.9) adds, perhaps rightly, VII.677–794, on "the little Infant" (136.18). His reference to "II, 873–880" should be to Book III.

immediate emotional reaction. Thus Robert is faced with physical convalescence, and a sense of worldly failure which he knows will bring disaster on his family. Margaret is faced with the absence of her husband and the approach of the disaster which this absence aggravates. The first passage from the Solitary's narrative shows him facing directly the deaths of his children and wife. Even more clearly, the Ellen of Book VI is, literally, faced with the dead body of her child and the indecent haste of the funeral party. In each episode, therefore, we have an example of Dennis's "ordinary Passion, whose Cause is clearly comprehended by him who feels it"; of his "Vulgar Passion ... which is moved by the Objects themselves ... As for example, Anger is moved by an Affront that is offer'd us in our presence ... Pity by the Sight of a mournful Object," and the like.[45] These episodes, then, are efforts of the "human and dramatic Imagination" (150.20–21), episodes which might be used in a drama; and since in each case the relevant passion may be moved either by events themselves or by "the Relation of" the events, and since, further, "all Men are capable of being moved by the Vulgar" (Dennis, i.338–39), it follows that Patty Smith must be lacking in some essential human characteristic if she fails to be moved by this relation of pathetic events.[46]

45/Dennis, i.216, 338. The anger of Ellen, in particular, is "moved by an Affront that is offer'd [her] in [her] presence." In Knight, ii.178, Wordsworth contrasts two epitaphs, the first of which is written in the third person, while the second has the "advantage" that "the Father ... speaks in his own person," and therefore "the situation is much more pathetic"; that is, in the second case the father is (or appears to be) faced with a "real" situation which calls forth his sorrow.

46/The expected reaction is usually conveniently indicated by the characters of *The Excursion*: see I.917 ff.; IV.7; and note especially VI.1053 ff., where the Solitary weeps at "the Relation" of a "mournful Object," though the Wanderer, to whom this sort of sorrow is "not sorrow, but delight" (*Prel.*, XII.245), and who "could afford to suffer With those whom he saw suffer" (*Exc.*, I.370–71), achieves the reaction of a more cultured sensibility (VI.1063–68, cf. I.605–9, 942–56). Wordsworth's surprise at Sara Hutchinson's failure to react to the figure of the leech-gatherer (see above, n.36) is surprise at her failure to be "instantaneously affected" by the "simple and direct" pathetic when she is "possessed of competent knowledge of the facts and circumstances"; the

The cases just examined seem similar to those postulated by Wordsworth in 1800 as the basis for the experimental poems of *Lyrical Ballads*: they represent "the essential passions of the heart ... our elementary feelings exist[ing] in a state of greater simplicity ... the great and simple affections of our nature" (18.6–10, 20.2). The case of the Solitary's "quarrel with his own conscience," according to Wordsworth, "tends more to meditative passion"; and we should therefore expect to find in his later utterances traces of emotions "complex and revolutionary," of "meditative ... pathos ... enthusiastic ... sorrow" (185.17–18); or, in Dennis's terms (i.216–17, 338), passions whose "Cause is not clearly comprehended by him who feels them," proceeding "from Thoughts, that latently, and unobserv'd by us, carry Passion along with them ... a Passion which is moved by the Ideas in Contemplation, or the Meditation of things that belong not to common Life."

The case of the Solitary differs from the others in that he is not personally involved in certain events which nevertheless call forth emotional reactions. He is involved, not with events, or with people, but with abstractions:

> "Society became my glittering bride,
> And airy hopes my children ...
> My Soul diffused herself in wide embrace
> Of institutions, and the forms of things."
>
> (*Exc.*, III.735–39)

Though no Frenchman, and though he has had no personal contact with France, he is emotionally involved in French affairs (III.741–45). When it is clear that France has failed such enthusiasts, he declines

---

grounds of his reproaches of Patty Smith are the same. One of the classes of poems which Wordsworth proposed in 1809, "Poems relating to human life," which includes poems grouped mainly under "Imagination" in the edition of 1815, is said to deal with "objects most interesting to the mind not by its personal feelings or a strong appeal to the instincts or natural affections, but to be interesting to a meditative or imaginative mind either from the moral importance of the pictures or from the employment they give to the understanding affected through the imagination and to the higher faculties" (*M.Y.*, i.335).

to renounce his views, and thus becomes not only emotionally involved in abstractions, but dishonestly so involved. He

> "seized
> All that Abstraction furnished for my needs
> Or purposes; nor scrupled to proclaim,
> And propagate, by liberty of life,
> Those new persuasions." (III.795–99)[47]

He endeavours to cut himself off from his own personal emotional tradition:

> "farthest from the walk
> Which I had trod in happiness and peace,
> Was most inviting to a troubled mind." (III.801–3)

In America he is resolved to

> "live
> No longer in subjection to the past,
> With abject mind" (III.873–75),

and, like the Wordsworth of 1793, who was

> "more like a man
> Flying from something that he dreads than one
> Who sought the thing he loved" (*Tintern Abbey*, 70–72),

the Solitary is now

> "like a fugitive, whose feet have cleared
> Some boundary, which his followers may not cross
> In prosecution of their deadly chase." (III.877–79)

47/The Solitary is in some sense a watered-down version of the Oswald of *The Borderers*, lacking his criminality, but (at any rate at first), like Oswald, seeing "that every possible shape of action Might lead to good" (*Bord.*, 1780–81). The crisis of each follows upon what each considers a betrayal. That Wordsworth felt some kinship between them is indicated by his use of the same phraseology to describe their meditations after crisis (*Bord.*, 1774–75; *Exc.*, III.700–1).

More important for the present problem: in this situation, his soul is "From the depths Of natural passion [*MS. variant*: personal feeling], seemingly escaped" (III.736–37). He refuses to act "naturally"; he

> "smiled
> At others' tears in pity; and in scorn
> At those, which [Nature's] soft influence sometimes drew
> From my unguarded heart" (III.809–12);

and eventually, he refuses to feel at all (III.892). "Natural passion," "personal feeling," which the Solitary feels at the loss of his family, is "simple," "human," "ordinary" feeling; his feeling for the abstract ideal of the Revolution is an enthusiasm both in the modern sense and in that defined by Dennis. For in so far as the Solitary's emotional progress is an "escape" from the "natural passion" which has brought him only distress, it involves emotions whose "Cause is not clearly comprehended by him who feels them."[48] In so far as it is concerned with the abstract catchwords of political activity, it involves "Thoughts, that latently, and unobserv'd by us, carry Passion along with them ... the Meditation of things that belong not to common Life."

It is thus easy enough to define, in Wordsworth's and Dennis's terms, the difference between the Solitary's situation and the others described earlier; but it is not wholly clear why the power of such a situation should be more difficult to communicate. Though the argument to Book IV promises one, there is no account of the audience's reaction to the narrative in *The Excursion*, except that the "not unfrequent ... strains Of native feeling" (that is, the "simple and direct" pathetic parts) were "grateful to our minds" and roused "compassion" (*Exc.*, IV.1–7). Nor is Dennis (i.339) very helpful: he says merely that "the Enthusiastick [Passions] are more subtle [than the Vulgar], and thousands have no feeling and no notion of them." And unless we are to say merely that the feelings of a man who does

48/Hence the Solitary's conscience appears to him in a vision of his dead wife, and memory (of "natural passion") is "like a plague" (III.847–55).

not understand them and their motivation are inevitably difficult to convey (which is possibly untrue and in any case unilluminating), we must look elsewhere for an explanation.[49]

Wordsworth cites certain other instances (which he does not specifically connect with the notions of power or the pathetic) in which he foresees difficulty of communication. The difficulty is ascribed, as we might expect in view of the mood of the Essay, to deficiencies in the reader; almost to what he called, some years earlier, "the pure absolute honest ignorance [of worldlings] with respect to the thoughts, feelings, and images, on which the life of my Poems depends" (76.19–77.2; May 1807). The *Immortality Ode*, he points out,

"rests entirely upon two recollections of childhood. ... A Reader who has not a vivid recollection of these feelings having existed in his mind in childhood cannot understand that poem. So also with regard to ... some of those images of sense which are dwelt upon [in *The Excursion*] as holding that relation to immortality and infinity which I have before alluded to; if a person has not been in the way of receiving these images, it is not likely that he can form such an adequate conception of them as will bring him into lively sympathy with the Poet. For instance one who has never heard the echoes of the flying Raven's voice in a mountainous Country, as described at

49/Some twentieth-century psychologies might provide a more ample vocabulary for discussion than does either Dennis or Wordsworth. For instance, a man may hate his father, and know the reason for his hatred, because his father beat him cruelly in childhood; or he may be unaware of the reason for his hatred, because he has a suppressed Oedipan desire to supplant his father in his mother's affections. These cases seem parallel to Dennis's "ordinary" and "enthusiastic" passions. The presentation of the second case by a writer who thought he understood Freudian psychology would presumably be no more difficult than that of the first, nor would its understanding be difficult for a reader similarly equipped. But the presentation of the second case would necessarily *differ* from that of the first, and perhaps in the direction of complexity; and if the reader were deficient in understanding of the Oedipan situation, in Freudian or other terms, his understanding of the artefact would be correspondingly more difficult. Wordsworth's presentation of the situation in *Goody Blake* and his explanation of it in psychological terms in the Preface to *Lyrical Ballads* (28.26–34) are like *Hamlet* and its well-known Freudian "explanation" by Ernest Jones; the play is, or is supposed to be, as mystifying without such an explanation as the situation of the effective curse in *Goody Blake*.

the close of the 4th Book will not perhaps be able to relish that illustration; yet every one must have been in the way of perceiving similar effects from different causes." (135.19–136.3)[50]

The difficulty lies primarily in the deficiency of the reader's factual knowledge and habitual associations;[51] or, as the reader might retort, in the poet's addiction to private imagery in which biographical and geographical accident is elevated to the rank of the essential. However this may be, the consequence is that the reader is unlikely to "form such an adequate conception of [such images] as will bring him into lively sympathy with the Poet"; that is, such an image will probably fail to "call forth and communicate *power*," since the reader has no common ground on which he can meet the poet, on which he can exert "a co-operating power" (184.16, 183.34). Yet such a basis may be found, since, even when the reader is deficient in the particular image involved, nevertheless "every one must have been in the way of perceiving similar effects from different causes." Granted a minimum basis for co-operation, co-operation is possible and power may in a measure be communicated: the reader unfamiliar with ravens in the Lake District may yet be moved, if he will, towards that common situation which is colloquially expressed as: "I see what he means – it's like" whatever "similar effects" arising from "different causes" may be within his experience. If he will not be moved, the case is hopeless, for his "imagination has slept; and the voice which is the voice of my Poetry without Imagination cannot be heard" (79.7–9). Such a manœuvre by the reader might be described

50/There follows the discussion of "ordinary or popular passion" cited above, which suggests that to Wordsworth the image of the raven is "imaginative and enthusiastic." Cf. Knight, ii.45: "it may happen, that the figure of one of the larger birds, a raven or a heron, is crossing silently among the reflected clouds, while the voice of the real bird, from the element aloft, gently wakens in the spectator the recollection of appetites and instincts, pursuits and occupations, that deform and agitate the world, – yet have no power to prevent Nature from putting on an aspect capable of satisfying the most intense cravings for the tranquil, the lovely, and the perfect, to which man, the noblest of her creatures, is subject."

51/The sublime is difficult to communicate because "the practice and the course of life" are "remote ... from the sources of sublimity" (185.22–23).

as "meditative ... treading the steps of thought" (185.17–20), whether the pathetic is involved or the sublime of "Far-stretching views into eternity" (*Exc.*, IV.1189).

In the case of the Solitary's narrative, similar considerations may apply. For the Solitary has been moved, in the incidents concerned, not by "natural passion" or "personal feeling," with which, since that is part of "general truth," the reader might be expected to have "lively sympathy"; but rather by particular historical events which the reader may not understand, and, moreover, by these events indirectly – by abstractions based on second-hand experience of the events. A corresponding effort of the reader's imagination, as with the image of the raven, is required: "the soul must contribute to" the "support" of the passion, "or it never becomes vivid, – and soon languishes, and dies" (184.12–13).

We return to the earlier question: why is the communication and evocation of power more difficult for an original writer than for a classic? The answer is now seen to lie in Wordsworth's conception of genius and originality. Originality may appear in the poet's subject-matter, or in his style, or in both. By 1815, Wordsworth, the stylistic experiments of 1798 well in the past, had reverted to a manner basically that of the eighteenth century, and is concerned with subject-matter, its commonplaceness or its originality; the longest discussion of any individual poet in the *Essay*, that of Thomson (172.15–175.18), is almost entirely concerned with that aspect of Thomson's verse.

The classic calls forth and communicates power more easily than the contemporary poet who is "original" in his subject-matter because the events and objects with which the classic deals are traditional, even commonplace. His subject-matter, even if his treatment of it is unfamiliar to the individual reader, is on the whole familiar – if not from real life, then from the tradition of literature. By such a subject-matter, whether it involves the pathetic or the sublime, "all men" are "instantaneously affected"; it has "effects immediate and universal" (185.2–6), or, as we might say today, the classic evokes responses from the reader which may be relied upon as inevitable because they are traditional. Wordsworth had argued for such a sub-ject-matter, even if it should be "truths whose very interest and importance have caused them to be unattended to, as things which could take care of themselves" (117.35–118.1), in the Preface of 1800 and in the *Essays upon Epitaphs*. Here, his concept of general truth is that wider one which he advanced in the Preface of 1802 and in other documents of that time (Chapter IV, sec. vi). Because "Genius is the introduction of a *new* element into the intellectual universe ... the application of powers to objects *on which they had not before been exercised*" (184.22–24), the occasions of power with which the original poet deals are necessarily new to all individual readers, and therefore less likely to be recognized as such.

The difficulty is real, but more complex than Wordsworth makes it. Various occasions, even the various occasions handled by one poet, will have various effects. I do not know that anyone before Blake saw a world in a grain of sand; yet it is probable that that image of power impresses immediately if it impresses at all, whereas no agreement seems to have been reached in a century and a half on the value, the power, or even the meaning of the overwhelmingly original Prophetic Books. Moreover, we must distinguish kinds of novelty: "the application of powers to objects on which they had not before been exercised" is an ambiguous definition of original genius. The difficulty which even the modern reader finds in many of Wordsworth's instances of power, as in Blake's Prophetic Books, lies not in their novelty so much as in their uniqueness: they are so far removed from general experience that their power can never be tested by the majority of readers. As we have just seen, Wordsworth is aware of this difficulty; it is, indeed, because he is aware of it that he adapts the theory of Dennis to his own poetry, in an attempt to illuminate the problem. He thought the difficulty might be overcome by the imagination of the reader, and, within limits, he was no doubt correct.

But, however precisely we manage to define such experiences of power in terms of Dennis's distinction between ordinary and enthusiastic passion, a difference is clear between the imaginative response of the reader to those experiences and his response to that general truth which is "not standing upon external testimony, but carried alive into the heart by passion; ... which is its own testimony" (50.21–22); which is "grounded upon the universal intellectual property of man, – sensations which all men have felt and feel in some degree daily and hourly; – truths whose very interest and importance have caused them to be unattended to, as things which could take care of themselves" (117.33–118.1). The original poet may, indeed, "widen the sphere of human sensibility" and apply his powers "to objects on which they had not before been exercised" (184.20–24), and yet be making use of general truth as these earlier documents define it, rather than of experiences as unique as those of Wordsworth upon the Penrith Beacon or listening to the cry of the Lake District raven. It is in this latter sense that Blake's *Songs of Innocence and Experience* are at once original and more successful than the Prophetic Books: they "widen the sphere of human sensibility" towards a possible innocence and towards an actual experience of evil, social, moral, and psychological, "truths whose very interest and importance have caused them to be unattended to, as things which could take care of themselves." Similarly, Donne's success in widening the sphere of human sensibility directs attention to many and various aspects of inter-sexual relationships, hitherto generally excluded, perhaps mainly by convention, from polite literature, but which any honest husband or lover will recognize as "truth which is its own testimony" or "sensations which all men have felt and feel in some degree daily and hourly."

In neither case does any time-lag in appreciation seem inevitable. In the case of Donne,[52] it does not seem to have existed; and this is

52/The genius of Blake was, of course, ignored in his own time, but his extraordinary method of publication may have been more to blame than his originality.

not surprising, since his success depends, not upon experience of a unique event or even upon imaginative sympathy with such an experience, but only on the reader's concession that a non-Petrarchan approach to erotic experience is acceptable; and for such a concession only a moment may be required. Indeed, without such an immediate acceptance of the power of the original poet (of whatever kind) by some individuals, who need not be the good critics described early in the Essay,[53] the poet would never succeed in gaining any general acceptance at all; the rate at which he gains it depends, no doubt, on the persuasive enthusiasm of such individuals, amongst other things which Wordsworth does not mention.

Thus, as we saw in the earlier discussion of the Essay's general argument, neither the proposition that time is necessarily involved in the solution of the difficulty which Wordsworth describes, nor its converse, that failure to communicate power immediately and generally is a test of the poet's genius, is true; and it is likely that only a poet of Wordsworth's extreme egotism, placed in circumstances such as those in which he found himself between 1807 and 1815, could have written such an elaborate defence of their validity. But the Essay remains valuable in its stress on the concept of power, since a consideration of that concept helps us to understand, if not always to justify, some of the qualities of Wordsworth's poetry which have puzzled critics. For he found the power which he valued in the commonplace, in the "ordinary sight," and sometimes in the unique private event; and when such an object or event could be presented with sufficient effect by a literal transcript of his experience, he was content to use such a transcript and allow it to work on the reader as the object or event had worked on himself.[54] To present it otherwise would, indeed, in at least some instances have weakened the effect.

53/Crabb Robinson was such a reader, though hardly a good critic.

54/"In answer to the common reproach that his sensibility is excited by objects which produce no effect on others," Robinson reported in 1815, Wordsworth "admits the fact and is proud of it ... [he] has a pride in deriving no aid from his subject. It is the mere power which he is conscious of exerting in which he delights" (*H.C.R.*, pp. 166–67).

In 1801 Wordsworth narrated to Charles James Fox an anecdote, pathetic enough, of a decaying couple in his neighbourhood: "She told my Servant two days ago that she was afraid they must both be boarded out among some other Poor of the parish ... but she said, it was hard, having kept house together so long, to come to this, and she was sure that 'it would burst her heart' " (35.21–25). The phrases reported seem commonplace,[55] but, according to Wordsworth, they sprang from "an almost sublime conviction of the blessings of independent domestic life" (35.28–29). In the situation and in the statement of it by the wife Wordsworth found power, and expected the power to be obvious to Fox. Some such power he must have found also in the woman of *The Sailor's Mother*, whose "appearance was exactly as here described" (Fenwick n., *P.W.*, ii.477), and in the other beggar woman whom he saw only through the eyes of his sister.[56]

It is to the records of such events and to those discussed earlier, rather than to the experimental poems of *Lyrical Ballads*, that we can best apply the arguments of an able critic for Wordsworth's "belief in the dignity of the subject as it is in nature" and for his search for "the only words which can convey the object or experience as nakedly as possible" (Sharrock, pp. 397, 401). The argument for a Wordsworthian theory which "represents an attempt to abolish any diction, any literary medium," however, covers only the case of poems like *Michael*; in other cases, "the only words which can convey the object or experience as nakedly," or at any rate as accurately, as possible may be highly figurative and "poetical." The aim is, in

55/The quotation-marks round "it would burst her heart" may indicate that Wordsworth thought this phrase unusual, perhaps an example of the metaphorical language of passion (48.1 ff.), or a revivifying (in the use of *burst* rather than *break*) of a dead metaphor. *O.E.D.*, however, quotes examples of the phrase in literary use up to the end of the sixteenth century (s.v. *burst*, sense 10, cf. sense 4), so that it was evidently an archaism of Standard English which survived in nineteenth-century dialectal use.

56/The sailor's mother was originally "Majestic ... as a mountain storm" (*P.W.*, ii [2nd ed.], 538); she was "like a Roman matron," marked by "strength" and "dignity," and roused "pride" and "lofty thoughts" in the poet; the woman of *Beggars* was "fit person for a Queen." These figures indicate the power which Wordsworth saw in the women.

both cases, that stated by Mr. Sharrock, but the means differ; indeed, at first sight seem antithetical. *Resolution and Independence*, we may note, is almost contemporary with the Preface of 1802 on which Mr. Sharrock bases his argument, yet contains, in quite early versions, perhaps the most complex poetic image in Wordsworth; and in these early versions especially, it contains also some of the most "unpoetical" writing he ever produced.[57] With Coleridge, we may call this juxtaposition an "INCONSTANCY of the *style*" (*Biog. Lit.*, ii.97; cf. ii.100); but the aim of each style is the same: to present the object or event itself with its power implicit. Such also is the aim of the second characteristic of Wordsworth's manner which Coleridge describes, "a laborious minuteness and fidelity in the representation of objects, and their positions, as they appeared to the poet himself" (*Biog. Lit.*, ii.101). Whether or not we agree with Coleridge and others that these characteristics are defects,[58] we can at least see them brought within the scope of a common purpose, on occasion, by the concept of power which the Essay expounds.

57/The minor comparisons noted above in *The Sailor's Mother* and *Beggars* correspond in effect to the complex simile of *Resolution and Independence*, 57–65. Indeed, the general effect of *The Sailor's Mother* is of a somewhat attenuated version of the situation of *Resolution and Independence*: a solitary figure met and questioned by the poet; unexpected dignity revealed; the poet lost in meditations which are, immediately or eventually, invigorating. Cf. the episode of the discharged soldier, *Prel.*, iv.400 ff.

58/See Havens, Chapter I, for an extended exposition of the Coleridgean point of view. In many of the examples of "matter-of-factness" there collected, there will, of course, be found no traces of "power" whatsoever, so that the comment of Havens (p. 14) on "the difficulty [Wordsworth] found in distinguishing the essential from the accidental" remains valid.

Nine ✳ Conclusion

Wordsworth's criticism is occasional, and therefore likely to lack such a formal system as may be seen in the work of a professional critic such as Hazlitt or in the scattered but copious and repetitive utterances of Coleridge. Yet it is obviously more original than a derivative work like Shelley's *Defence*, and more formalized than the pregnant but undeveloped *obiter dicta* of some other Romantics, such as Keats; and it is possible to trace in it a logical process of development: a growth in clarity and in mastery of the subject, accompanied by an increasing sense of relevance to the subject; that is, Wordsworth's kind of poetry, how it is made and what is its expected effect upon the reader. That some of the writing we have analysed (the general argument of the *Essay, Supplementary to the Preface* most notably) is wrong-headed and tendentious arises usually from the occasion; but where Wordsworth is concerned with poetry, his own or others', rather than with the defence of his reputation, he is illuminating more often than not.

The early part of this development we have already traced in Chapter VI, in an attempt to see the points of resemblance and of difference between the Preface to *Lyrical Ballads* and the *Essays upon Epitaphs*. This stage provides an approximate model of the kind of development which follows: it is a progress, by instalments, towards mastery and clarity, whereby a concept hinted at in an early work is more fully developed in a later, and (if necessary) irrelevances, difficulties, and inconsistencies are silently abandoned. What is gained in one document, as it were by the way, and as if the author were aware of it not as a formal critical tenet but rather as a "natural," instinctive way of talking about poetry, becomes in a later document consolidated and expounded as a formal critical concept.

Thus the second version of the Preface to *Lyrical Ballads* (1802) expands what in the first was the merest hint of poetry as expression rather than mimesis, of the poet as emotionally involved with his subject rather than a spectator and reporter of the emotional behaviour of others. The difficulty of writing dramatic poetry in an "expressive" medium is faced, and in the doctrine of "selection" and in the theory of metre poetry is seen as artefact rather than the mere effusion of the passion from which it takes its origin. This argument is unsatisfactory at various points: the concern over dramatic expression is not specifically linked to the doctrine of "emotion recollected in tranquillity" and the "spontaneous overflow of powerful feelings," and metre was originally offered, in 1800, as artifice to be set against the "naturalness" of "the real language of men" or "the language of prose," rather than as a control upon the possibly overpassionate character of that utterance.[1] But in this second version of the Preface, the gain[2] is the new stress upon the emotional involvement of the poet, however ill that interpolated emphasis accords with the basic argument of the Preface of 1800.

In the *Essays upon Epitaphs*, the basic tenet, emphasized by the deliberate choice of a particular illustrative genre which demands it, is the emotional involvement of the poet. Thus what was new in the Preface of 1802, at any rate in the degree of emphasis, becomes a formal basis of argument in the *Essays upon Epitaphs*. Moreover, difficulties of the Preface's argument are abandoned or solved: because the monument is a more or less permanent physical object, open to the inspection of all, a corresponding permanence and uni-

1/See 49.29–50.3, 57.36–37, 55.9 ff., 38.4–5, 45.29 ff.; Chapters II and IV.

2/I use this word to denote the step taken in the general direction of Wordsworth's progress, which is from mimesis to expression, from cool observation to passionate involvement, or (as we might risk saying) from Classic to Romantic.

versality of literary appeal are required in the epitaph inscribed on it; but the means by which these are to be achieved is not defined in the clumsy sociological terms of the Preface. It would be possible to say that the issue is shirked, but at least the embarrassments of the solution proposed in the Preface are avoided. The difficulty of accommodating an expressive poetic to dramatic utterance is played down, because dramatic utterance is not essential to the epitaph, because a stiff formality in its use, when it is used at all, is envisaged, and because the epitaph which uses it is likely to be not quite of the highest rank. Again, in the Essays the reconciliation of effusion and artefact is seen as real, and not contrived as it was to some degree in the Preface: the epitaph is presented as artefact both as literature and in its mere physical form, words carved upon stone.

To the concept of general truth which the Preface states first in 1800 and which it amplifies in 1802, the Essays add a balancing concept of individuality. In the comparatively narrow sense which is relevant to the epitaph, this amounts to little more than "a distinct and clear conception, conveyed to the Reader's mind, of the Individual" who is the subject of the poem; but it is the individual seen in a particular context which gives significance to the presentation: "his character as, after death, it appeared to those who loved him and lament his loss" (101.8–11). Here, then, is a new concept of the poet's kind of truth: not so much the presentation of "characters of which the elements are ... such as exist now and will probably always exist" (20.19–21), as of the significance of particular things in particular contexts – the vision of the poet brought to bear upon an object, a person, or a character, so that, looked at in one way, in the poet's way, rather than in another, it means more (in fact something more general) than itself.[3] In the presentation of this kind of truth the process of selection as the Essays define it is of major importance (Chapter VI, sec. iv).

3/"... it is the slightly variant or novel way of seeing which largely justifies the poet's effort" (David Perkins, *The Quest for Permanence* [Cambridge, Mass., 1959], p. 25).

The gain of the *Essays upon Epitaphs,* apart from their clarification of some of the concepts of the Preface to *Lyrical Ballads,* is the introduction, again by the way, of the concepts of reconciliation of opposites and of the related faculty of the Imagination. The introduction of these concepts, though clear on inspection, is, as we observed earlier (Chapter vi, secs. viii, ix), so nearly a matter of instinct that the word *imagination* occurs only once in the Essays in its characteristic Wordsworthian (or Coleridgean) sense. The next document in our survey, the Preface of 1815, is, obviously, largely concerned to offer a formal exposition of the concept of Imagination; and, again, what was added in the earlier document by the way has become the basis of argument in the later.

The gain which we might have expected in the Preface of 1815 is hardly to be seen there, but rather in the contemporaneous *Essay, Supplementary to the Preface.* The Preface is concerned to define the Imagination by illustrating its processes. The gain of the Essay is that, in a context almost purely controversial, it begins to define the materials upon which the Imagination works. These are barely mentioned in the Preface: "the plastic, the pliant, and the indefinite ... inherent and internal properties" (152.24–153.10). That part of the Essay which in these pages has been regarded as operative is concerned with the concept of *power* as the subject-matter of the greatest poetry and as the material of the poetic Imagination. The discussion is difficult because, as before, the concept is introduced casually, like the expressive poetic of the Preface of 1802 and the virtually unnamed concept of the Imagination in the *Essays upon Epitaphs.* The term is, as the discussion in Chapter viii above witnesses, scarcely defined in the Essay; had Wordsworth continued to write formal criticism, we might have expected a formal exposition of the concept in some later document. But we may gather something of Wordsworth's meaning from the Essay itself, from letters of similar date, and rather more from the analogues to the power of great poetry, or of the subject-matter of great poetry, which appear in Wordsworth's autobiographical verse and in the prose fragment on the Sublime and Beautiful. The concept involves, also, one which was touched upon in the *Essays upon Epitaphs*: the power of the individual as the poet presents it, reconciled with and tempered by the sense of the general. For the scenes and the events of power such as were used earlier to illustrate this concept – natural scenes in themselves, such as the Simplon Pass; the leech-gatherer and his effect upon the poet; the great human spirit of Michael – must be presented, in the first instance, as individual scenes and events: individual not so much in that they are or may be actually unique, as in that the poet sees them in a unique fashion, from a unique viewpoint which he labours to present to the reader; either (as we saw earlier) "in the most naked simplicity possible," or with the aid of more or less "art"; but in any case with a constant aim (Chapter VIII, sec. v), which is to present the scene or the event to the reader so that he sees it with the unique vision of the poet. But, as the individuality of the subject of an epitaph is to be balanced and reconciled with "the common or universal feeling of humanity" (101.7), so the individuality of the scene or event of power as the poet uniquely sees it is to be given general significance: the Simplon Pass and all its elements are "types and symbols of Eternity"; Michael, a type of paternal love at its best; the leech-gatherer, of resolution and independence. And even "the echoes of the flying Raven's voice in a mountainous Country," as described in the fourth book of *The Excursion*, may yet be perceived, indirectly, by a perception that it comes within a category of generalized "similar effects," as a source of power (135.33–136.3). Thus "the poet conceives and produces – that is, images – individual forms in which are *embodied universal ideas* or *abstractions*" (*H.C.R.*, p. 191); the individual, the unique vision, becomes a symbol, which "always partakes of the reality which it renders intelligible; and while it enunciates the whole, abides itself as a living part in that unity of which it is the representative."[4]

Wordsworth produced no formal literary criticism or aesthetic theory after the documents of 1815. His next work in prose, the

4/Coleridge, *Statesman's Manual* (London, 1839), pp. 230–31.

Letter to a Friend of Robert Burns (1816), is concerned with literature, but from the point of view of the ethics of biography and of book-reviewing. The *Guide to the Lakes* in its various forms and editions shows the same artist's mind as we have observed in the works discussed above, but the aesthetics of natural scenery is not its major concern. His other prose works after 1815 are even more strictly occasional and practical in their intention. Indeed, it would be surprising if we were to find any advance in Wordsworth's thinking on poetry and aesthetics beyond the documents of 1815 (unless, as was observed above, it were a fuller exposition of the concept of *power*); for these documents more or less complete the description, begun in 1798 with the Advertisement to *Lyrical Ballads*, of the poetics of his own verse. Beyond this we could hardly expect Wordsworth to proceed.

* Index

This book

was designed by

ANTJE LINGNER

under the direction of

ALLAN FLEMING

and was printed by

University of

Toronto

Press